Michael Graves

ARCHITECTURAL
Monographs 5

Michael Graves

NEW YORK

ARCHITECTURAL Monographs 5

Subscriptions and Editorial Offices
7/8 Holland Street, London W8
Tel. 01-937 6996

Publisher
Dr Andreas C Papadakis

Editor
David Dunster

Editorial Board
Alvin Boyarsky, Robert Maxwell,
Robert Stern, James Stirling

ACKNOWLEDGEMENTS

The Editor would like to thank Karen Vogel Wheeler of Michael Graves' office for all her assistance and work in assembling material, and Carol Constant for assisting with initial layouts.

The photographs of the Hanselmann House taken by Tom Yee appear by courtesy of Condé Nast Publication Inc. Copyright © 1973 by the Condé Nast Publications Inc. Photographs of the Alexander House taken by Bill Maris are Copyright © 1974 The Hearst Corporation. Photographs by Laurin McCracken, Balthazar Korab and Norman McGrath are also gratefully acknowledged. Other photographs are by Michael Graves.

The following have worked in Michael Graves' office and contributed to the projects shown here.

Bruce Abbey	Madlen Goldstine	Laurin McCracken	Henry Smith-Miller
Kenneth Behles	Jose Gonzalez Barahona	Pedro Mendoza	James Swan
Christopher Bene	Nicholas Gonser	Peter Mickle	Thomas Szumlicz
Ronald Berlin	Ruth Goodman	Bruce Miller	Sara Jane Tsakonas
Ted Bickford	Stan Haas	Thomas Navin	Max Underwood
Peter Carl	Lawrence Haines	Robert Nichols	Ronald Vanard
Ellen Cheng	G. Steven Harris	G. Daniel Perry	Peter Waldman
Christopher Chimera	Suzanne Kolarik	Mig Perkins	Gloria Walters
Mark Cigolle	Randall Korman	Thomas Pritchard	Seth Warner
Linda Joy Cohen	Benjamin Kracauer	David Reading	Karen Vogel Wheeler
Caroline Constant	Eric Kuhne	Paul Robertson	Robert Carey White
Stephen Corelli	Charles Lagreco	Nonya Schwartz	Timothy Wood
Michael Farewell	Diane Legge	Masaharu Seno	Konrad Wos
Patricia Fingerhood	Stephen Levine	Gordon Smith	
Laurel Fitch	Peter Lokhammer	Sylvia Smith	
Wanatha Garner	Bruce MacNelly	Terrence Smith	

First published in the United States of America in 1979 by

RIZZOLI INTERNATIONAL PUBLICATIONS, INC.
712 Fifth Avenue/New York 10019

© 1979 Architectural Monographs and Academy Editions
All rights reserved
No parts of this publication may be reproduced in any manner whatsoever without permission in writing from the publishers.

The opinions expressed by writers of signed articles appearing in this publication are those of their respective authors for which the editor and publisher do not hold themselves responsible.

Printed and bound in Great Britain

Library of Congress Catalog Card Number: 78-68511
ISBN: 0-8478-0215-9

Contents

7   Foreword

8   *Michael Graves*
    Alan Colquhoun

18 Selected Buildings and Projects

97 *Freud and Russell at the Wherehouse*
    Peter Carl

105 List of Buildings and Projects

106 Bibliography

107 Résumés: French
             German
             Italian
             Spanish

Selected Buildings and Projects

18 Union County Nature and
    Science Museum
20 Hanselmann House
24 The Newark Museum Master Plan
26 Benacerraf House
28 Rockefeller House
30 Keeley Guest House
32 Medical Office Ear, Nose and Throat
    Associates
36 Snyderman House
40 Investment Office Gunwyn Ventures
44 Alexander House
48 Drezner House
    Sklute House
49 Mezzo House
50 Murals:
    XV Triennale Exhibition
    Professional Office Transammonia, Inc.
51 Wageman House
52 Claghorn House
56 Housing for the Elderly Competition
58 Warehouse Conversion
64 Crooks House
68 Furniture, Lamp and Sconce Sketches
70 The Newark Museum Carriage House
    Renovation
72 Schulman House
76 Chem-Fleur Factory
80 Kalko House
82 Plocek House
86 Fargo-Moorhead Cultural Center
90 Abrahams Dance Studio
94 'Roma Interrotta' Exhibition

Front cover:
Detail from Fargo-Moorhead Cultural Bridge
Back cover:
Gunwyn Ventures office interior
Photograph: Norman McGrath
Frontispiece:
Warehouse Conversion courtyard entrance
elevation

Foreword

Michael Graves was born in Indianapolis in 1934. Educated at Harvard and a Prix de Rome scholar at the American Academy, Rome, he has been a professor of architecture at Princeton since 1962. In 1972, the publication of *Five Architects* brought him to international prominence. Despite the recent economic depression, more than enough work has been assembled to merit inclusion in these pages as a kind of interim *oeuvre complète*. While all the work bears his indelible stamp, he would be the first to acknowledge that it has been work produced under the banner of his name, as the acknowledgements show. Karen Vogel Wheeler must be singled out, however, for her assistance in the preparation of this issue of the magazine.

A measure of the quality of Graves' work can be gauged from the serious contributions both Alan Colquhoun and Peter Carl in their essays make to the level of architectural criticism. Two further points seem germane to the publication of Graves' architecture. The first concerns the level of technical control over the building. Graves was noticed first because his buildings exhibit a complexity that photographs hardly document. This complexity was not achieved because the client's budget was high, but by thoroughly exploiting the means of construction of the American building industry. While his work may be architecture with a capital A, his professionalism as an architect, constrained as all are by brief, site and budget, is of the highest order. Architecture as art does not necessarily mean therefore that the building is carelessly assembled, for in Graves' hands the means of construction is both put to the acid test of articulation of an idea, and simultaneously integrated with that idea so that it becomes its servant.

My second point concerns the recent developments in the work, and is more in the nature of a question than a comment. It is to do with the validation of borrowing from the past.

The sensuousness of materials of construction and technical restrictions of what is and what is not buildable play parts in the realisation of any building. To paint a surface of a building is always to lay some code over that building, whether it is a code referring to the systems out of which that building is constructed — an obvious and recent example would be the Centre Georges Pompidou — or whether is is a code depicted in a mural placed at some significant point of the building — as in the Snyderman House or the offices for Gunwyn — in which the conceptual elements are presented again not in three dimensions but in two. This coding in Graves' work consists of at least two sets of categories, one the area which interests Peter Carl, that is the deepest level of exploration of what it means to build, and the other which is the nature of those elements which combine to make a building. In the latest works, the Plocek House, and the cultural complex for Fargo and Moorhead, the keystone as a form is employed, as Colquhoun argues, as an absent element, as *trompe l'oeil*, and as signifying a flat arch. This 'play' with the keystone is therefore possible because the keystone does not exist as an element in the material construction of the building, but instead exists as an element in the intellectual construction.

Is it then that Graves feels some nostalgia for the classical vocabulary, without wishing to engage the mode of construction of his buildings as an element which could be expressive in itself? This question might be clarified if another attitude is posed to it. Moretti, in his article written in 1952 called 'The Value of Profiles' and translated and published in *Oppositions* 4, proposes that *'the variation of light (reveal) the everlasting palpitations of an ancient façade, diverse from hour to hour, as the sun's course shapes it (the cornice) in harmony with the world . . . the form of a cornice conveys the reasons for a façade and reveals it vehemently . . .'*

The question then becomes, to what extent is the idea that a building be united at every level of its elements of plan, form, surface and detail, now under attack? There can be no doubt that Graves can build what he draws. The question must be left as such until the completion of those most recent works still on the drawing board imposes the acid test of occupation.

Michael Graves
Alan Colquhoun

Criticism occupies the no-mans-land between enthusiasm and doubt, between poetic sympathy and analysis. Its purpose, except in rare cases, is not to eulogise or censure, and it can never quite grasp the essence of the work it discusses. It must try to reduce the work's apparent originality and expose its ideological framework, without turning it into a mere tautology.

This applies particularly to the work of Michael Graves, with its appearance of being *sui generis* and its sensitivity to outside influences which it immediately absorbs into its own system. This essay, therefore, will attempt to discuss his work in terms of three broad contexts: the American tradition, the tradition of modern architecture, and the classical tradition. It is not suggested that a discussion of his work in these terms will exhaust its meaning. It will merely provide a rough and ready scaffold — a way of approaching the work obliquely.

Graves' work is so clearly related to the international Modern Movement that it is at first sight difficult to see in it any reference to purely American traditions. But some of the ways in which it differs (and differs profoundly) from European interpretations of the Modern Movement see traceable to specifically American sources. Graves' apparent rejection of modern architecture as a social instrument—and his insistence that architecture communicates with individuals and not classes—does not operate in a social void. His work is made possible by social conditions which are probably unique to the USA at the present moment (though they existed in Europe between 1890 and 1930). The chief of these is the existence of a type of client (whether institutional or private) which regards the architect not only as a technician who can solve functional problems, or satisfy a more or less pre-formulated and predictable set of desires, but also as an arbiter of taste. In this role he is called upon not only to decide matters of decorum; like the modern painter, he is expected to say something 'new', to propound a philosophy. No doubt this applies only to a minority of clients (and even these are probably often puzzled at the results); but their very existence explains how an architect as intensely 'private' as Michael Graves can insert himself within the institutionalised framework of society despite the absence of a clearly defined 'market'. If his work reflects the nostalgia for 'culture' which is characteristically American and which, as Manfredo Tafuri has pointed out,[1] can be traced back at least to the City Beautiful movement, it depends on the existence of a type of client who has similar—though less well defined—aspirations. In Europe the critique of a materialistic modern architecture has usually taken place under the banner of a betrayed populism. It is perhaps only in America that it could be launched in the name of intellectual culture. Certainly the importance in Graves' work of the French tradition—its assimilation, initially through the example of Le Corbusier, of the Beaux-Arts discipline of the plan, has its origins in a purely American tradition going back to Richardson and McKim.

But there also exists a technological condition peculiar to the USA which seems especially favourable to Graves' architecture and which relates to the social insofar as it depends on the fact that most of his commissions are for private houses or additions. This is the balloon frame—a system of construction whose lightness and adaptability gives the designer great freedom and allows him to treat structural matters in an ad hoc way. Without this form of construction an architectural language like that of Graves, which depends on a blurring of the distinction between what is real and what is virtual and between structure and ornament, would hardly be conceivable. By using a system of construction which provides so few constraints, Graves is able to treat structure as a pure 'idea'. The regular grid, for example, which is such an important ingredient of his work, is relieved of those positivistic and utilitarian qualities which it still had for Le Corbusier in the Maison Domino, for example. For Graves' structure has become pure metaphor; he thus reverses the postulates of the Modern Movement in which the split between perception and calculation resulted in an emphasis on instrumentality.

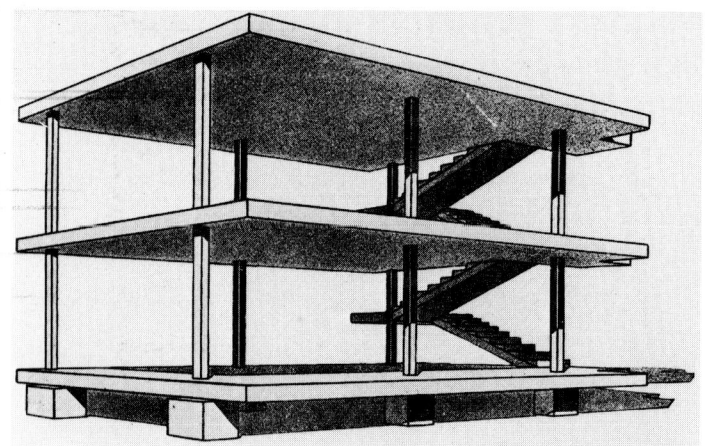

1 Le Corbusier, Maison 'Dom-ino' 1914
2 McKim, Mead and White, Newport Casino 1878-81
A frame construction freely manipulated
Photograph: Valkenberg

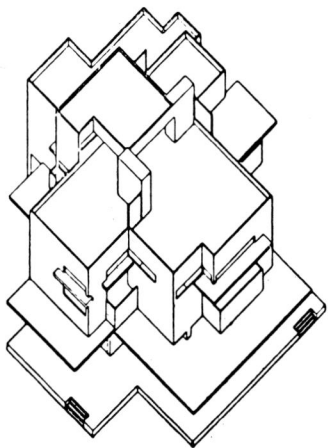
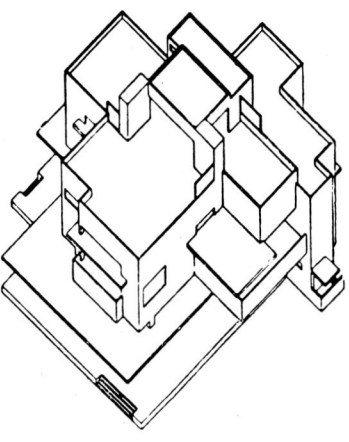

The openness and transparency of Graves' houses are made possible by the use of the frame, while their complexity and ambiguity is made possible by the fact that the frame can be manipulated at will. These are qualities which his work shares with the Shingle Style, even more than with its Shavian counterpart, and seem characteristic of later nineteenth-century American domestic architecture. In Europe the houses of the Modern Movement were relatively box-like. The Neo-Plasticist projects of Van Doesburg and Mies van der Rohe were the exception, and it is these projects, as Vincent Scully has pointed out, that have such a striking resemblance to the houses of Frank Lloyd Wright, with their hovering planes and strong vertical accents. If the houses of Graves also have closer ties with Neo-Plasticism than with the more typical houses of the European movement it may be that, as in the case of Wright, there is a coincidence between cubist spatial principles and an American tradition which, in its response to climate, in its attitude toward nature and in a certain kind of sociability, creates an intermediate zone between the private realm of the house and the public realm of its environment. Not only the openness of the nineteenth-century American house, but also the proliferation of verandahs, porches, and bay windows and the frequent placing of these on the diagonal, suggest a parallel with the way Graves weaves secondary spaces in and out of the periphery of the cage, or superimposes a diagonal fragment on an otherwise orthogonal *parti*.

All this is perhaps to say no more than that the picturesque nineteenth-century house is a precursor of a modern architecture which combines cubist devices with an anecdotal and episodic elaboration of the programme. This should surprise us no more than similar connections in the other arts, for instance the fact that modern music took over from romantic music its rejection of classical symmetry and classical cadence.

In the context of contemporary American architecture, there are two figures with whom one is tempted to compare Graves. Among the New York Five architects, with whom Graves has become associated, it is Peter Eisenman with whom he seems to have the greatest affinity. In the mid-sixties, when they worked together on a competition for the upper west side of Manhattan, they shared the same influences—notably those of the Como School—and both attempted to construct a new architectural language out of the basic vocabulary of the Modern Movement. But from the start they diverged—Eisenman towards a syntactic language of exclusion, Graves towards a language of allusion and metaphor. This semantic inclusiveness has led Graves to direct historical quotation, which now puts his work at the opposite pole to that of Eisenman. But in the work of both one finds an architecture in which the ideal completely dominates the pragmatic, even though in the case of Graves—in contrast to Eisenman—the point of departure is always the practical programme, the distribution of living spaces. But these quotidian considerations are merely a point of departure; they are immediately ritualised and turned into symbols. With Eisenman— the semantic dimension is conceptual and mathematical; with Graves it is sensuous and metaphysical.

Graves' later work might seem to bear some resemblance to (and even the imprint of) the work of Robert Venturi, with his parodistic use of traditional motives. But this similarity is superficial. Graves shows no interest in what seems to be Venturi's chief concern: the problem of communication in modern democratic societies and of 'architecture as a mass medium'. If Venturi wants to bridge the gap between 'pop music and Vivaldi', Graves remains exclusively a 'serious' composer for whom the possibility of communication is predicated on the existence—even in a fragmentary form—of a tradition of high architecture. This no doubt explains Venturi's preference for the romantic and populist overtones of vernacular architecture against that of Graves for the architecture of the classical and academic traditions.

3 Van Doesberg, House 1922
4 Frank Lloyd Wright, Robie House, Chicago 1906 Ground floor plan

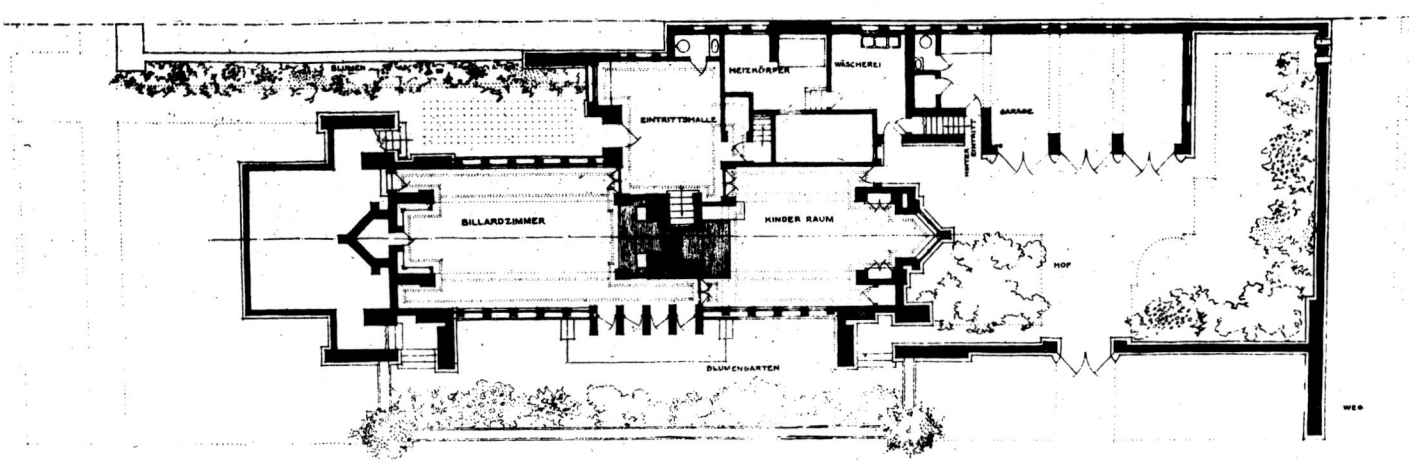

Though the degree of dependence Graves' work has on American traditions is perhaps arguable, its affiliations with the Modern Movement are beyond dispute. The nostalgic quality of these affiliations has been stressed by other critics, but it should not be forgotten that Graves belongs to a generation for whom the Modern Movement still represented all that was vital and creative in architecture. To return to the 1920s and Le Corbusier was not an eclectic choice but a return to sources. What was new about this return was its rejection of functionalism and its claim that architecture had never exploited the formal and semantic possibilities of modernism as the other arts had. There was also the conviction that the 'new tradition' of avant-garde art constituted a historical development from which it was impossible to turn back.

It is certainly true that the development of the avant-garde marks a radical break with the form of artistic language which existed until the latter part of the nineteenth century. Traditionally, language was always thought of as describing something outside itself, in the 'real' world. The difference between natural language (considered as an instrument rather than a poetics) and artistic languages was merely that in the latter the form was an integral part of the message—the 'how' was as important as the 'what'. At whatever date we put the moment when the epistemological foundations of this 'rhetorical' world began to disintegrate, it was not until the end of the nineteenth-century, and in the context of avant-garde art, that the content of a work began to become indistinguishable from its form. External reality was no longer seen as a *donnée* with its own preordained meanings, but a series of fragments, essentially enigmatic, whose meanings depended on how they were formally related or juxtaposed by the artist.

By returning to the sources of modern architecture Graves attempted to open up a seam which had never been fully exploited, as it had been in cubist painting. In his work, the elements of *techné* and the architectural elements (windows, walls and columns) are isolated and recombined in a way which allows new metonymic and metaphoric interpretations. At the same time rhythms, symmetries, perspectives and diminutions are exploited in a way which suggests the need, in discussing his work, for a descriptive vocabulary such as existed in the Beaux-Arts tradition, and still exists in musical criticism, but which is generally lacking in modern architectural discourse. Within this process no semantic distinction exists between functions and forms. They reinforce each other to produce meanings which extend in an unbroken chain from the most habitual and redundant to the most complex and information-laden.

To respond to Michael Graves' architecture it is essential to understand the 'reduction' this process involves. It is this which makes his work specifically 'modern'. It dismantles the preconceptions which would allow one to have a ready-made idea of what a 'house' is and insists that the observer or user carries out a reconstruction of the object. Graves' elementarism is related both to the architecture of the Modern Movement and to modern art in general. It is tied to an elementarisation resulting from industrialisation and the disappearance of craft, and it strives for the condition of the *tabula rasa*, the primal statement.

5

5 Juan Gris, Bottle, Newspaper and Fruit Drink 1917
Coll: Kunstmuseum, Basel

The reconstruction of the object, made necessary by this process of analysis and reduction, involves the use of codes which are themselves meaningful and internally coherent. But Graves is not interested in the way in which these syntactically organised and semantically loaded elements already form a system whose meaning has been ideologically internalised. For him all the elements must be reduced to the same condition of 'raw material'. They have become de-historicised and 'potential', and must be reconstructed consciously as a 'structure'. He is interested in how such a structure works perceptually as the product of conflicts and tensions in the psyche of the individual. He demonstrates the *process* by which meanings are generated and this leads him to a language whose articulation depends on oppositions, fragmentation and the visual pun.

In this process of reduction Graves does not attempt (as Peter Eisenman does) to strip the elements of their connotations. Columns, openings and spaces

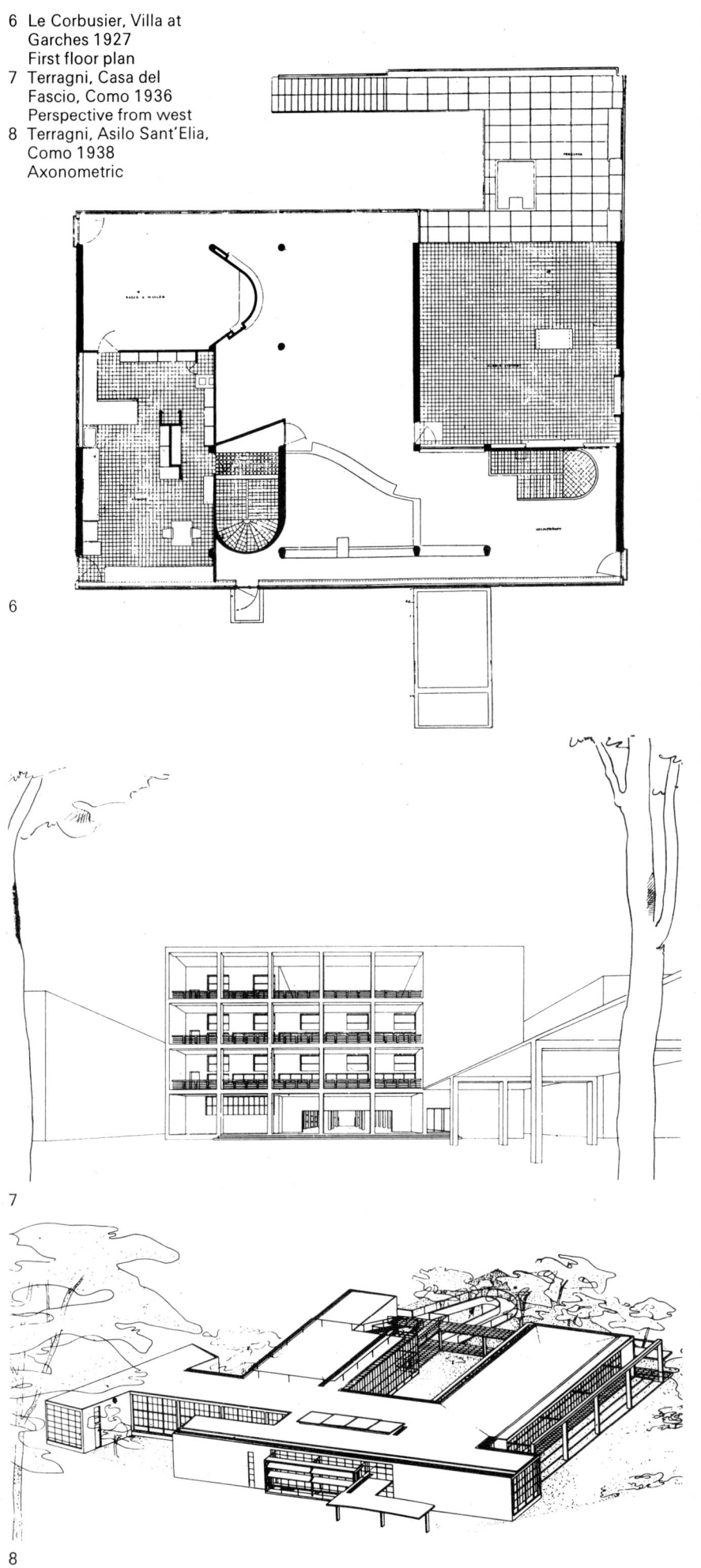

6 Le Corbusier, Villa at Garches 1927
First floor plan
7 Terragni, Casa del Fascio, Como 1936
Perspective from west
8 Terragni, Asilo Sant'Elia, Como 1938
Axonometric

all retain their qualities of body image and the meanings which have accumulated around them. Not only do the basic architectonic elements have meanings which relate to their functions, but their very isolation also allows them to become metaphors. There is, indeed, a danger that these metaphors may remain private and incommunicable; in his earlier work this danger is increased because of the reliance on relatively abstract forms. Where meanings are clear in his earlier work, they tend to be those which have already become established in modern architecture.

The most fundamental source of Graves' work (and it is this which links him with the other members of the so-called New York Five) is Le Corbusier. In Le Corbusier's work there is always a tension between the figurations and symmetries of the French classical tradition and the infinite improvisations demanded by modern life, which are made possible by the neutral grid. It is this tension which Graves exploits. But he superimposes on this Corbusian system—whose chief vehicle is the 'free plan'—an open three-dimensional cage which was seldom used by Le Corbusier. The vertical planes of Graves' work are closely related to the work of Giuseppe Terragni—to such buildings as the Casa del Fascio and the Asilo Infantile at Como, with their open structural cage, their delicate layering of structural planes and their frequent absorption of the frame in the wall surface. The transparency of the cage enables Graves to provide an adumbration of the building's limits without destroying the flow of space between inside and outside. The dialectic between solid and planar elements and the structural grid becomes a basic architectural theme, not only in plan but also as perceived in three dimensions and dominates the whole plastic organisation in a way that it seldom does in the work of Le Corbusier.

Apart from these purely architectural sources, Graves' work is directly related to Cubist and Purist painting. His own work as a painter is closer to his architecture than that of Le Corbusier was to his. For Le Corbusier it provided a lyrical outlet to some extent constrained by the logical and systematic researches of the architect, but Graves develops parallel themes in both painting and architecture, among which one finds the typically cubist notion of a world built out of fragments, related to each other not according to the logic of the perceived world but according to the laws of pictorial construction. His buildings are, as it were, projections into real three-dimensional spaces of a shallow pictorial space and his spaces are frequently made up of planes which create an impression of Renaissance perspective or the successive planes of the Baroque theatre.

Although the dominance of the three-dimensional frame suggests, as in Neo-Plasticism, the parity between all three dimensions, in Graves' work the plan is still thought of as possessing figural qualities which actually generate the vertical and spatial configurations, in the manner of Le Corbusier and the Beaux-Arts. It is in the development of the plan that the influence of his painting can be felt most strongly. The paintings suggest collages built up out of fragments which create diagonal fault lines or, as if with torn paper, trembling profiles suggestive of the edges of bodies. These elements reappear on his plans and create a nervous interplay of frag-

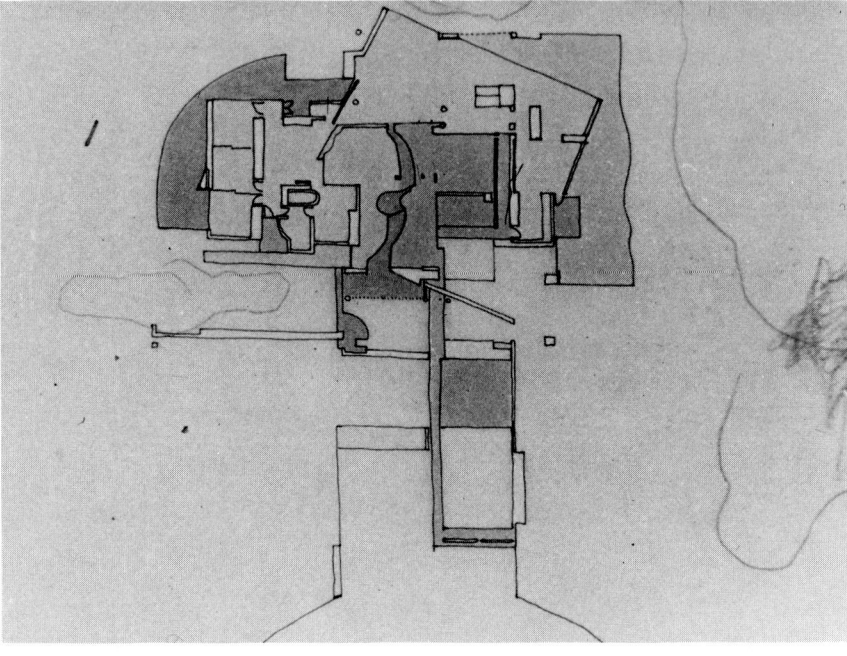

mentary planes, a web of countervailing spatial pressures, inflected with slow curves or overlaid with diagonal figures.

Unlike the plans of Le Corbusier, with their muscular, vertebral sense of order, Graves' plans tend to be dispersed and episodic and often resemble, perhaps fortuitously, the plan of Chareau's Maison de Verre with its multiple centres, complex spatial subdivisions and gentle inflections. There is, in Graves' plans, a sense of almost endless elaboration and half-statement, every function being the clue for syntactic complexity or mataphorical qualification.

This elaboration is not arbitrary. It comes from an extreme sensitivity to context which is perhaps its chief difference from the tradition of the Modern Movement, with its attempt to create the architectural types of a new order in polemical contrast to the existing built environment. I have said that many of Graves' projects are additions. These additions draw attention to their difference from the existing buildings, they do not ignore them. The old house is considered as a fragment which it is possible to extend and qualify in a way unforseen in the original. In the Benacerraf House, for example, the wall separating the original house and the extension is removed and the cage of the addition penetrates the living spaces of the existing house to form a transparent veil which transforms the original space and overlays it with a new spatial meaning.

But sensitivity to context is equally apparent in completely new structures. The houses respond to the natural environment, itself modified by the building. The more typical houses of the Modern Movement tended to respond to the gross features of the environment (particularly orientation) by setting up elementary oppositions; for example, that between an open side which was fully glazed and a closed side which was solid. Graves uses this basic opposition as a compositional point of departure, as can be seen in the Hanselmann House of 1967, where the theme open/closed is almost obsessively stated and is reinforced by a ritualistic frontalisation and the displacement of the front façade to form an additional plane of entry.

9 Graves, Gunwyn Office, Princeton 1972
Entrance hall and mural by Graves
and
Dreisner House 1970 sketch plan
Fragmentary planes appear in both painting and *parti*
10 Chareau, Maison de Verre, Paris 1928
Second floor plan, compared with Graves, Snyderman House 1972
Ground floor plan

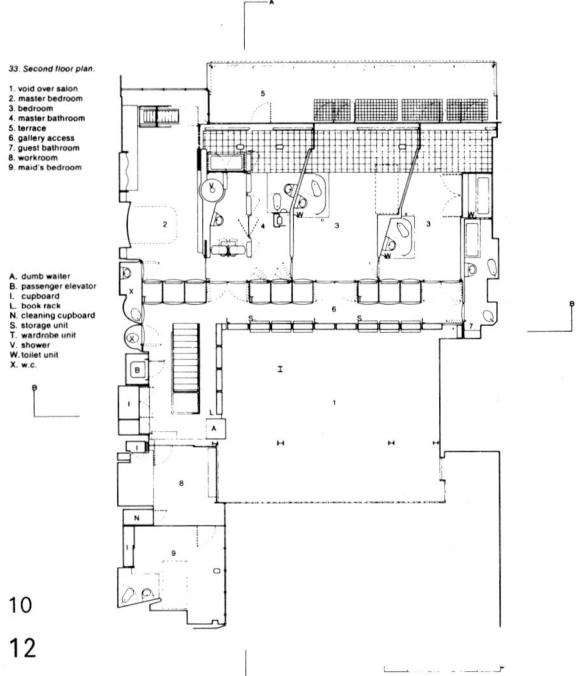
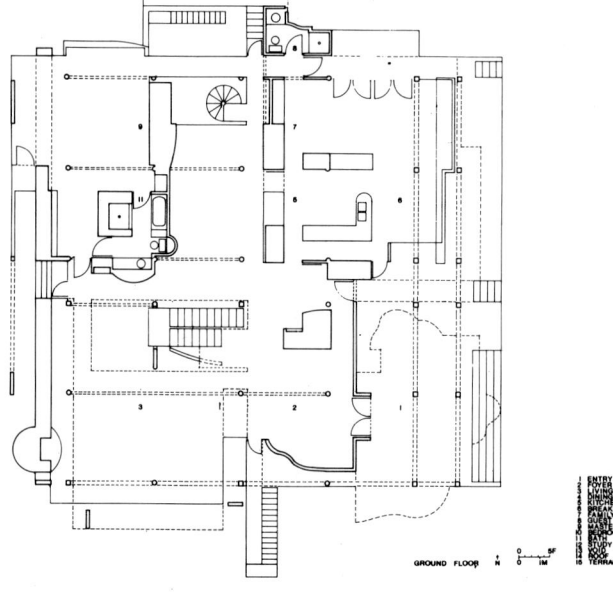

But in other works, for instance the Snyderman House of 1972, the opposition closed/open is used with greater subtlety, qualified by a number of conflicting contextual demands. The 'closed' surface is punctured by a variety of openings and its function as a limiting plane is actually enhanced by its greater transparency. The way in which this and other diagrammatic expressions of opposition are modified in the design process is illustrated by comparing the sketches for the Snyderman House with the final design. In the early sketches the plan consists of two equal axes at right angles, the east-west axis being bounded on the west by a solid wall punctured by only one opening and on the east by an open surface with fragmentary obstructions (the plane of entry). In the final design these ideas are retained but are overlaid with counter-statements. The west wall becomes a perforated screen. At the same time the east-west axis is strengthened by a caesura in the structural grid related to the staircase, while the north-south axis is suppressed. A diagonal is introduced by the erosion of the south-east corner and the skewing of the second floor accommodation—a diagonal which is reinforced by raising the south and east façades to three storeys. These moves suggest entry from the south-east corner and act in contrapuntal opposition to the plan's biaxial symmetry. The house is no longer a statement of simple oppositions, but an overlay of several *different* oppositions, each element separately inviting contradictory interpretations.

Other ways in which Graves' buildings differ from more orthodox modern buildings can be seen by analysing the Gunwyn office conversion at Princeton of 1972. The elements used in this design are those one might expect to find in a typical 'systems approach' building of the West Coast—tubular steel columns, exposed I-beams, standard lighting tracks and standard office furniture. The basic imagery is industrial, efficient and smooth. But there is another language superimposed on this. Whereas according to functionalist practice the systems should be logically independent, Graves (starting, as always, from Le Corbusier's poetic use of mechanical forms but going further into a world of free fantasy) deliberately overlaps them to produce ambiguities which gently subvert their primary and unequivocal meanings and give rise to less obvious correspondences.

The space of the office is complex, with various penetrations through three storeys. A hatch to the second-floor office projects over one of these voids. Its wafer-thin work top is carried on a bracket attached to the column on the *opposite* side of the void, which thus reaches out to receive an unexpected but hardly onerous burden and at the same time provides the hatch with a frame borrowed from the nearby tubular balustrade at floor level. Similar ambiguities are created when the glass-brick wall to the office is prised open and an I-beam inserted to support its upper half. This I-beam, seen from alongside the office, appears as a jagged fragment mysteriously projecting from a column. Most of the columns are circular, but when they occur in a wall they turn into pilasters and merge with the wall surface above. All these fragments and transpositions have a local, internal logic of their own. Their shock effect is due to the way they undermine expected hierarchies. The fragments are differentiated by means of colour, for the most part brilliant but intermixed with grass greens, sky blues and flesh pinks. Just as these colours suggest elements of nature, so does the metaphorical play of functional elements have anthropomorphic, and sometimes surreal, overtones relating mechanical functions to our own bodies and making us question reality.

Graves' buildings, in the phase of his work most directly influenced by the Modern Movement, consist of a large number of variations on a limited number of themes. The most persistent idea is that of the open frame defining a continuous space partially interrupted by planes and solids. Not only is horizontal space continuous but vertical penetrations occur at crucial points to create three-dimensional continuity. Through this space the frame is threaded, creating a dialectic between a rational *a priori* order and a circumstantial, sensuous and complex plastic order. This is in essence the 'free plan' of Le Corbusier, but developed with greater complexity in a repetition, transformation and interweaving of formal themes reminiscent of musical structure. Tensions develop round the periphery of the building and there is maximum exploitation, by means of layered screenings and shallow recessions, of the plane of the façade—the intense moment of transition between the 'profane' world outside the house, and the 'sacred' world inside.

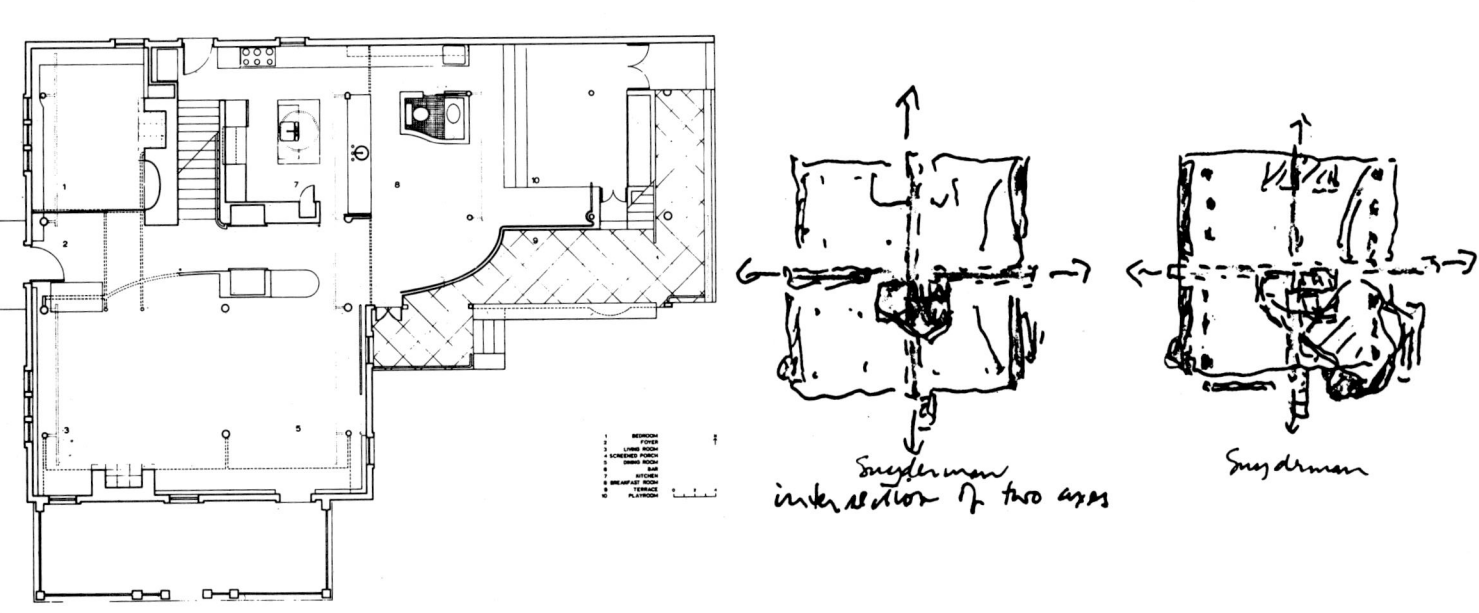

11 Graves, Benacerraf House 1970
Ground floor plan, and Graves, Snyderman House 1972
Sketches
Benacerraf unifies extension and original, but in Snyderman ideas are overlaid and juxtaposed

Graves' work cannot be called 'classical' in any strict sense. But his thought is permeated with a kind of eighteenth-century deism and a belief that architecture is a perennial symbolic language, whose origins lie in the nature and our response to nature. He finds support for these views from modern writers such as Mírcea Eliade. His frequent use in his writings of the words 'sacred' and 'profane' shows that he regards architecture as a secular religion, which is in some sense revelatory.

In his earlier work the symbolic images and metaphors are very generalised and drawn from a repertoire of abstract forms chiefly derived from Le Corbusier and Terragni. This language is autonomous within an architectural tradition and operates through the use of certain graphic codes, the most important of which is the plan.

But during the early 1970s Graves seems to have become dissatisfied with the expressive possibilities of this language and, above all, of the plan as an abstraction; this coincides with a radical change of style. The attitude behind this change is expressed in the following programme notes for a students' project:
'The design of a guest house addition to an existing villa is given . . . to focus the students' attention on the perceptual elements of a building, the wall surfaces and the spaces they describe . . . the plan is seen as a conceptual tool, a two-dimensional diagram or notational device, with limited capacity to express the perceptual elements which exist in three-dimensional space.' [2]

Graves' buildings have always laid stress on these 'perceptual elements'—especially on the function of the plane as a method of stratifying space and as symbolic of the spaces which it defines or conceals. But in his earlier projects the solid and planar elements in themselves were reduced to zero degree of expressiveness, in accordance with the functionalist precept of minimum interference with the industrial product as 'ready-made'.

In his more recent work these elements have begun to be semantically elaborated. They are no longer the minimal ciphers which go to form a rich metonymy; they become overlaid with meanings belonging to the architectural tradition. Columns develop shafts and capitals; openings are qualified with architraves and pediments; wall surfaces become ornamented. A new dimension of purely architectural metaphor is added to the functionalist and natural metaphors of his earlier work.

It is possible that these ideas developed initially less from a process of deduction than from particular design problems. The use of figural elements seems, for example, to be connected with his habit of extracting the maximum of meaning from a given context. In the Claghorn House of 1974—which seems a pivotal work—the humble motif of a chair rail with bolection mouldings is used as a way of linking the new to the old. This seems to have been suggested by the fact that the existing house had few spatial qualities but a strong nineteenth-century flavour. This carrying through of motifs is similar to the use of the frame in the Benacerraf House. But here the process is reversed. Instead of the new extending its language back into the old, the thematics of the old are reused in the new. As if in sympathy with this, the outside of the addition has a

12 Graves, Claghorn House 1974
In the interior, above, the bolection moulding marks the junction of existing and new. The same moulding appears in the mural, below.
Transammonia Inc., New York 1974

13 Graves, Crooks House
1975
Parti sketch and
elevation

14 Graves, Plocek House
1977
Preliminary elevation
and plan

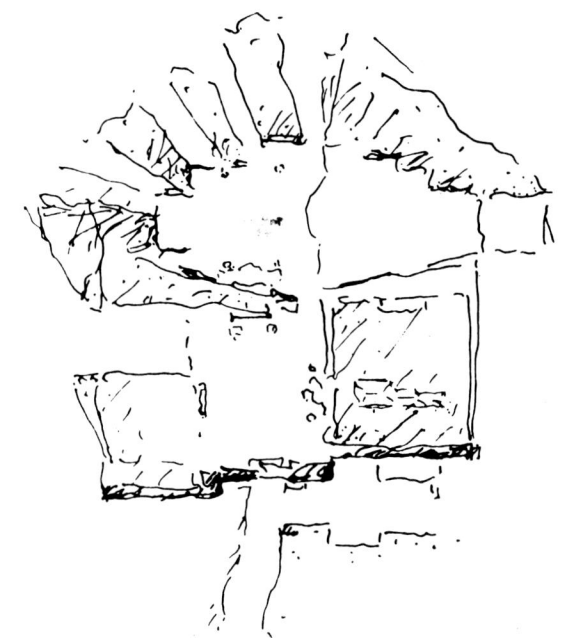

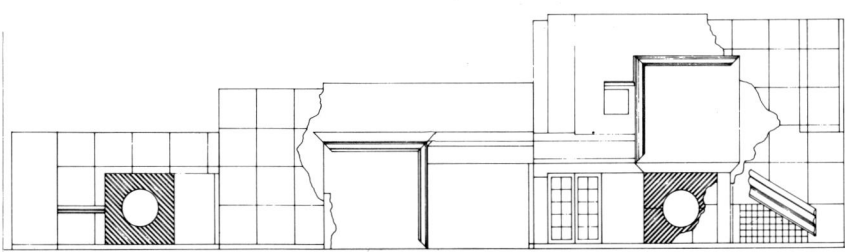

13

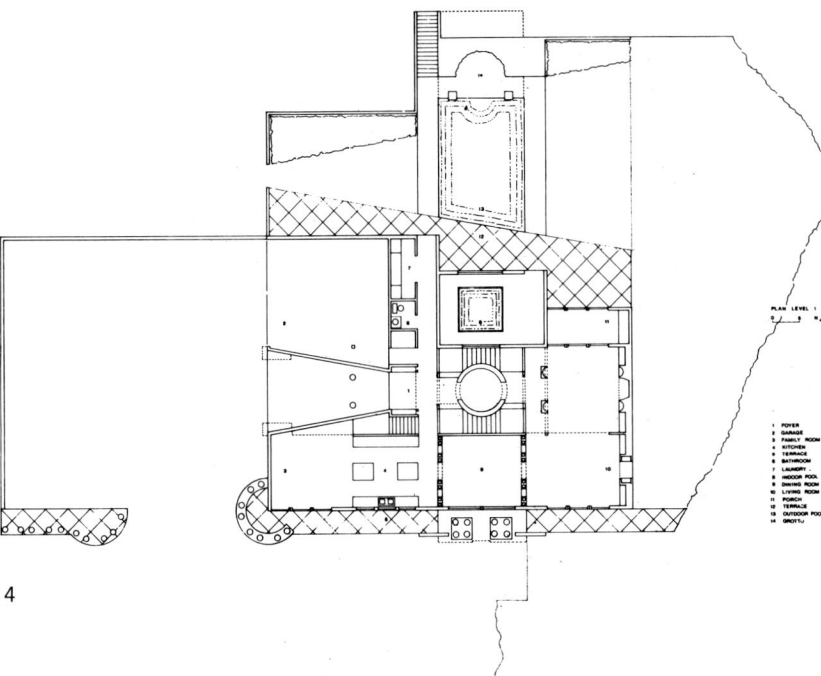

14

heavily figural quality, with a broken pediment and a wall trellis, turning what would have been an inconsequential statement into one which is dense with parabolic meanings. At the same time, sombre colours echoing the period taste of the old house replace the clear colours of the earlier work.

At about the same time, architraves and other figural elements appear in Graves' paintings, underlining the fact that the change to a figurative, ornamental architecture has not altered his method of composition with its dependence on *collage*. It is like the change from analytical to synthetic cubism. Traditional figures are introduced into the architecture as quotations and fragments, as were the functionalist motifs of the earlier work. Because these figures already exist in our memory, and because they are ornamental and not structural, they can be transposed, split up, inverted or distorted without losing their original meanings. The chief sources of this 'metalanguage' are Italian Mannerism, eighteenth-century 'romantic classicism', and the later Beaux-Arts. But in developing a language of ornament which is simple and allows for repetition, Graves has recourse to the language of Art Deco— that 'debased' style which tried to unite the more decorative aspects of Cubism with a remembered tradition of architectural ornament.

In Graves' earlier buildings the fundamental element is the frame or grid, creating an abstract field in which the planes and volumes locate themselves. It is impossible, in such a system, for the wall to develop any density; its function is simply to modulate space. In his more recent work the wall—or the wall fragment—takes the place of the frame as the main organising element. Two consequences follow from this. Firstly, the space is no longer continuous but made up of discrete spatial figures bounded by walls or colonnades. The walls develop thickness and the negative, solid spaces are read as *poché*. Figural space is seen as being carved out of solid mass. During the preliminary stages of the design, the plan is allowed to suggest the spatial composition independently of its three-dimensional consequences; thus, in the Crooks House, the early sketches show no distinction between house walls and garden hedges. According to the code of the plan, they both define space in terms of void and solid, figure and *poché*. But this results in a metaphorical relationship between house and garden; topiary defines internal spaces, whose 'ceiling' is the sky. We see here the ambiguity between fully-enclosed space and semi-enclosed space that has always been a feature in Graves' buildings.

The second consequence of the new importance given to the wall is that the shallow layering of space in the frontal plane of the building, which was previously created by parallel and separate planes suspended in the cage, is now flattened onto the wall surface itself. The wall becomes a bas-relief with layers of ornament built up or peeled away. Fragments of architectural motifs are assembled to create a balanced asymmetrical whole.

The massive architectural elements that occur on the façade are frequently distorted and transposed. Thus, in the studies for the Plocek House, several simultaneous interpretations of the same figures are invited. The main entry is monumentalised by the presence of two giant columns supporting a flat arch. But this monumentality is subverted by

15 Gibbs, St Martin in the Fields 1722
Door moulding
Photograph: David Dunster

16 Graves, Fargo-Moorhead 1977
Bridge study

contradictions. The traditional flat arch with voussoirs is established, but subjected to a figure-ground reversal by the removal of the keystone. The expected pyramidal composition is reversed; the centre is a void between the masses on either side, which become a 'split pair'. The voussoirs are read both in their normal sense as radiating wedges on a flat plane and as the receding lines of a *trompe l'oeil* perspective. The columns are structurally redundant in voussoir construction. Their role as pylons constricting and guarding the entrance is reinforced by the absence of capitals and the insertion of an architrave between them and the arch. Such transformations can be seen as an extension of the Mannerist permutation of a repertoire of figures where two systems of meaning are superimposed and the paradigmic relations are stated explicitly in the same object, for example, in the 'Gibbs surround'.

In his earlier work metonymic meanings had to be created by the relationship between elements which were themselves relatively mute. As soon as established architectural figures become the basic counters relationships are established, not between irreducible forms but between the semantic contents existing in the figures. Graves' buildings now become *bricolages* of recognisable figures complete with their historical connotations. For example, on the bridge of the Fargo-Moorhead project there is an overt reference to Ledoux's barrel-shaped 'House for the director of the river Loue' in the Saline de Chaux; this image is conflated with a frozen waterfall, reminiscent of the ornamental *urne à congélations*.

But it is the way in which Ledoux has reduced the classical repertoire to pure geometrical figures that enables his forms to release primary and archetypal sensations. The historical reference by itself would not be enough. Graves' work therefore depends on eighteenth-century sensationalist theory, not on pure historical associations.

Perhaps the most important single aspect of Graves' work lies in the attitude it reflects towards nature. His work contains a continual dialectic between architecture as the product of reason, setting itself against nature, and architecture as a metaphor for nature. The drama of this dialectic is played out in the architecture itself. The open structure characteristic of his earlier work allows the virtual space of the building to be penetrated by outside space and itself frame the natural landscape. Thus defined by its structural elements, the building remains incomplete—as if arrested in the process of marking out a habitable space. References to the primitive act of building are filtered through the language of Cubism and advanced technology (itself a metaphor since the actual technology is mostly pre-industrial). The round column, isolated against the sky, suggests the tree as primordial building material; free-form profiles either on plan, or (as in the Benacerraf House) in elevation, suggest the presence of nature within the man-made world of the building. There are references to a domesticated nature, as in the use of perforated steel beams with their suggestion of pergolas. An all-pervading nature is also evoked by the association of colours with the primary aspects of nature—sky, earth, water and vegetation. The earlier buildings recall both conservatories and bowers or arbours, which protect man from nature out of nature's own materials.

In the later work, Graves' classicist preferences are for garden structures (topiary and trellises) or for those architectural motifs which are associated with a mythologised nature—rustication, grottos, cascades, ruins. The fragmentation of the buildings suggests the presence of natural obstacles to conceptual completeness and the inability of man to establish order in the face of time and chance. One

17 Ledoux, Director's House on the River Loue
18 Ledoux, Royal Saltworks, Arc-et-Senans 1776 Detail of an opening Photograph: David Dunster

has the impression of an arcadia which is not only irretrievable, but also somehow flawed.

These are the qualities which unite the two phases of Michael Graves' work and allow him to use the language of Cubism or of the classical tradition to recreate an architecture out of its primordial elements; to offer a new and intense interpretation of architecture itself and of man's cultural predicament in relation to nature.

Graves' work is a meditation on architecture. This is to say much more than that it is concerned exclusively with the aesthetic. Such a concern is perfectly compatible with the problem of construction, which, in the case of a Le Corbusier or a Mies, is the *sine qua non* of aesthetic choice and is based on the (aesthetic) principle of economy of means. With Graves this problem is excluded; architectural meaning withdraws into the realm of 'pure visibility'; the substance of the building does not form a part of the ideal world imagined by the architect. Structure becomes a pure representation. The objective conditions of building and its subjective effect are now finally separated. Architecture is created and sustained in the psyche, and its legitimate boundaries are established by voluntary judgment acting on an imagination nourished by history.

The difference between these two systems of representation, and the different status which they attribute to the 'real', can be seen if we compare two works by the engineer Gustav Eiffel. The tower and the Statue of Liberty represent the two poles towards which structure gravitates at the end of the nineteenth century. In the first case, structure is the sufficient and necessary condition of meaning; in the second, the structure is purely 'enabling' and plays no part in the object as a sign. So long as one accepts the traditional distinction between sculpture and architecture the paradoxical relation between these two attitudes remains obscured. But it becomes apparent the moment one sees both sculpture and architecture as modes of representation, where meanings are derived either from the traditional subject of sculpture—the human form—or from architecture itself. Both the human form and its 'house' are perceived as cultural 'traces', not as natural and objective 'referents'. If architecture becomes the subject of representation, this representation necessarily includes the memory of the 'problem' of structure.

This system of representation is the exact opposite of the 'classical' process by which the ephemeral was translated into the durable, according to which durability as such was a value, and materiality a symbol of the transcendental. With the instrumentalisation of structure, the mythic is re-channelled, and, in the Modern Movement, takes up its abode in instrumentality itself. In the architecture of Michael Graves, the alternative route is taken. The myth becomes pure myth, recognised as such, and the architectural sign floats in the dematerialised world of *gestalt*, and the de-historicised world of memory and free association.

Notes
1 Manfredo Tafuri, 'American Graffiti: Five x Five = Twenty-five', *Oppositions* 5.
2 M. Graves, 'The Swedish Connection', *Journal of Architectural Education*, Sept. 1975.

Union County Nature and Science Museum
1967
Mountainside, New Jersey

This museum in the Watchung Mountains of northern New Jersey was intended to house exhibitions of local flora and fauna. Its programme required a lecture room, amphitheatre, greenhouse and exhibition space for permanent and changing installations. The building is organised in several zones, progressing from the enclosed lecture room for visitor orientation near the entrance, to more open exhibition space, to the semi-enclosed open-air amphitheatre (not built) and finally to the park-like setting of the reservation in which the museum is located. Sequential layers, corresponding to the structural grid, frame views to the landscape which gradually become more open as one moves toward the outdoor. This serial, scenographic organisation also allows future additions to the building to continue the architectural promenade. The axonometrics show the complete building of which only the auditorium and foyer were built.

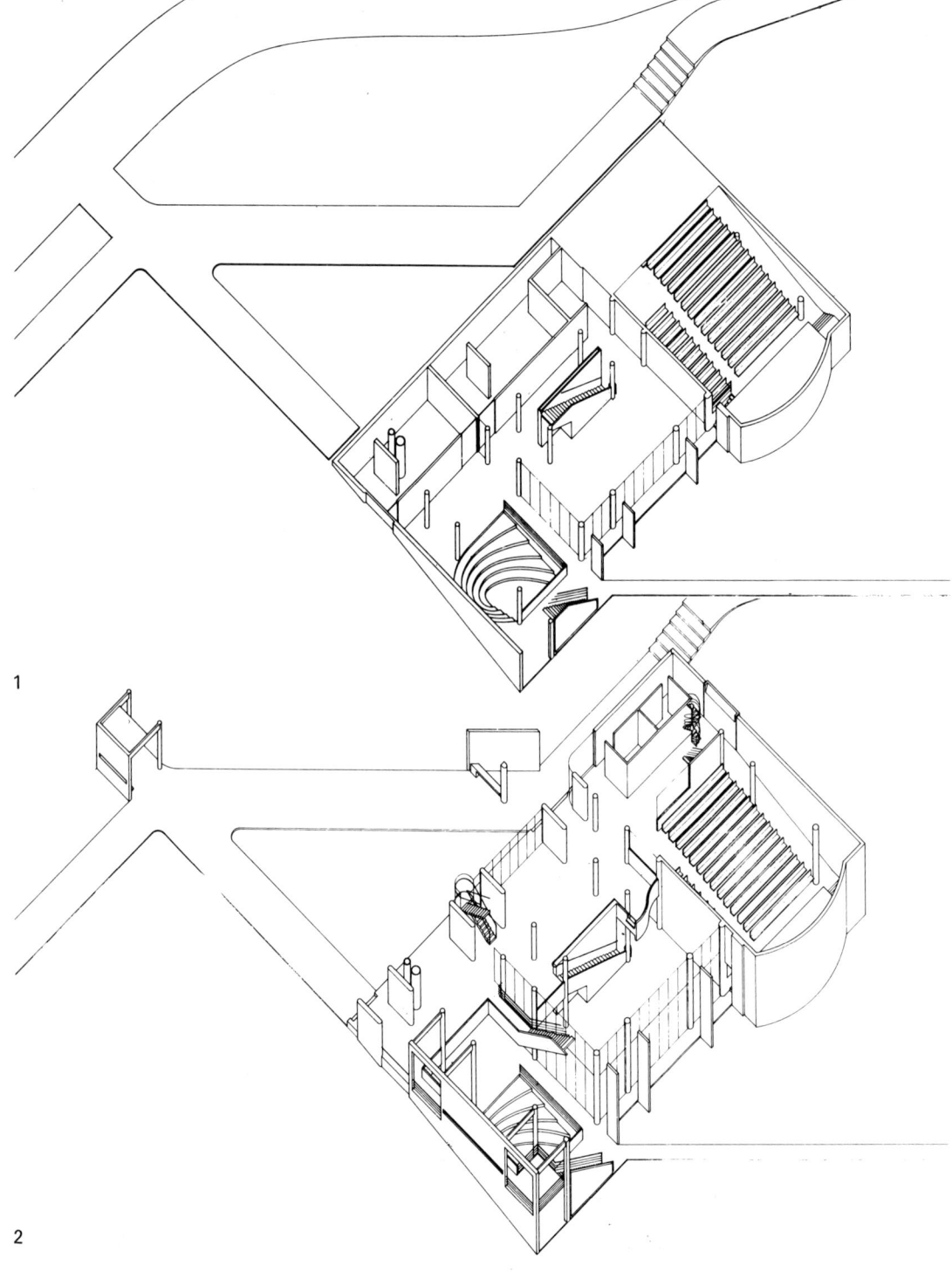

1 Axonometric: lower level
2 Axonometric: entrance level

UNION COUNTY MUSEUM

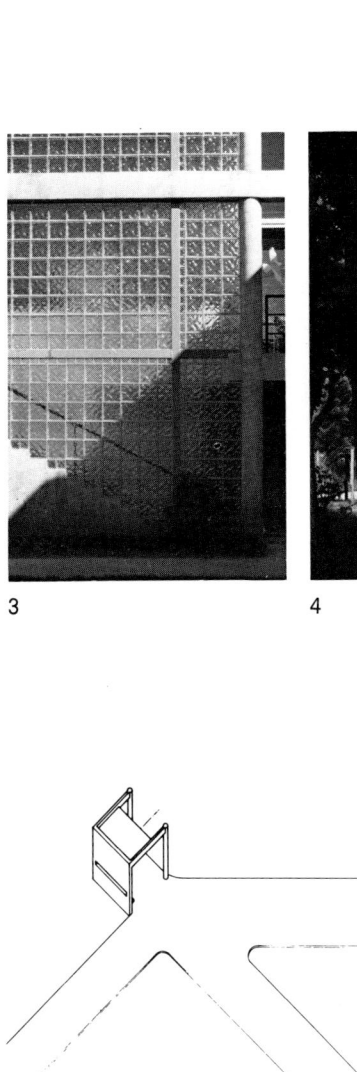

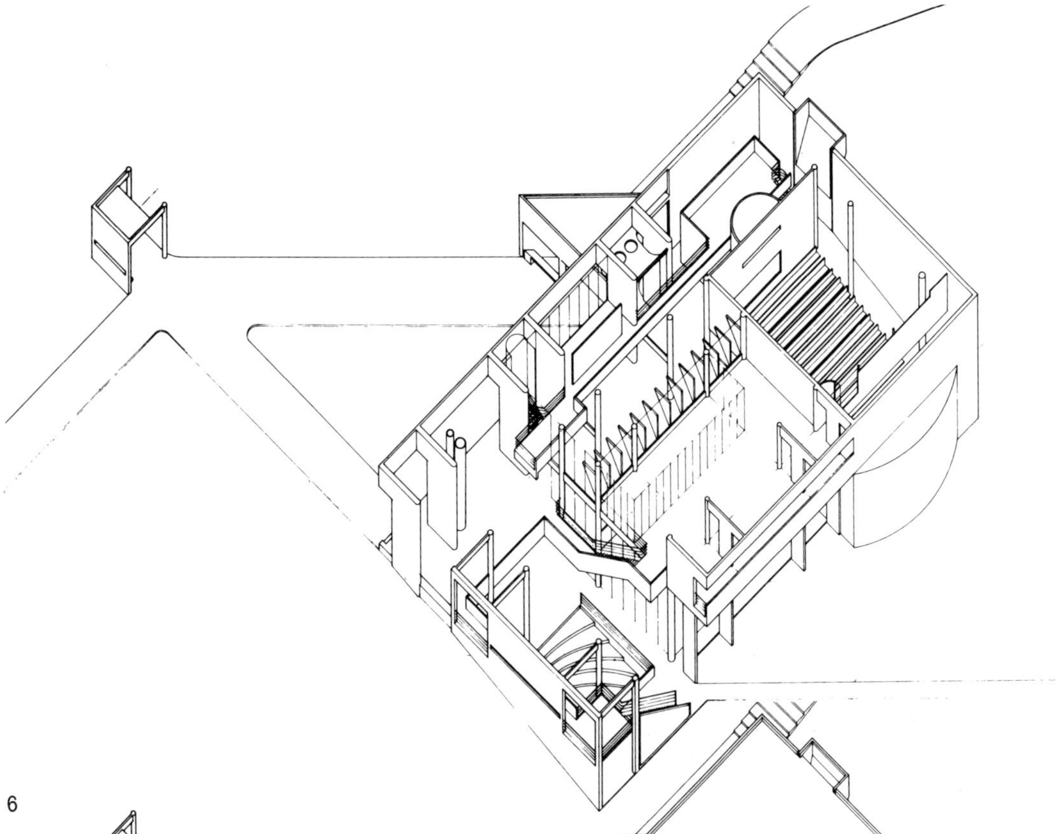

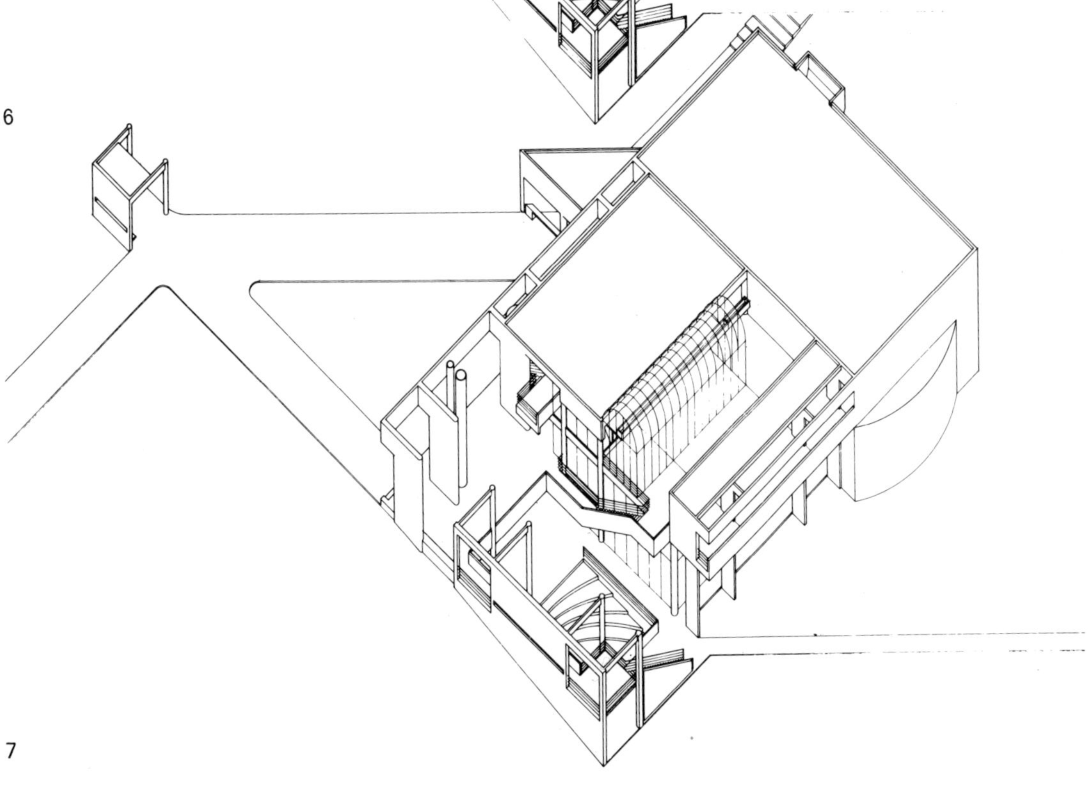

3 Garden wall
4 Garden entrance façade
5 Detail: stairway to upper level offices
6 Axonometric: upper level
7 Axonometric: roof level

Hanselmann House
1967
Fort Wayne, Indiana

This house for a family of two adults and four children is located on a corner site which is entered adjacent to a stream running diagonally through the property. The house is a double square in plan and volumetrically a double cube, with one open and the other enclosed. The house is understood frontally by the layering of three principal façades. The first of these, consisting of a pipe-rail frame and the front plane of a studio house (which have not been built), defines the outer edge of the house's precinct. It acts as a gate, receiving the stair between the ground and the entrance level. The main volume of the house is entered at the second primary façade located at the centre of the composition. This point of entry is also reflected in the distortion of the roof terrace plan, above. The third façade, which is the densest, is the rear wall of the house containing the mural. The imagery of the mural, painted by the architect, identifies elements of the house's composition and of the surrounding landscape. An outdoor terrace on the ground level relates to the diagonal of the stream and implies a larger compositional frame in which the idealised geometry of the house is seen in opposition to the natural landscape.

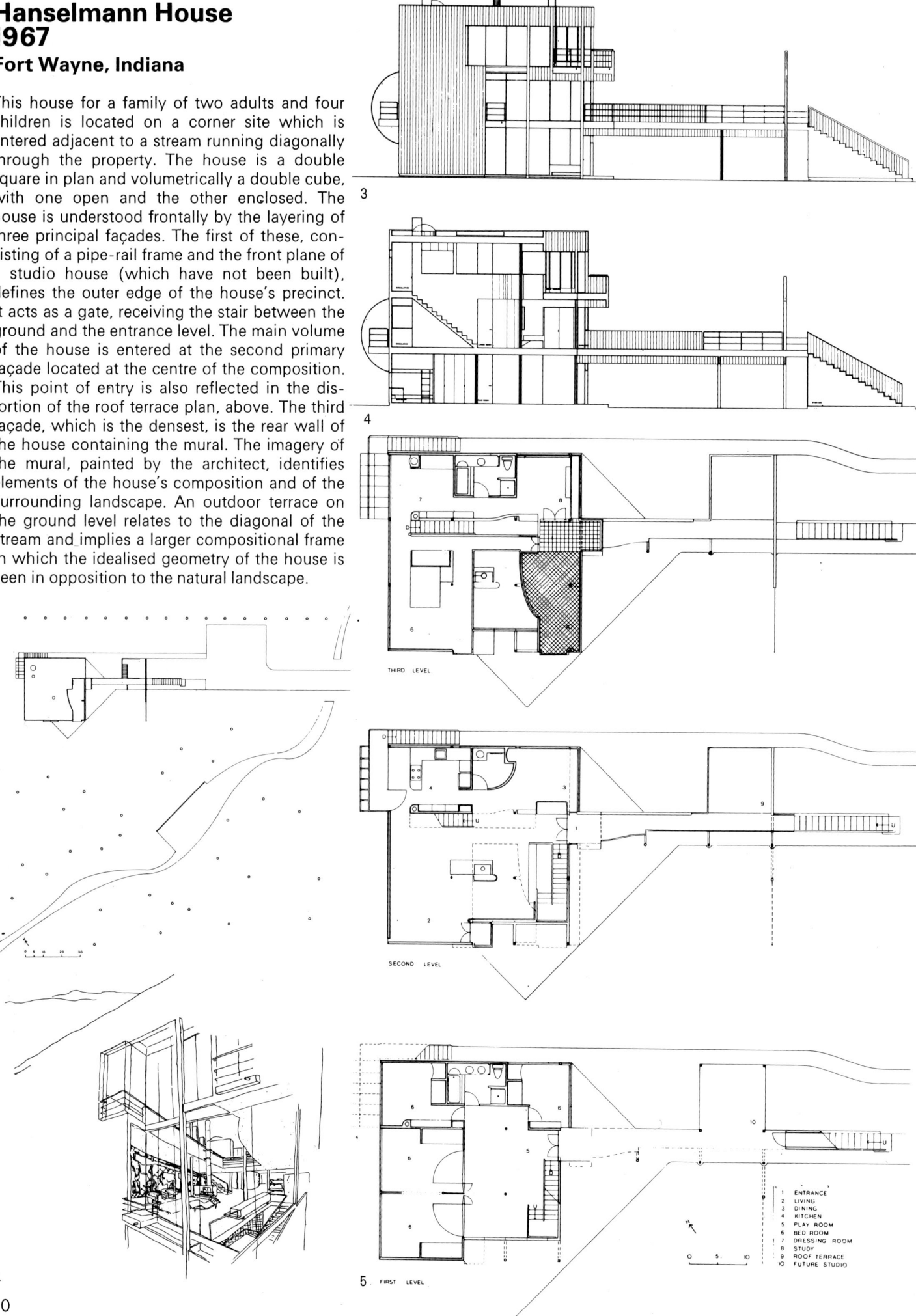

HANSELMANN HOUSE

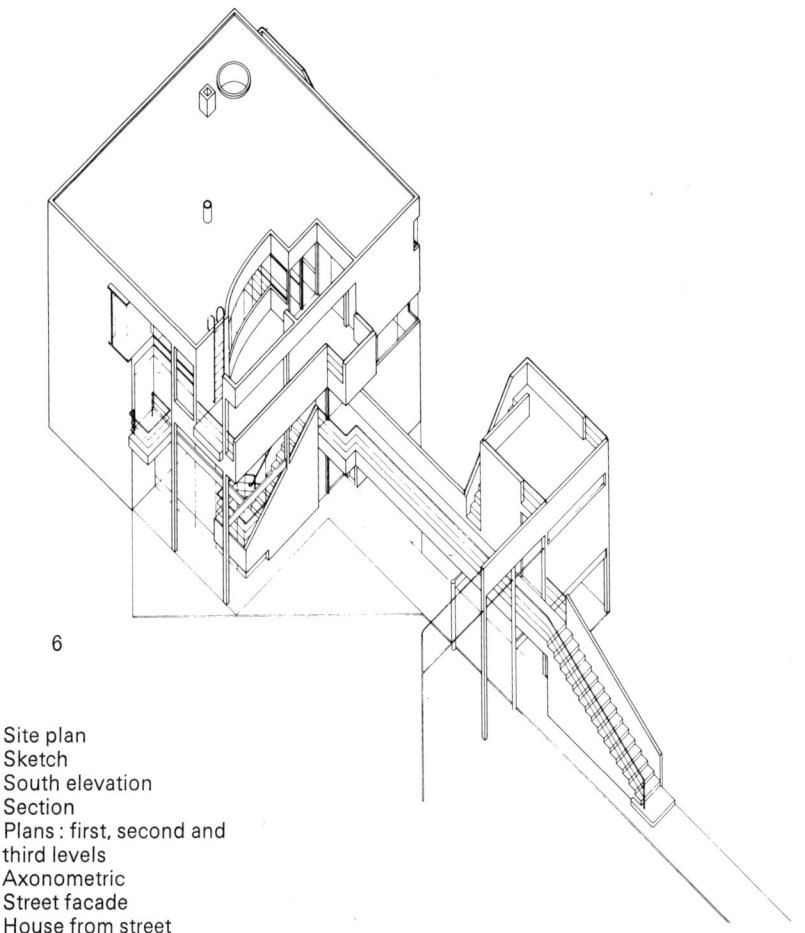

1 Site plan
2 Sketch
3 South elevation
4 Section
5 Plans: first, second and third levels
6 Axonometric
7 Street facade
8 House from street
  Photograph: Jim Offerle

HANSELMANN HOUSE

9 Entrance to living room
10 Street façade
11 Living room with mural
12 Living room
Photographs 9–12:
Tom Yee

9

10

HANSELMANN HOUSE

11

12

The Newark Museum Master Plan 1968
Newark, New Jersey

The Newark Museum master plan expands existing facilities with new gallery spaces, administrative offices and an amphitheatre. The existing buildings are organised by the new construction which consists of a series of linked pavilions surrounding the garden, allowing the various activities to function independently or as part of the larger organisation. The garden is developed as an outdoor room which contains artifacts such as large-scale sculpture.

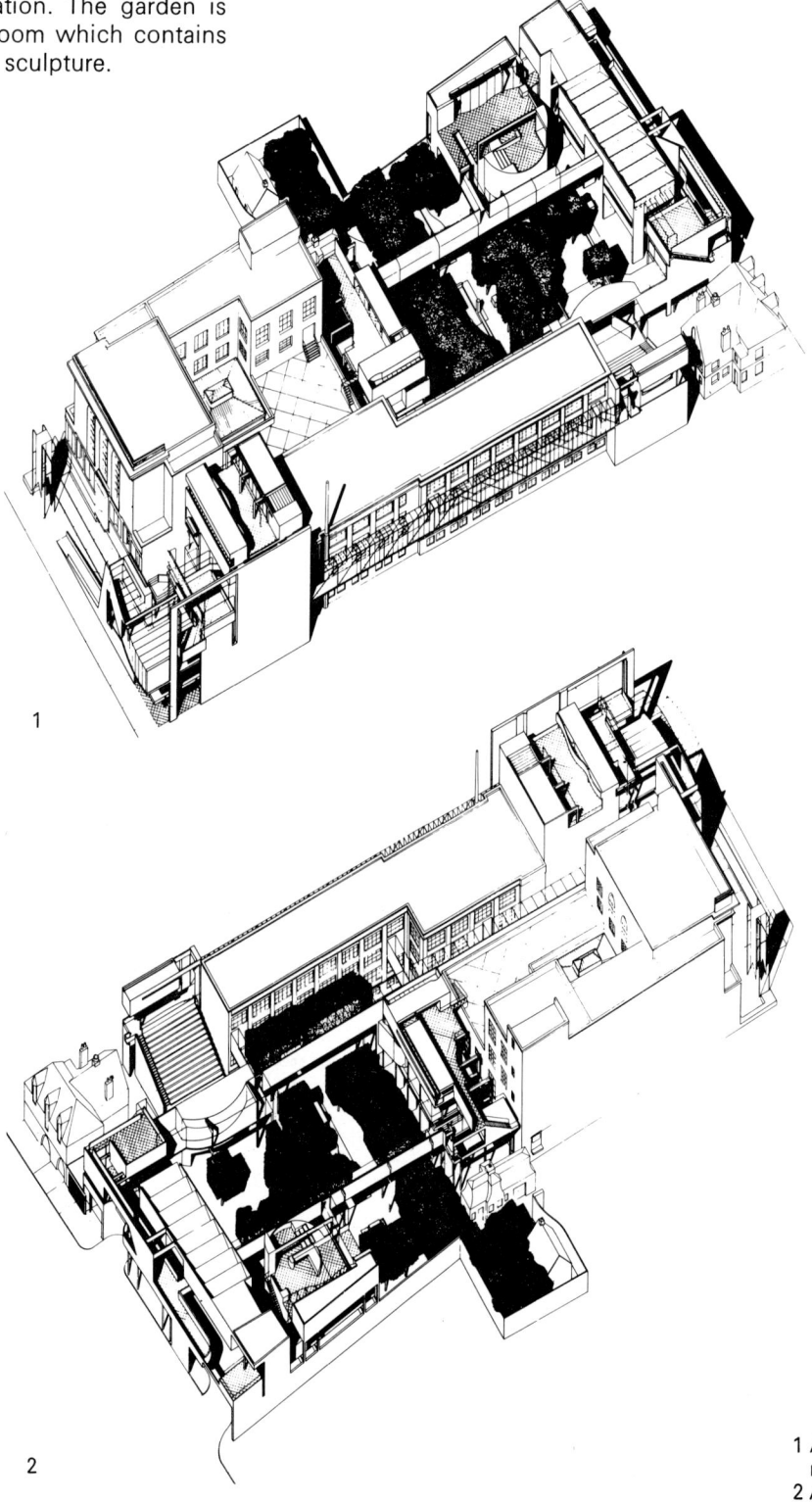

1 Axonometric: view from north
2 Axonometric: view from south

NEWARK MUSEUM

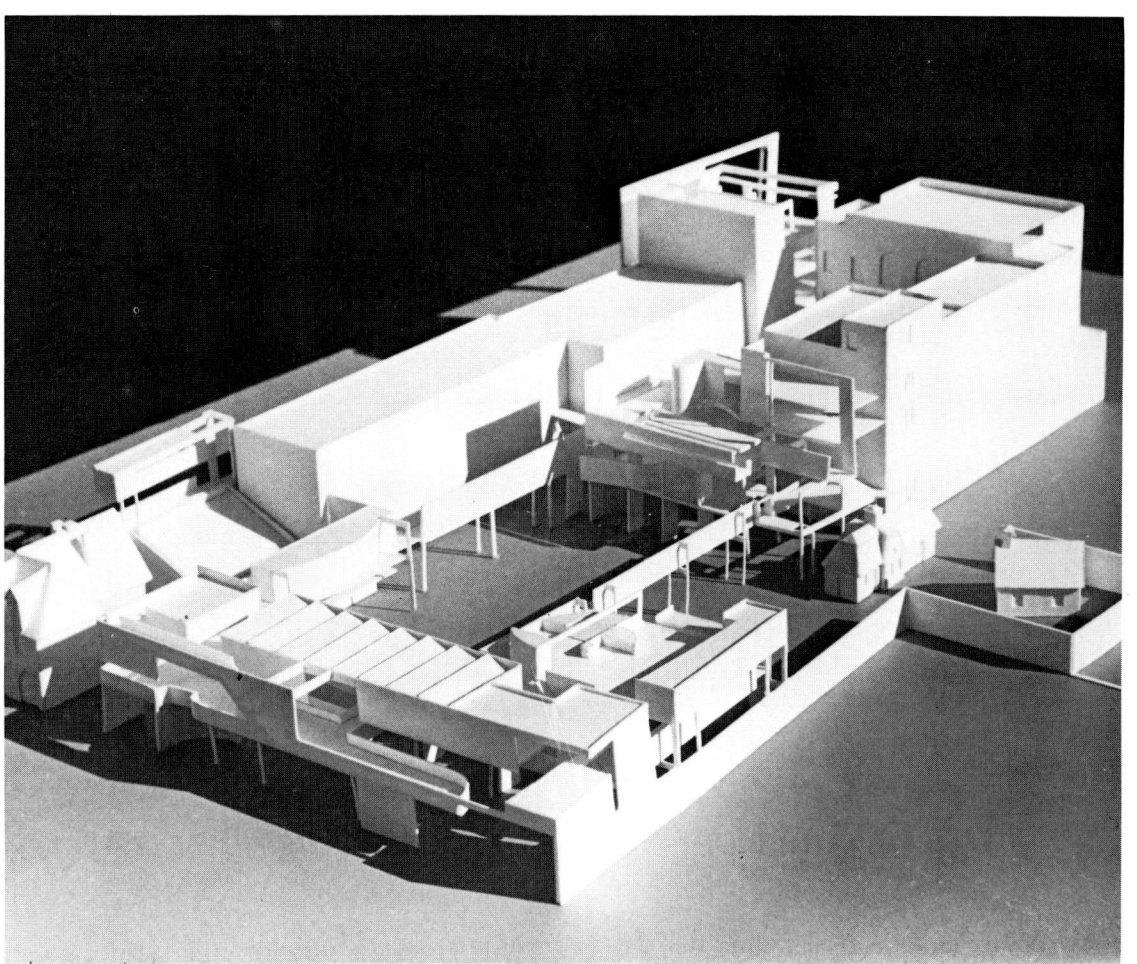

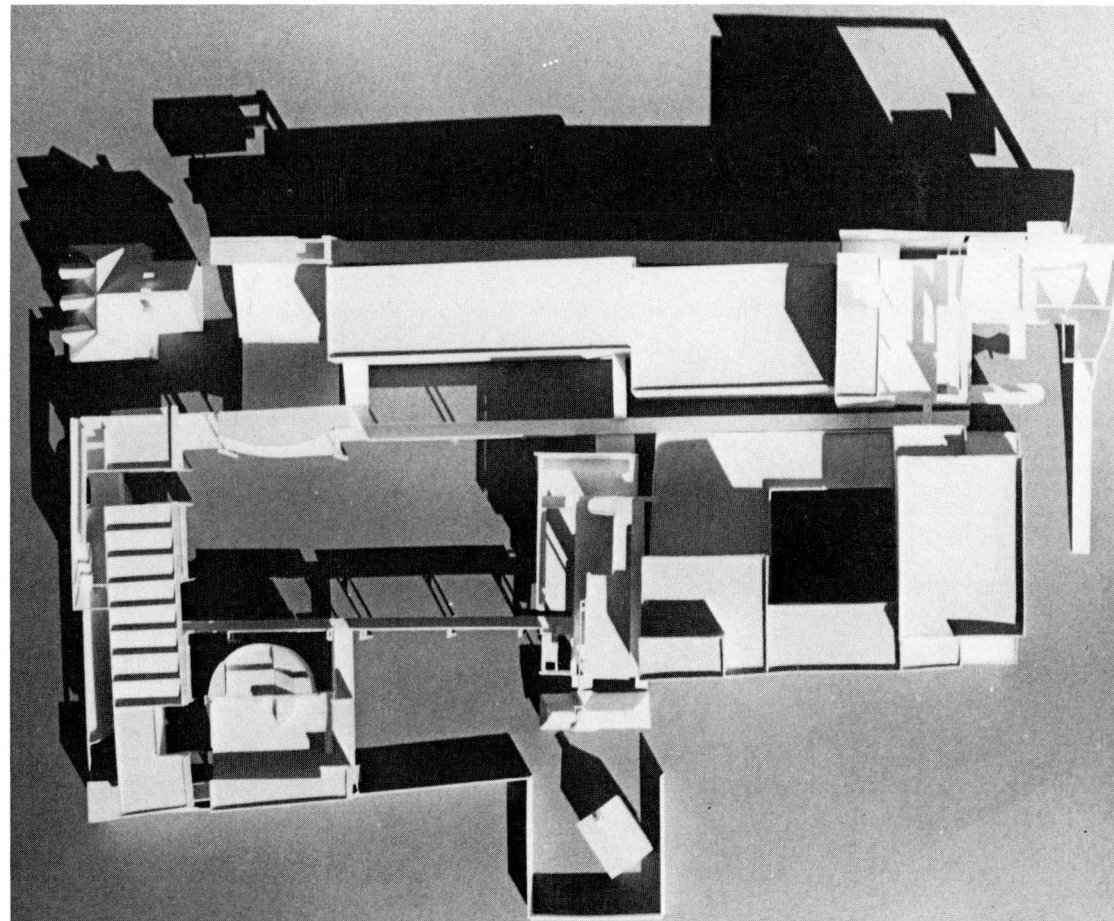

3 Model, showing south and west sides
4 Model

25

Benacerraf House
1969
Princeton, New Jersey

The Benacerraf House addition was intended both as a free-standing pavilion in the garden and as a logical continuation of the original house grid. The new composition momentarily terminates the existing main axis from the street and turns it toward the garden and the preferred light. The south façade, now primary, articulates a dialogue between nature and manmade artifact that is both actual and metaphorical. It acts as a sunscreen for the addition's roof terrace and at the same time, through the lyrical, curvilinear profile of its opening, reinterprets characteristics found in nature. The opening frames one's view to the garden and the sky and can be seen a representation of a treeline or clouds. On the same façade, the beam which supports the second storey is equivalent in height to a hedgerow along the south border of the garden; painted green, the beam implies an association with the hedge in order to engage the space held between.

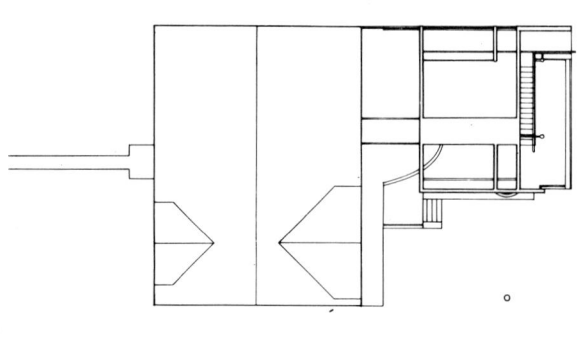

3

1

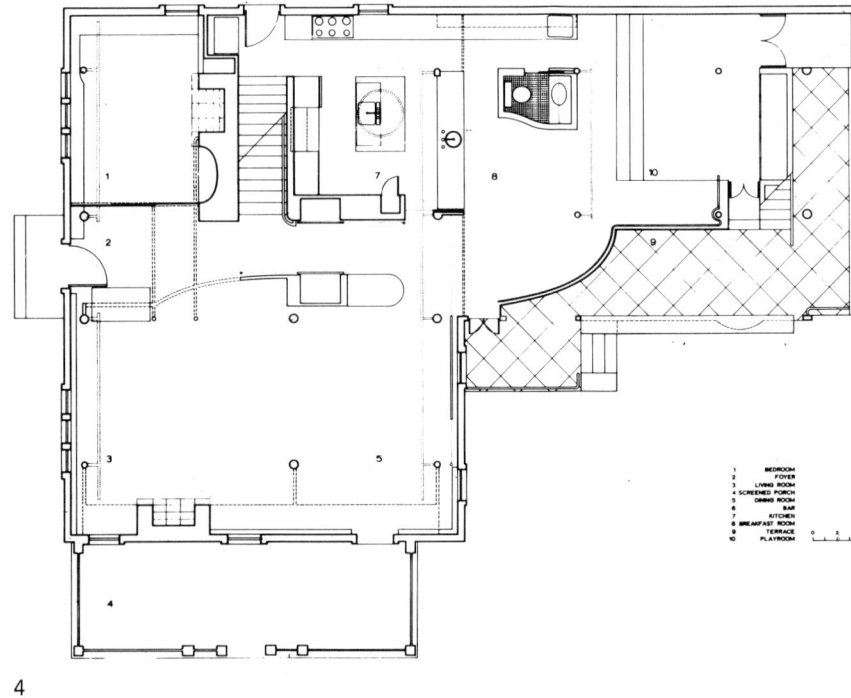

4

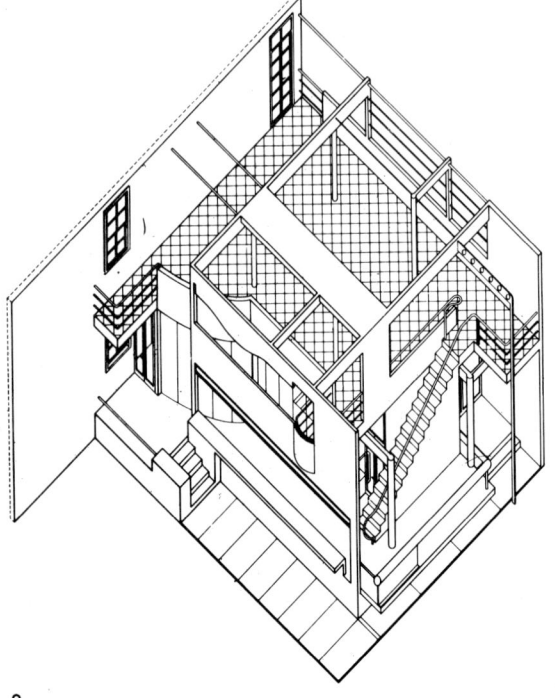

2

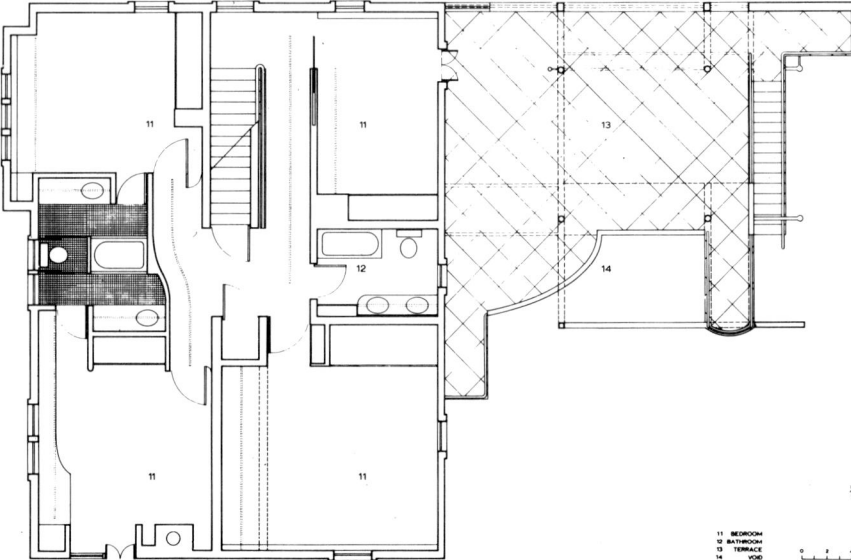

5

BENACERRAF HOUSE

6

1 Detail: roof terrace
2 Axonometric
3 Site plan
4 Ground floor plan
5 Upper floor plan
6 Three quarter view
　Photograph: Laurin
　McCraken
7 South façade
　Photograph: Laurin
　McCracken

7

Rockefeller House
1969
Pocantico Hills, New York

The Rockefeller House was designed as a residence for a family of six on a steeply sloping site with a distant view to the Hudson River. The house was to include separate sleeping quarters for four children, maids' quarters, guest room, swimming pool and large outdoor recreation areas within the immediate grounds of the house.

The building is organised so that the driveway passes through the west façade into the precinct of the house and ascends to the entrance at the high point of the site. Family areas are located on the entrance level and bedrooms on the ground level below. Both the roof and the ground have been developed as terraces for large outdoor social events.

In the composition, the landscape and the building are treated as interacting forces. The west façade serves as a datum for an interdependency of house and site that is both actual and conceptual. As the entry façade, it marks the edge of the house's domain and implies a building mass behind it into which natural elements, such as the figural void of the enclosed court, the pool and the rock outcropping, are seen to intrude. The guest pavilion has in turn been pulled away from the mass of the house, assuring the privacy and separateness that this element requires.

The west façade also acts conceptually as the edge between the natural and the man-made. The lyrical, freely disposed elements within the plan represent on a metaphorical level the introduction of natural characteristics into the rational grid of the house.

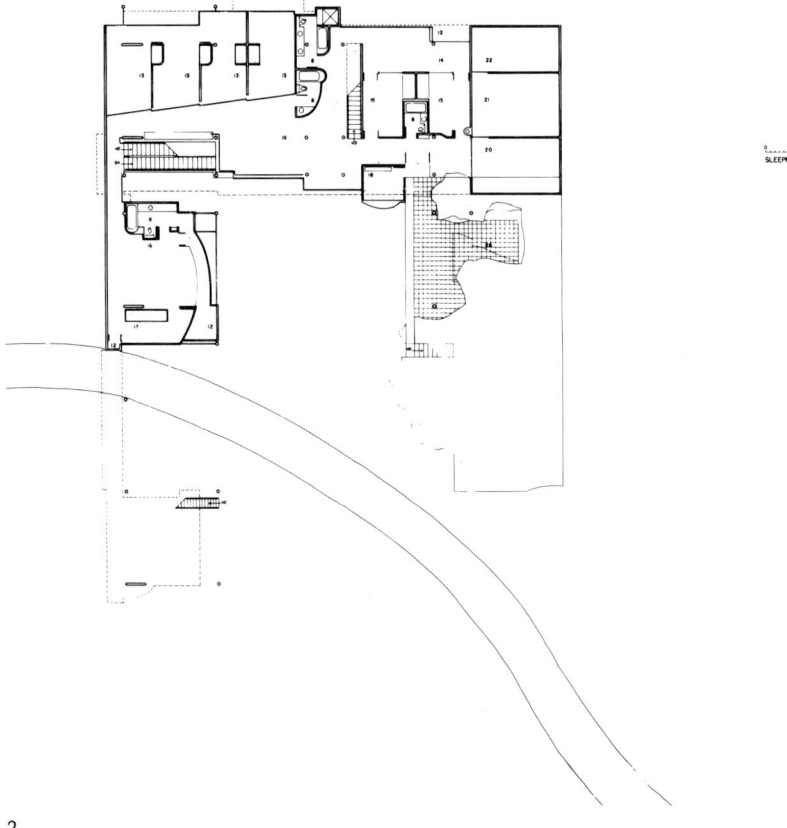

2

1

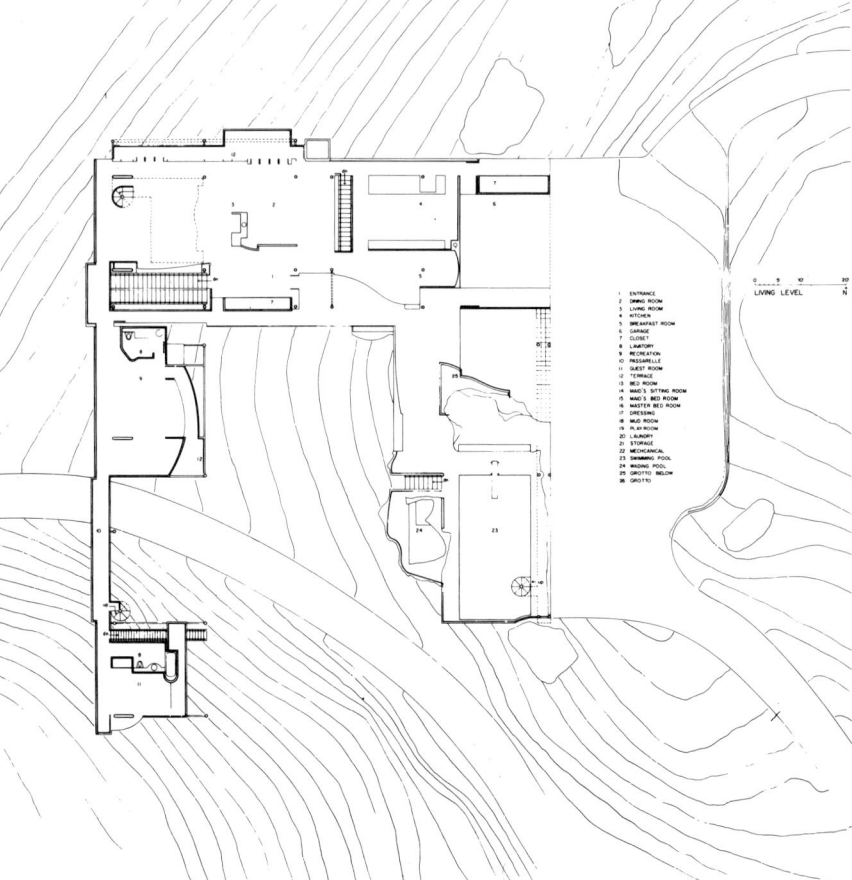

3

ROCKEFELLER HOUSE

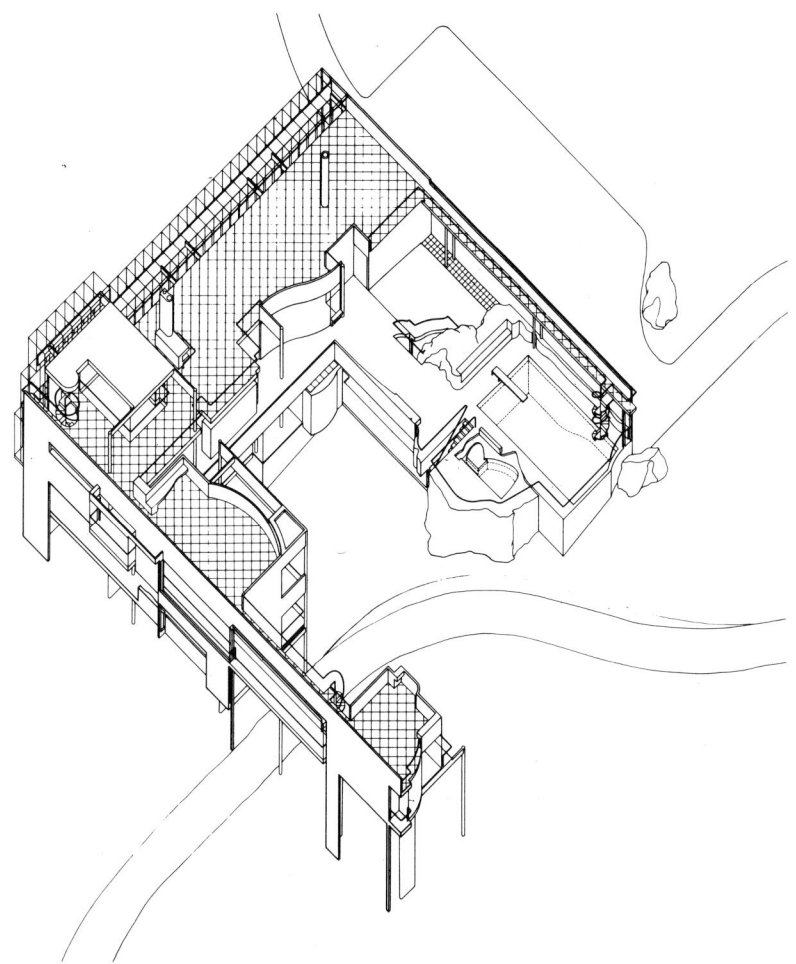

1 Model : roof plan
2 Plan : sleeping level
3 Plan : living level
4 Axonometric
5 Model viewed from west

4

5

Keeley Guest House
1972
Princeton, New Jersey

This addition, located on the garden side of an existing house, contains a writer's studio and a guest room for a university professor and his wife. It is intended to be both a free-standing pavilion in the garden and a logical extension of the original house. The studio is located at ground level in order to place it in the garden and connected to the main house by a covered walkway, allowing it to be a direct extension of the social spaces of the house. The guest room is made more private by its location on the second floor. The third level terrace can be used for sunning.

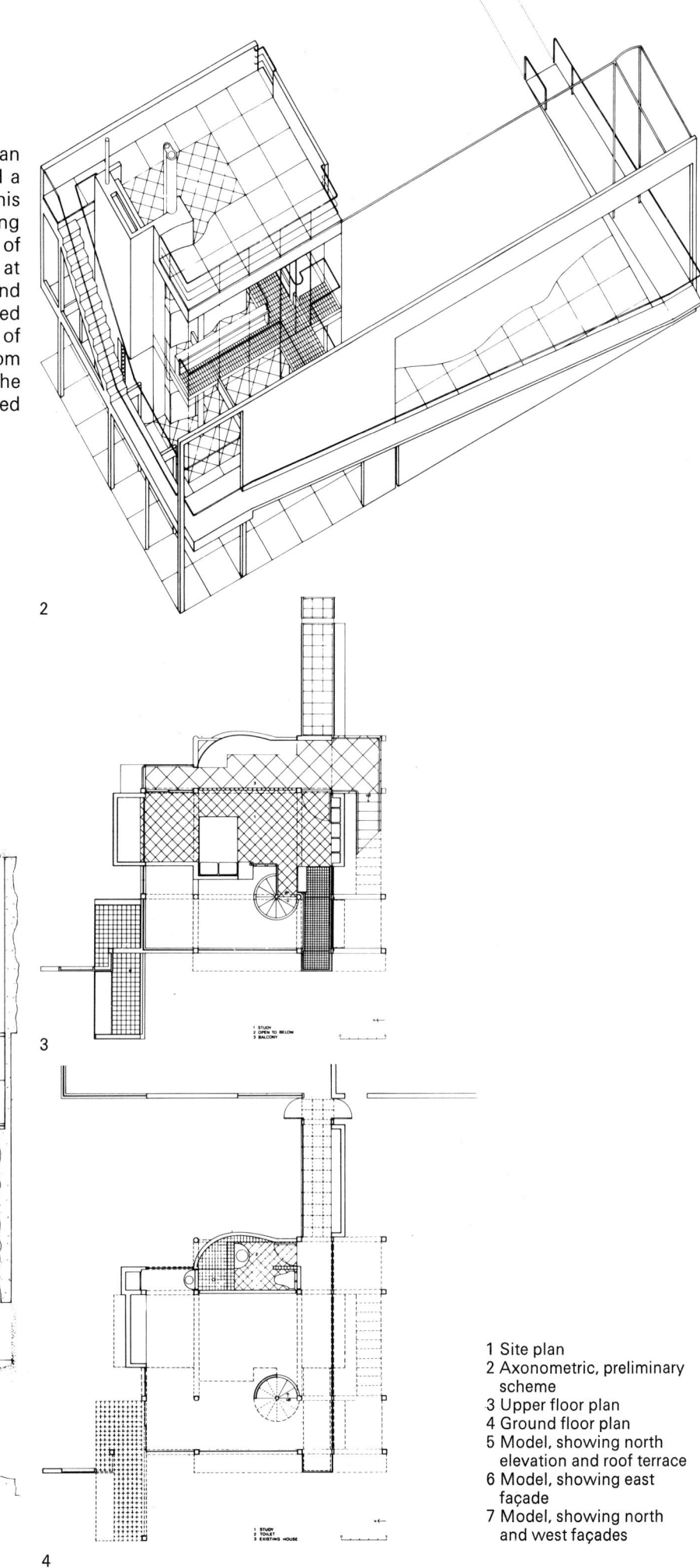

1 Site plan
2 Axonometric, preliminary scheme
3 Upper floor plan
4 Ground floor plan
5 Model, showing north elevation and roof terrace
6 Model, showing east façade
7 Model, showing north and west façades

KEELEY GUEST HOUSE

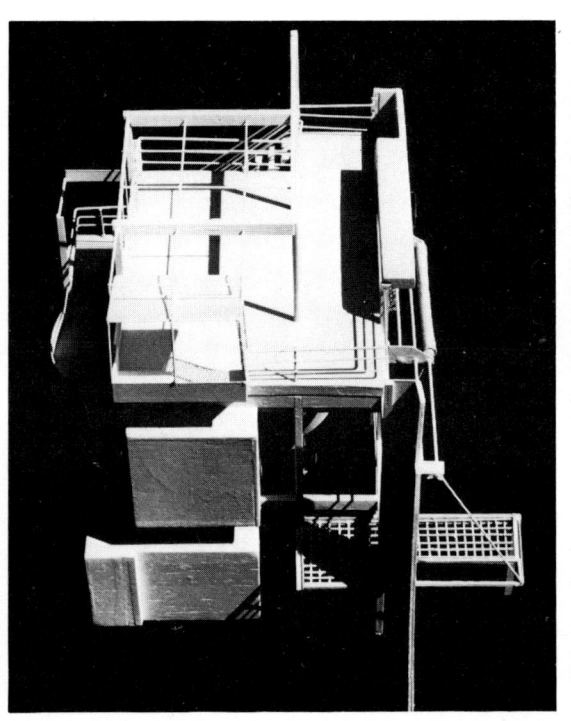

5

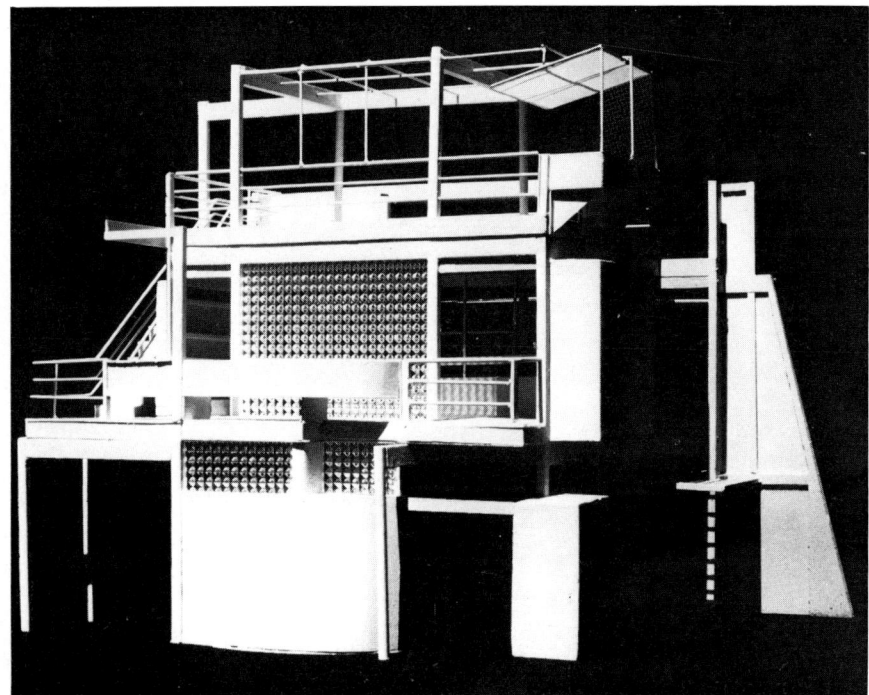

6

7

Medical Office
Ear, Nose & Throat
Associates
1971
Fort Wayne, Indiana

In this project, a single open space on the ground floor of a 1920s medical office building in Fort Wayne has been renovated for a medical group. The space, which is eleven feet high, has been subdivided by a series of lower, linked pavilions. The eight-foot height of these pavilions allows the large space, with its regular, gridded lighting, to be seen as continuous while providing smaller, more intimate rooms for particular functions such as reception, examining rooms and doctors' offices.

The patient's path through the office is a circular progression from the entry and waiting area to the examination and treatment centre and back, past scheduling and bookkeeping. The treatment centre, with the examining rooms grouped around a central nurses' station, is rotated in plan to emphasise its programmatic importance. Each of the examining rooms is completely enclosed to provide acoustical separation from the main space, while skylights in their ceiling allow a sense of the space beyond. Murals painted by the architect are located in each of the examining rooms and in a curving alcove opposite the nurses' station. The murals extend the interior spaces visually by allowing the viewer to identify with the totemic objects placed in them.

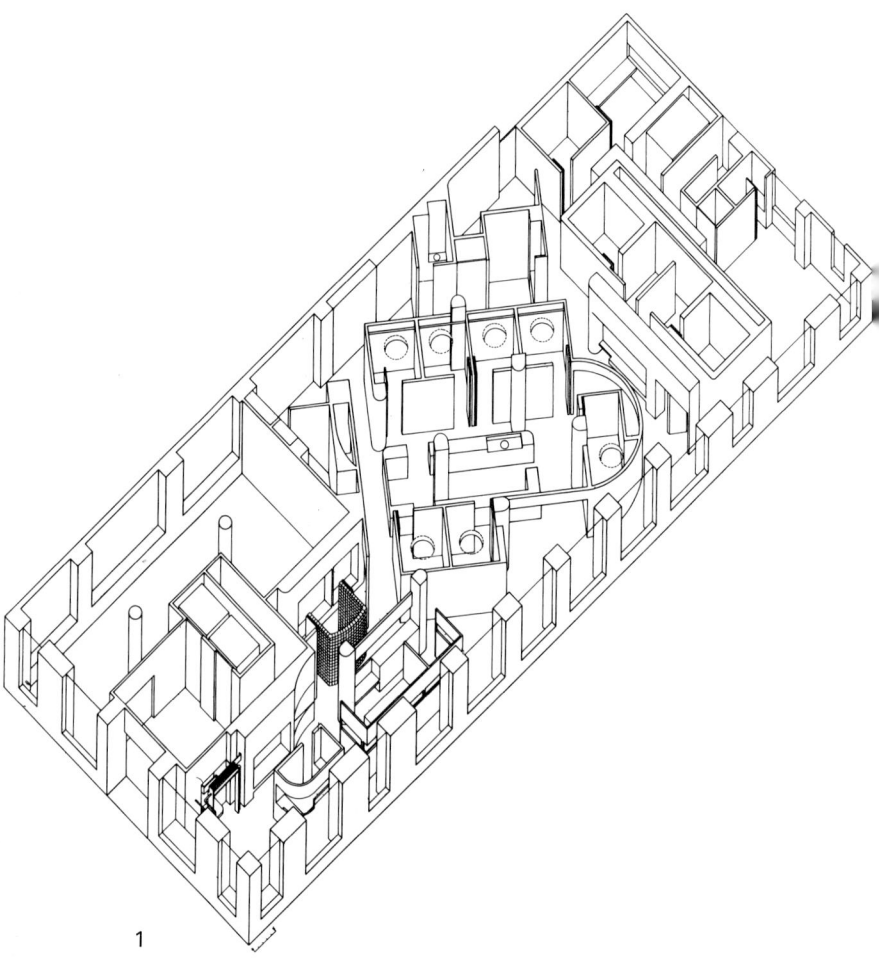

1

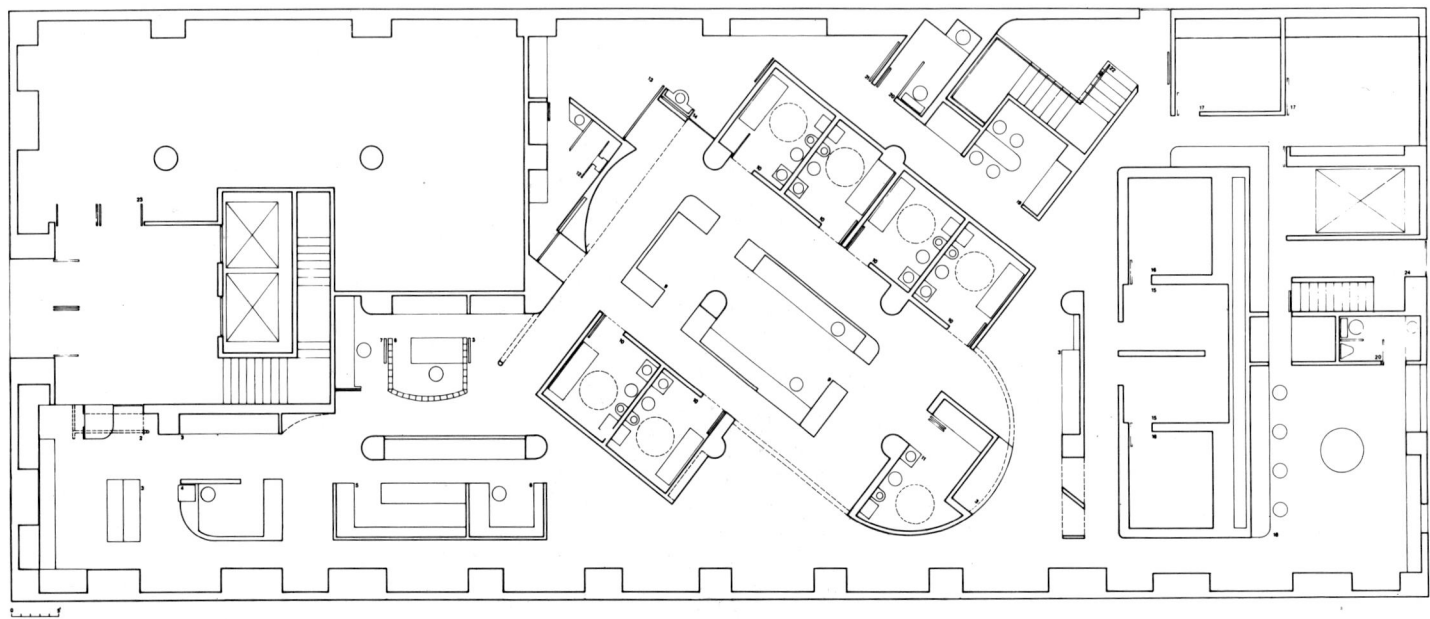

2

MEDICAL OFFICES

1 Axonometric
2 Plan
3 Entrance to waiting room
4 Office wall detail

MEDICAL OFFICES

5 Nurses' station mural
6 Nurses' station
7 Nurses' station mural and examining room
8 Examining room
  Photograph: Balthazar Korab
9 Examining Room
  Photograph: Balthazar Korab
10 Examining room

5

6

7

MEDICAL OFFICES

8

9

10

Snyderman House
1972
Fort Wayne, Indiana

The Snyderman House is located on a heavily wooded forty-acre site in Fort Wayne. The site is distinguished by a pond and a flat plateau opposite each other on an axis perpendicular to the natural entrance to the area. The house stands at the intersection of these two axes, with the main entrance in the east façade.

The programme required a private residence for a family of six. The children's rooms were designed to convert to a guest suite in the future. The plan is composed in four quadrants. The main stair occurs at the intersection of the two axes, just as the house itself occupies this special position in relation to the larger site. The rooms are organised both to take advantage of the appropriate exposure to the sun and to establish a progression from the entrance to the most private spaces. By its east-west alignment, the building, as man-made, is put in an ideal position in relation to the sun whose path from the front façade to the back traces both the course of a day's activities in the rooms and the movement from collective to more individual private spaces.

Throughout the design, there is an interaction of opposed elements—flat and curved, interior and exterior, public and private—which is derived from an understanding of the house in its natural setting. The interaction between man-made and natural occurs at a metaphorical level and also permeates the built composition. The 'natural' is taken to mean that which shows the attributes of nature—irregularity, lyricism, movement. Similarly, 'man-made' becomes synonymous with idealised form, geometry, stasis. The curved forms of the guest suite and its oblique orientation, for instance, are seen in opposition to the idealised square of the house, in keeping with its programmatic separateness. Polychromy is used to refer to both natural and man-made elements. The colours modify the perfection assumed in the white frame and make allusions to the adjacent landscape.

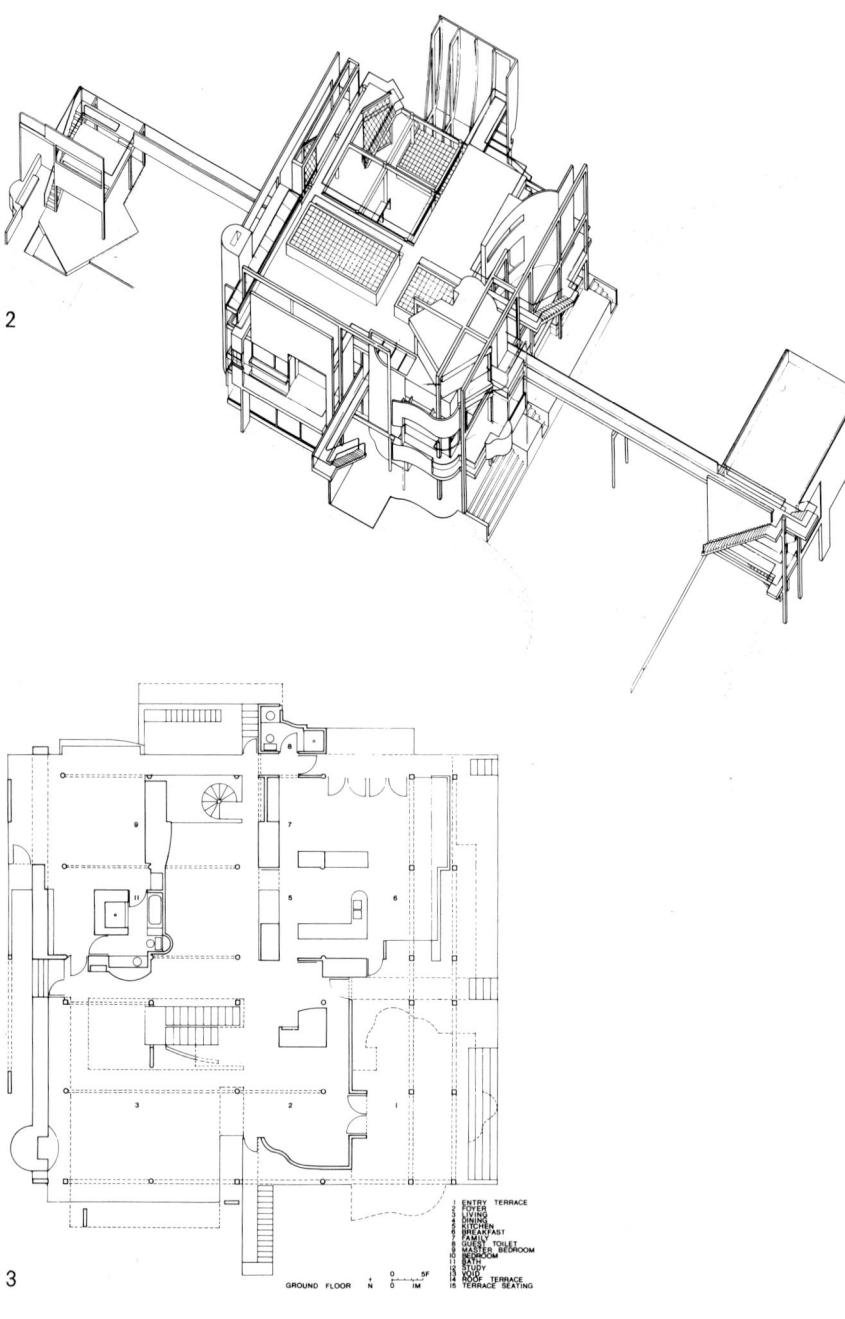
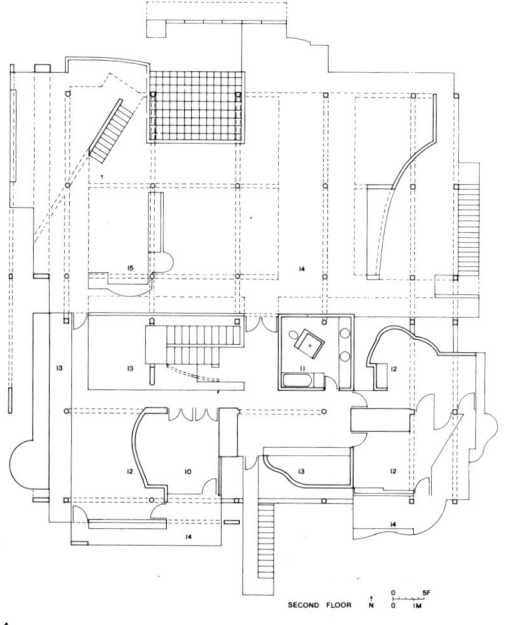
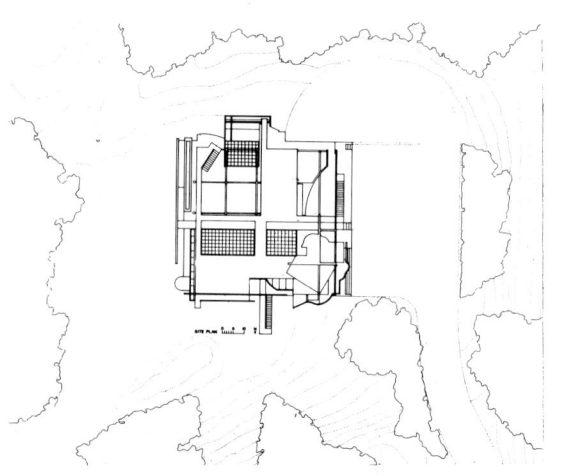

1 Site plan
2 Axonometric, preliminary scheme
3 Ground floor plan
4 Upper floor plan
5 West elevation
6 East elevation
7 North elevation
8 South elevation

SNYDERMAN HOUSE

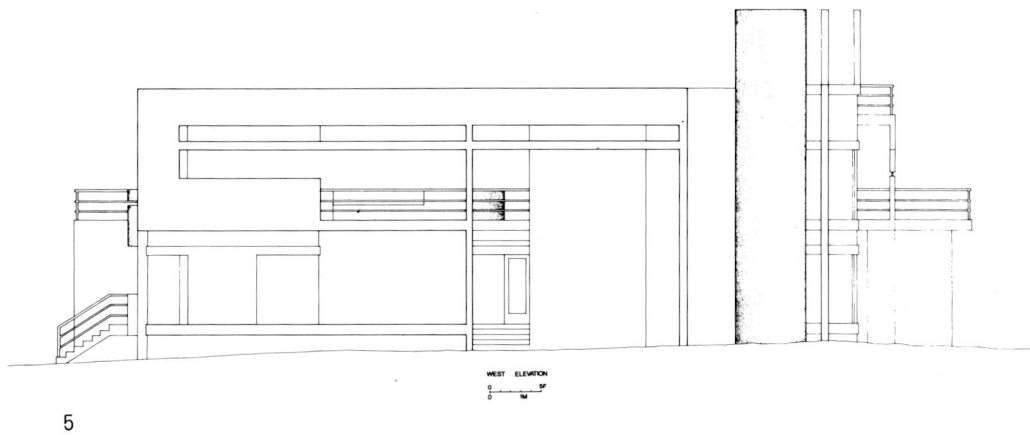

5

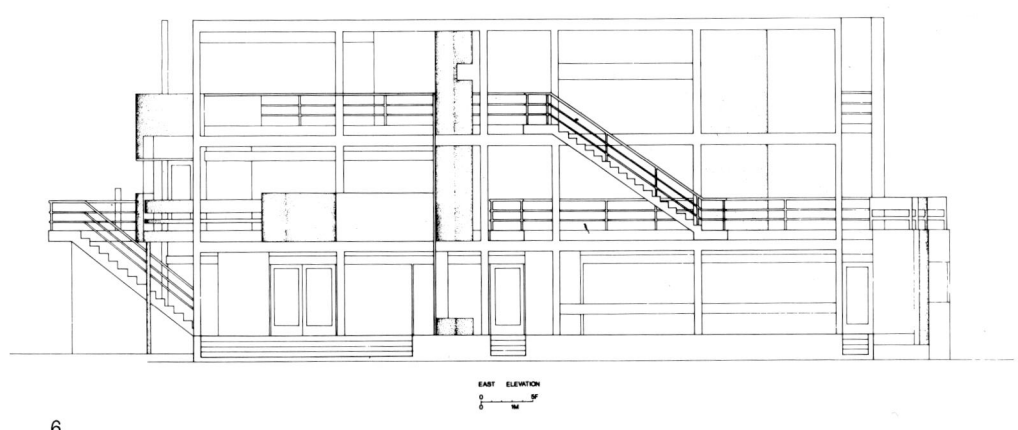

6

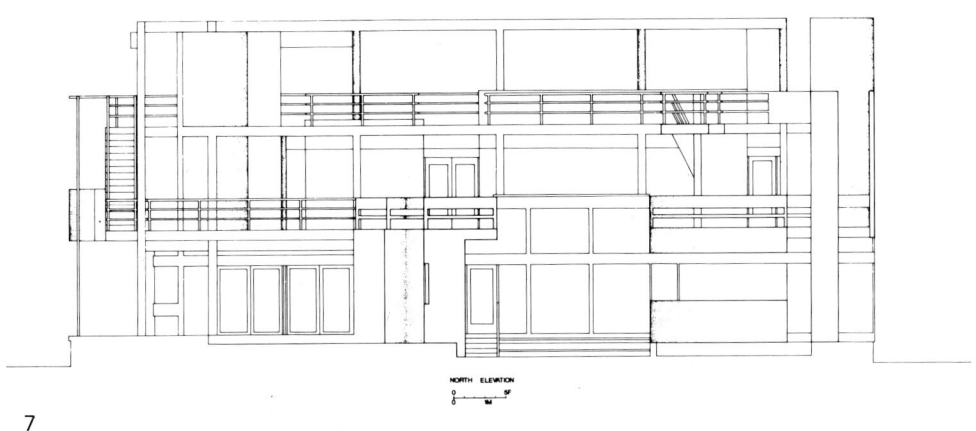

7

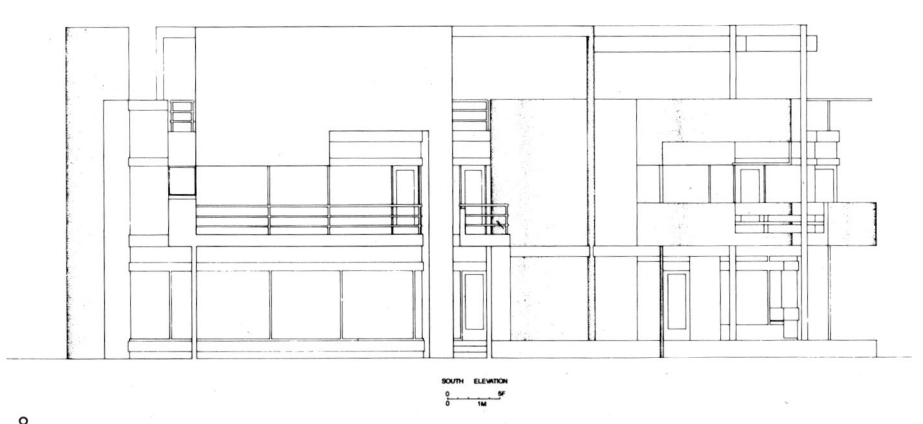

8

SNYDERMAN HOUSE

9

10

SNYDERMAN HOUSE

11

9 South façade
10 East façade
11 Detail of south façade
12 Stair
13 Dining room with mural

12   13

Investment Office
Gunwyn Ventures
1972
Princeton, New Jersey

The upper three floors of an existing nineteenth-century office building in Princeton were renovated for a capital investment firm. The clients required separate offices for the three principal partners, with provision for two future junior partners. All were to share centralised secretarial services and a conference room which was intended to be the most private space.

Major sections of the structure between the second floor and the roof were removed and an independent system of columns and beams erected within the resulting volume. The open plan arrangement placed within this spatial context allows privacy where required without disrupting an overall reading of the open space. The zones of activity are distributed hierarchically along the main axis; the conference room is placed at the head of the axis on the street edge.

A mural painted by the architect gives visual extension to the space and unites the two stories of open offices adjacent to it. References to the landscape both in this mural and in the polychromed elements throughout the space provide a metaphorical dimension to the scheme, which complements the openness of the plan and suggests that a continuity exists between the interior spaces of the new office and the outdoor roof terrace beyond.

1

2

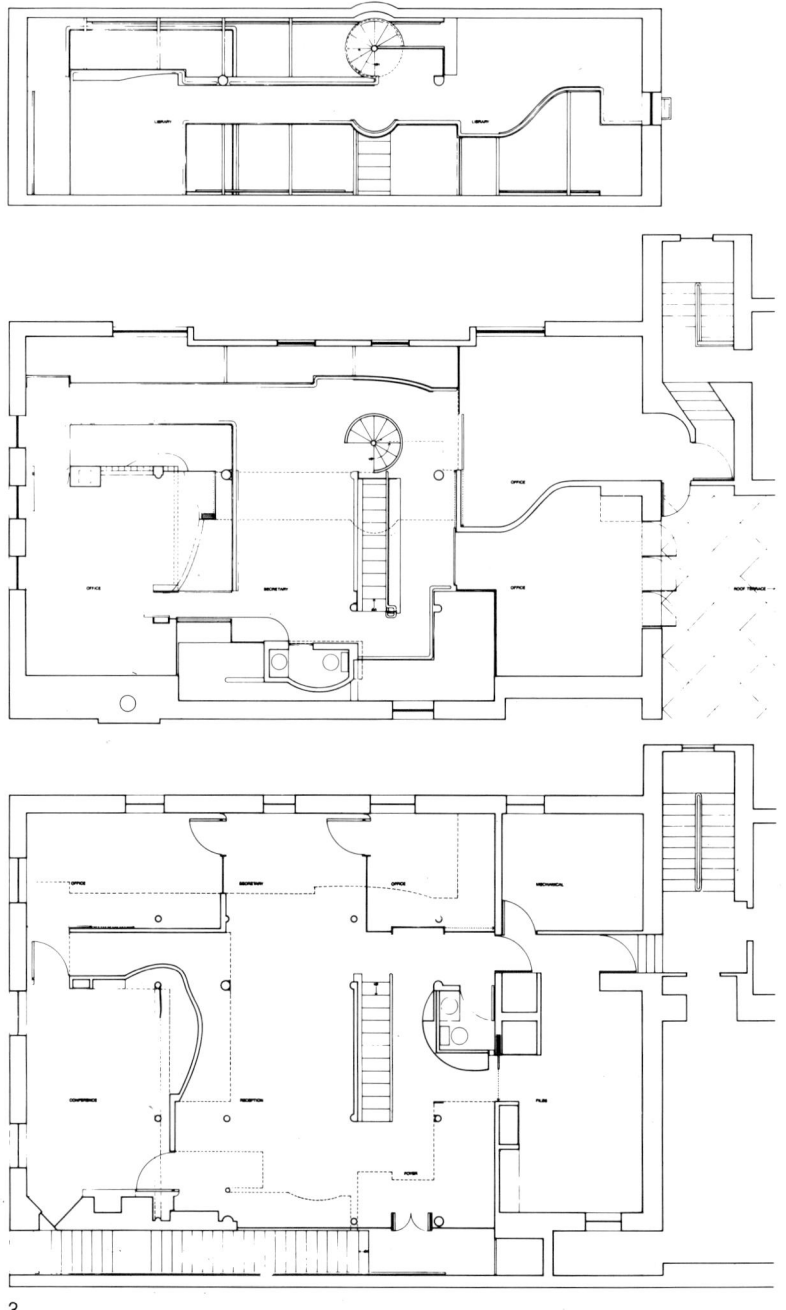
3

GUNWYN VENTURES

1 Entrance looking to upper levels
  Photograph: Norman McGrath
2 Exterior of building
  Photograph: Laurin McCracken
3 Plans of first, second and third levels
4 Axonometric: level 2
5 Axonometric: level 1

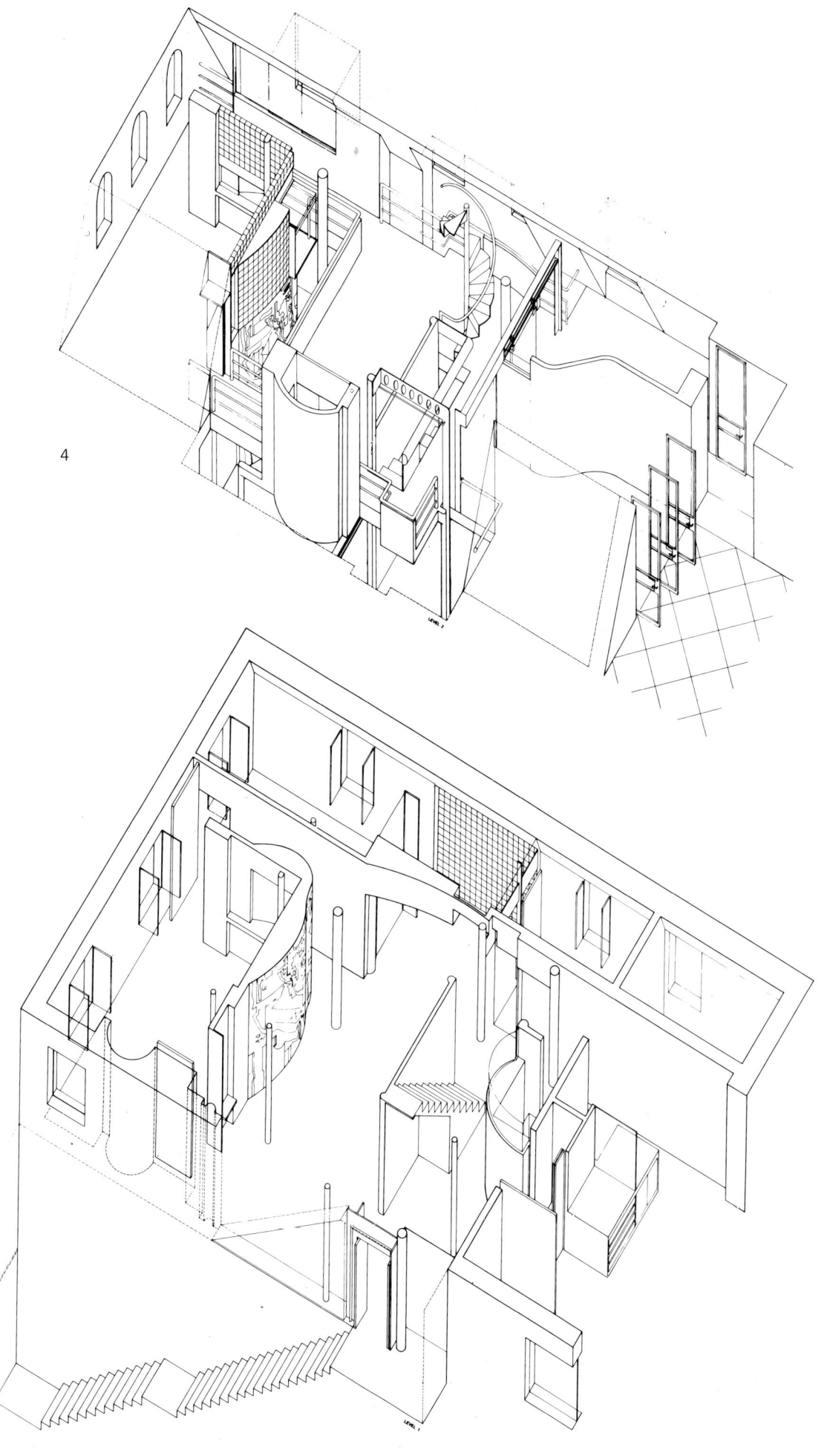

GUNWYN VENTURES

6 Office interior
7 Interior view
8 Interior view
9 Partner's office door
10 Interior view
11 Interior view
12 Third level
Photographs 6-12:
Norman McGrath

6

7

8

GUNWYN VENTURES

9

10

11

12

Alexander House 1971 and 1973
Princeton, New Jersey

This addition to a 1930s neo-colonial house includes a kitchen, breakfast room, potting sink, desk and sitting room within one 900 square foot space on the ground floor.

The original house, like many of neo-classical descent, has a quadripartite plan with a central entrance hall. The addition, similar in size to one quadrant of the original house, has its own four-part organisation and its own centre. As one moves from dining room to kitchen to breakfast room to garden along the new central axis, the spaces become more open and light-filled. The picturesque quality of the breakfast room's curving glass block wall is sympathetic to the nature of the garden beyond.

An open trellis-like frame extends the garden façade and partially encloses the existing porch. The steel 'window' above the frame is a reference to the primary window of the master bedroom located on the main house behind it. Similar to an open casement, the 'window' implies the opening of the bedroom to the garden view.

A separate addition on the second floor includes a guest room and a library whose mural, painted by the architect, extends the interior space by suggesting aspects of the garden landscape beyond.

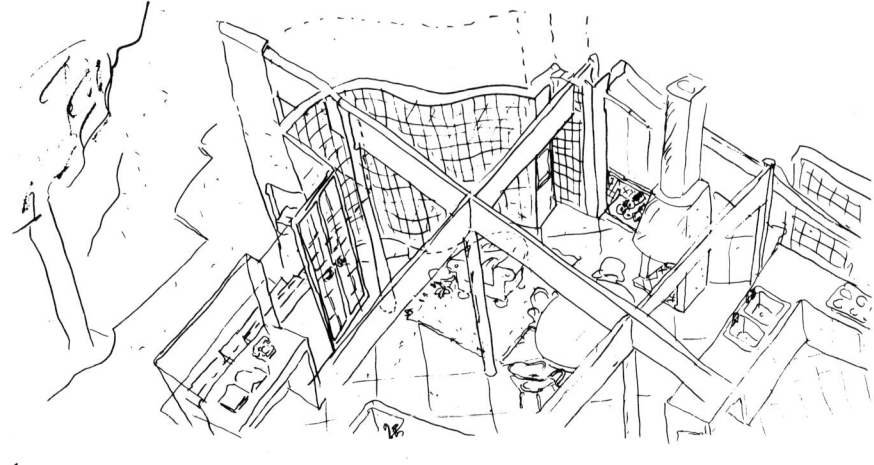
1

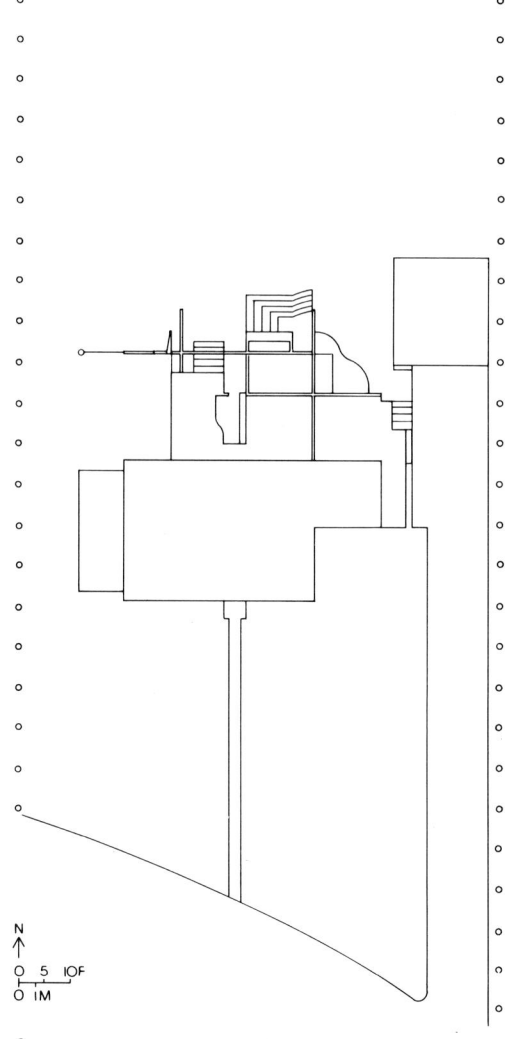
2

1 Sketch of breakfast room
2 Site plan
3 Upper floor plan
4 Ground floor plan

ALEXANDER HOUSE

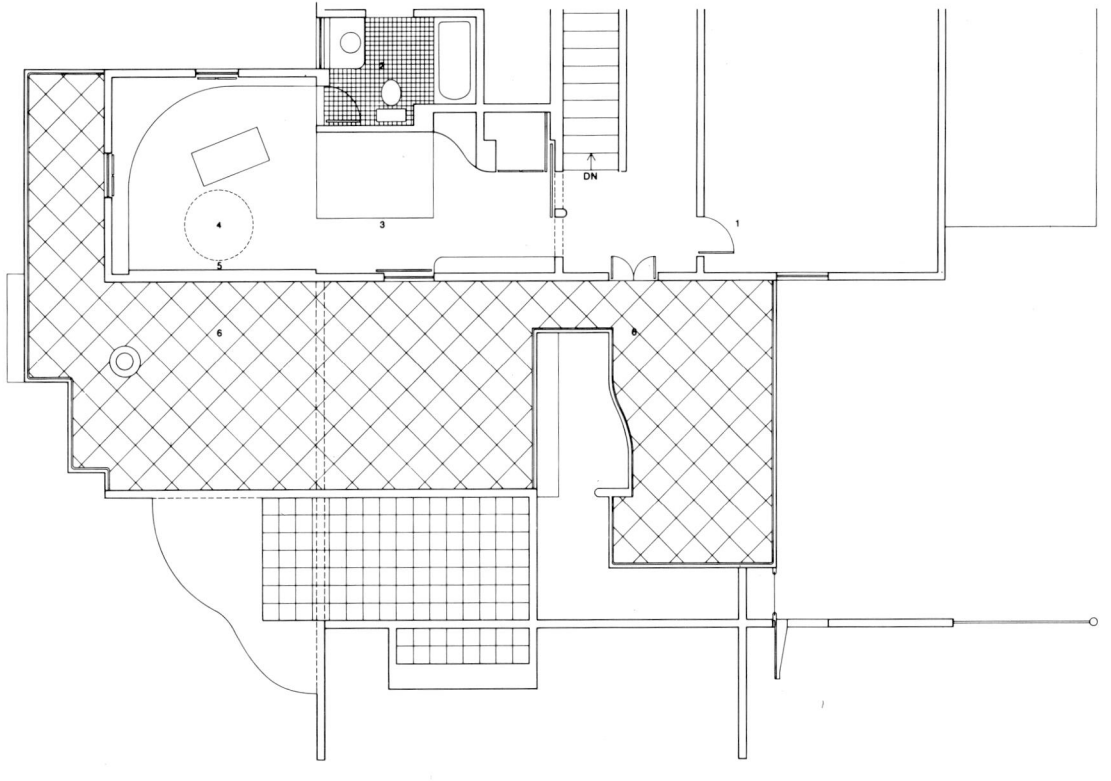

1 EXISTING BEDROOM
2 EXISTING BATH
3 GUEST
4 LIBRARY
5 MURAL WALL
6 ROOF TERRACE

3

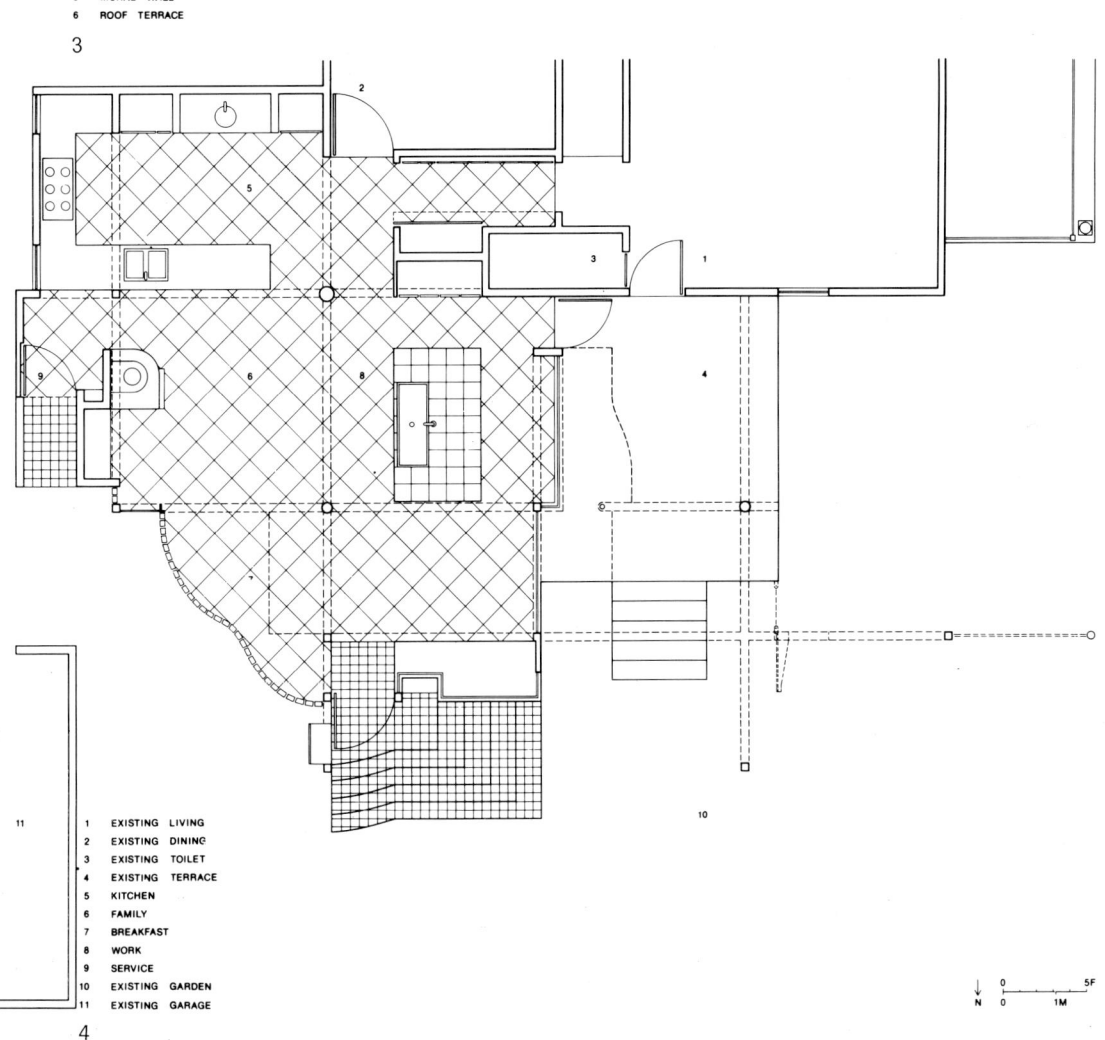

1 EXISTING LIVING
2 EXISTING DINING
3 EXISTING TOILET
4 EXISTING TERRACE
5 KITCHEN
6 FAMILY
7 BREAKFAST
8 WORK
9 SERVICE
10 EXISTING GARDEN
11 EXISTING GARAGE

4

ALEXANDER HOUSE

7 Breakfast room
  Photograph: Bill Maris
8 Sitting room
  Photograph: Bill Maris
9 Bay window desk
10 Window open to garden view
11 Library with mural

ALEXANDER HOUSE

9

10

11

47

Drezner House
1970
Princeton, New Jersey

Sklute House
1970
Bucks County, Pennsylvania

The site for the Drezner House is located at the end of a residential cul-de-sac. From the point of entry, two site influences are registered in the plan. One is a projection of one's frontal orientation to the site through the house to the private garden beyond, and the other, at an oblique angle to the first, refers to an existing clearing which is the most significant element of the otherwise densely wooded site. These two gestures are understood in the plan through their mutual influences which produce a spatial transparency where they are superimposed.

The Sklute House, like the Mezzo House which was designed at approximately the same time, establishes an equity between the building and the site in order to gain an identification with its particular setting. The building was to be built on the brow of a hill in a circular clearing once made for a campground. Though rather small, the house is made to appear large by its relationship to the topiary hedge and by the counter gesture of this composition to the wooded site surrounding the clearing.

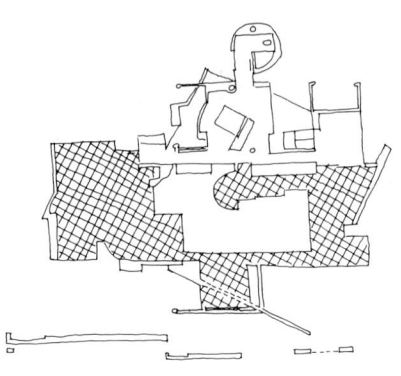

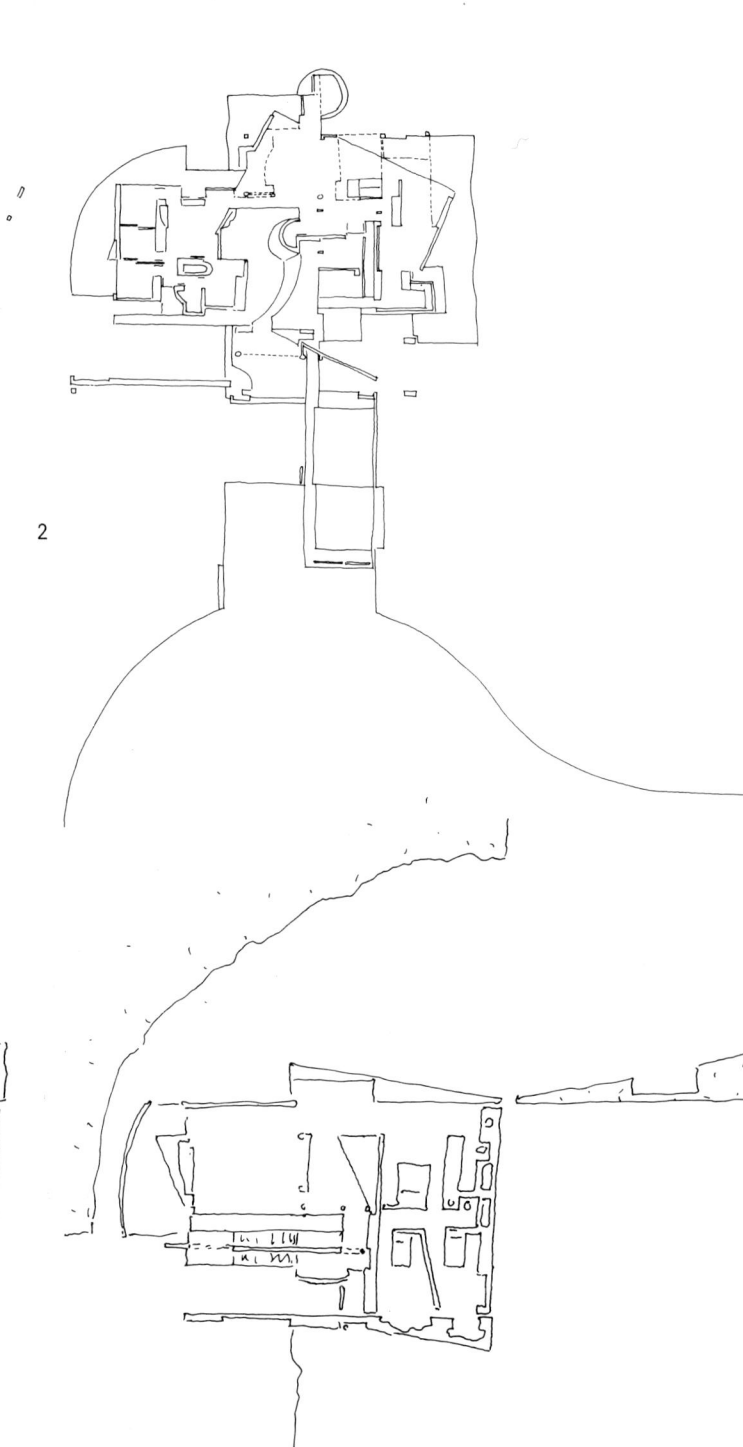

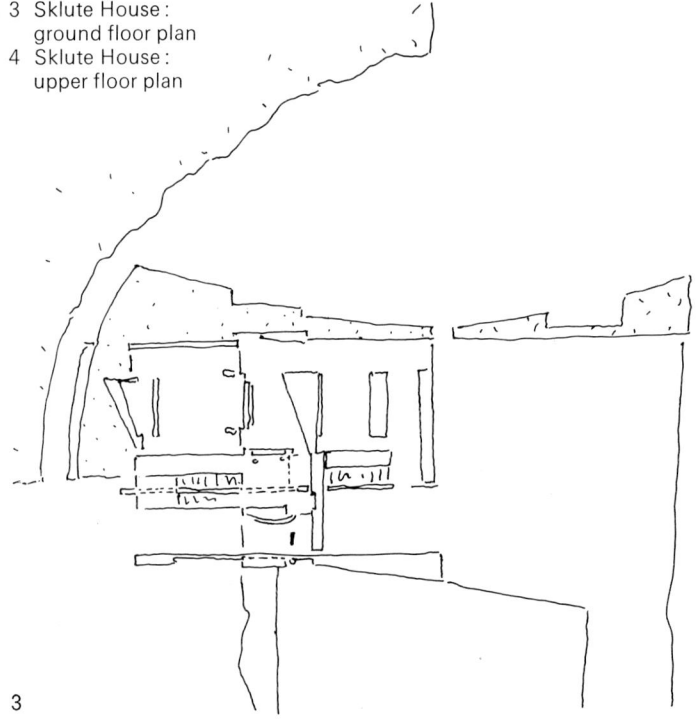

1 Drezner House: upper floor plan study
2 Drezner House: ground floor plan study
3 Sklute House: ground floor plan
4 Sklute House: upper floor plan

Mezzo House
1973
Princeton, New Jersey

The Mezzo House is located on a steeply sloping site, entered at an upper level from the street and progressing downhill to a stream. The clients required that the major living areas be located on the lowest level, most removed from the street and therefore most private. In order to establish the 'door' at this level, adjacent to the kitchen and social sections of the house, an exterior stair was located at one end of the scheme, thus bypassing the upper level bedrooms and more private activities of the house without bisecting the plan.

If the stairway is assumed to retain its classical role as a centralising motif, the landscape can be seen in equity with the house itself. The oblique orientation of the slope relative to the street implies an enclosive gesture toward the garden and produces a means to identify the house with a broader landscape by drawing the adjacent site into the composition.

2

1

3

1 ENTRY
2 FOYER
3 LIVING
4 KITCHEN
5 FAMILY
6 LAUNDRY
7 GARAGE
8 BATHROOM
9 DINING
10 BEDROOM
11 PLAYROOM
12 DRESS
13 VOID
14 TERRACE

4

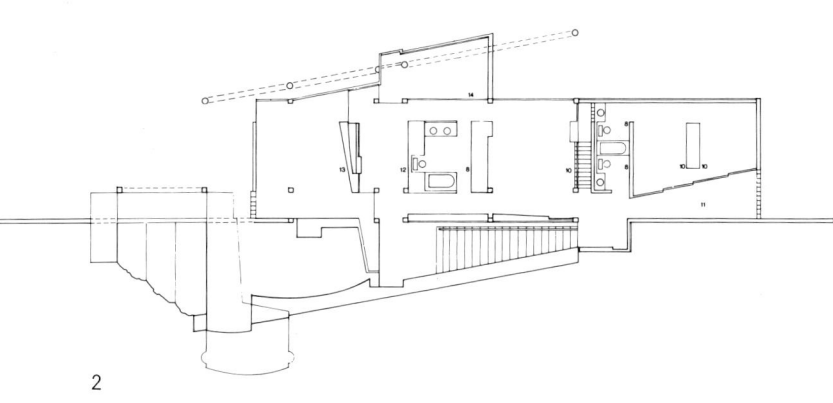

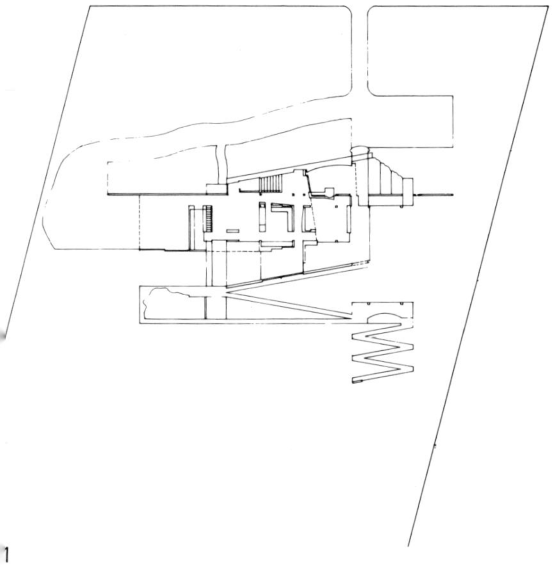

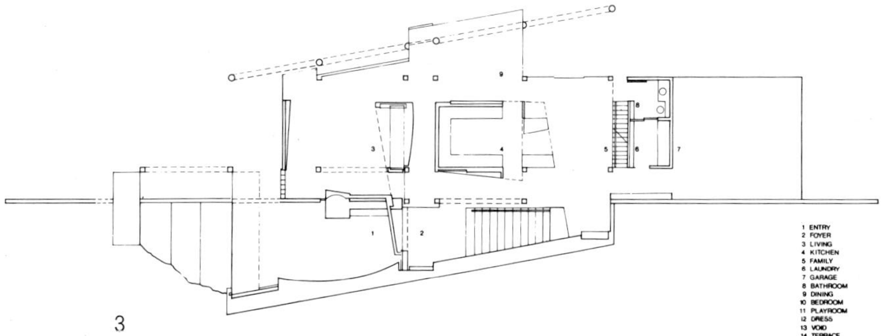

1 Site plan
2 Upper floor plan
3 Ground floor plan
4 Axonometric

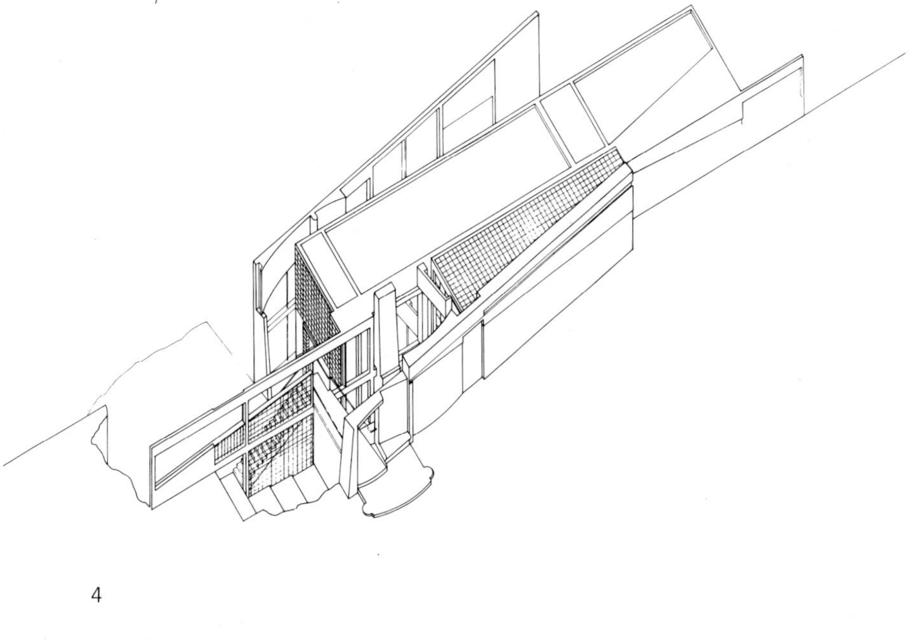

Murals

XV Triennale Exhibition 1973
Milan, Italy

Professional Office Transammonia, Inc. Murals 1974
New York, New York

The murals draw not only on the general context and spatial relationships of painting but also on the larger architectural and landscape settings in which they are located. Sources of elements are generally derived from remembrances of nature with references to man's own relationship to his surroundings, both natural and built.

TRIENNALE
This mural was installed in the exhibit for Triennale XV in Milan, designed by Aldo Rossi. The mural contains references to general themes found in the juxtaposition of architecture and landscape, such as the framing characteristics which these two elements offer each other. Further, there are particular suggestions of the Italian landscape as remembered and as quoted from other painters such as Giorgio Morandi.

TRANSAMMONIA
The three murals painted for the Transammonia offices derive their general base from the gridded network of the existing structure. Their particular interests are derived from two sources: from the historical context of surrounding buildings and from the local modern context of the interior designed by Charles Gwathmey. The murals identify these two architectures within the frame of the painted space and comment on their juxtaposition.

1

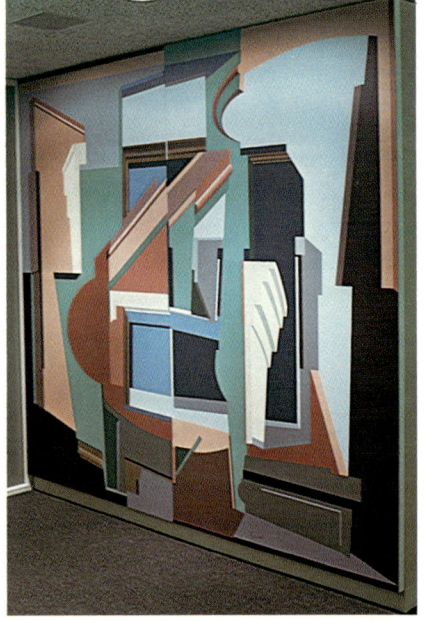

2   3

4

1 Triennale mural
2 Transammonia mural 1
3 Transammonia mural 2
4 Transammonia mural 3

Wageman House
1974
Princeton, New Jersey

In this project the garage of an existing house is converted into a studio on the ground floor and a master bedroom and bath above. A new street façade extends across the front, enclosing a private garden for the studio between the original house and the new wall.

This new façade attempts to organise the disparate volumes of the two-storey addition and the existing one-storey house and provides a new entrance in the area between garage and house. The depth of the forecourt is indicated on the façade by a ground-like dark green panel. Above this panel, the molding set at an angle is coincident with the cornice of the original house, suggesting that the new façade be read as garden wall enclosure.

This molding, together with the panels of diminishing size, sets up a perspective drive toward the entrance. The symmetrical location of the gridded panels further emphasises the 'centre'. In the earlier scheme, the suggestion of a split pediment is used to call attention to the importance of the entrance.

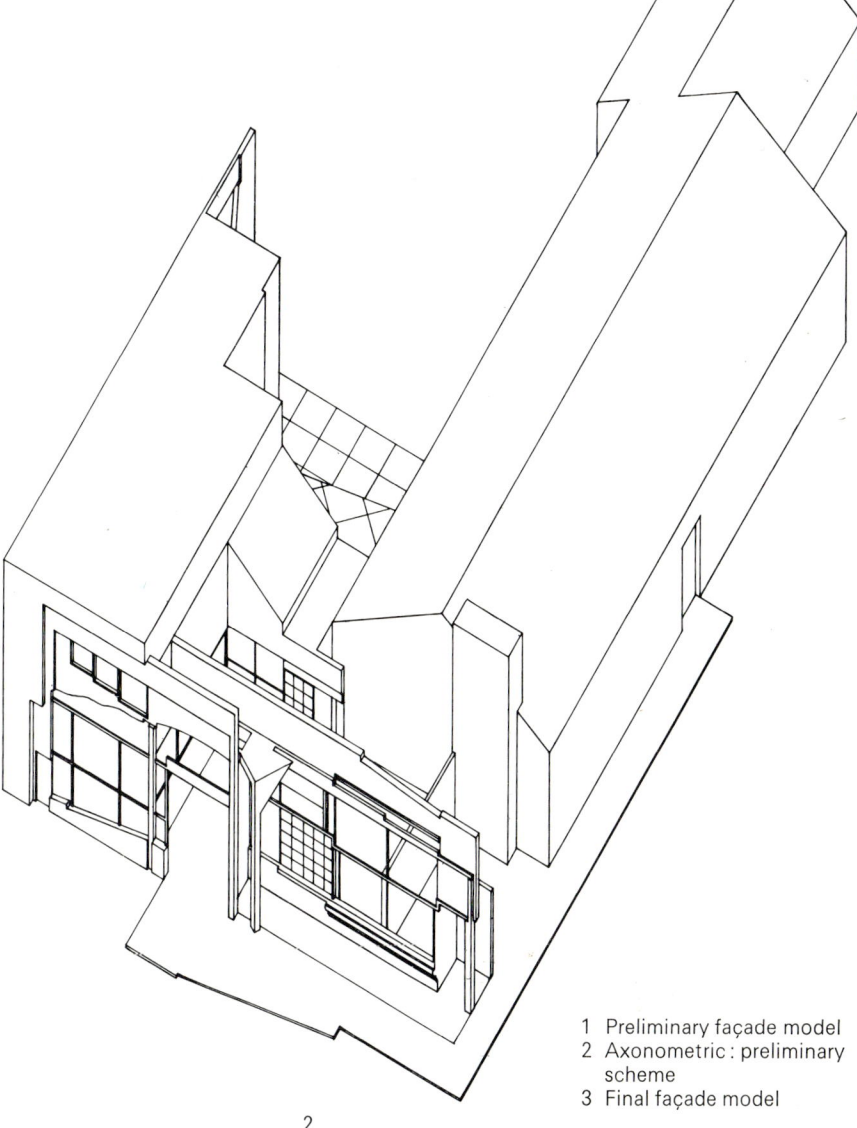

1 Preliminary façade model
2 Axonometric: preliminary scheme
3 Final façade model

Claghorn House 1974
Princeton, New Jersey

The Claghorn House, an 1890s white clapboard Queen Anne style building, is located on a half-acre lot in Princeton. The addition, which includes a kitchen, breakfast room, bar, china pantry, garden room and porch, links the house to its rear garden.

Each of these functional areas is given a different space, defined by explicit structural elements such as columns, beams and screens. The spaces are organised in layers that progress from enclosed to more open as one moves toward the garden. On the kitchen side of the addition, there is a china pantry and bar which is used as a sitting area, a sunlit cooking area and a breakfast room overlooking the garden through a large window. On the deck side, the garden room is separated from the dining room by segments of the original wall, painted terracotta (as if it were a masonry bearing wall) to define the room's outer edge. The garden room has a glass wall leading onto the deck. The dropped ceiling over the garden room and the diagonal tiling on the dining room wall provide perspective connection with the kitchen.

Over the deck, a cruciform post and beam construction divides the space into quadrants and forms a gate or frame over the porch stairs. The crossing suggests enclosure by making a window-like gesture to the sky; the underside of the beam crossing is painted blue to reinforce that reference. The deck is also linked conceptually to the ground by the use of plinth-like planters alongside the stairs.

The addition is related visually to the original house by the use of direct references to its classical and neo-classical antecedents. These references, often quite literal, take the form of traditional devices like latticework suggestive of sun-filled garden structures, broken pediments symbolising man's occupation of the centre and string coursing alluding to one's assumption of the floor as transposed ground plane. These are reinterpreted here to reinforce their symbolic and actual roles or meanings as elements of architecture. The use of colour refers to the antecedents of the older house and also so to nature, particularly to the surrounding garden.

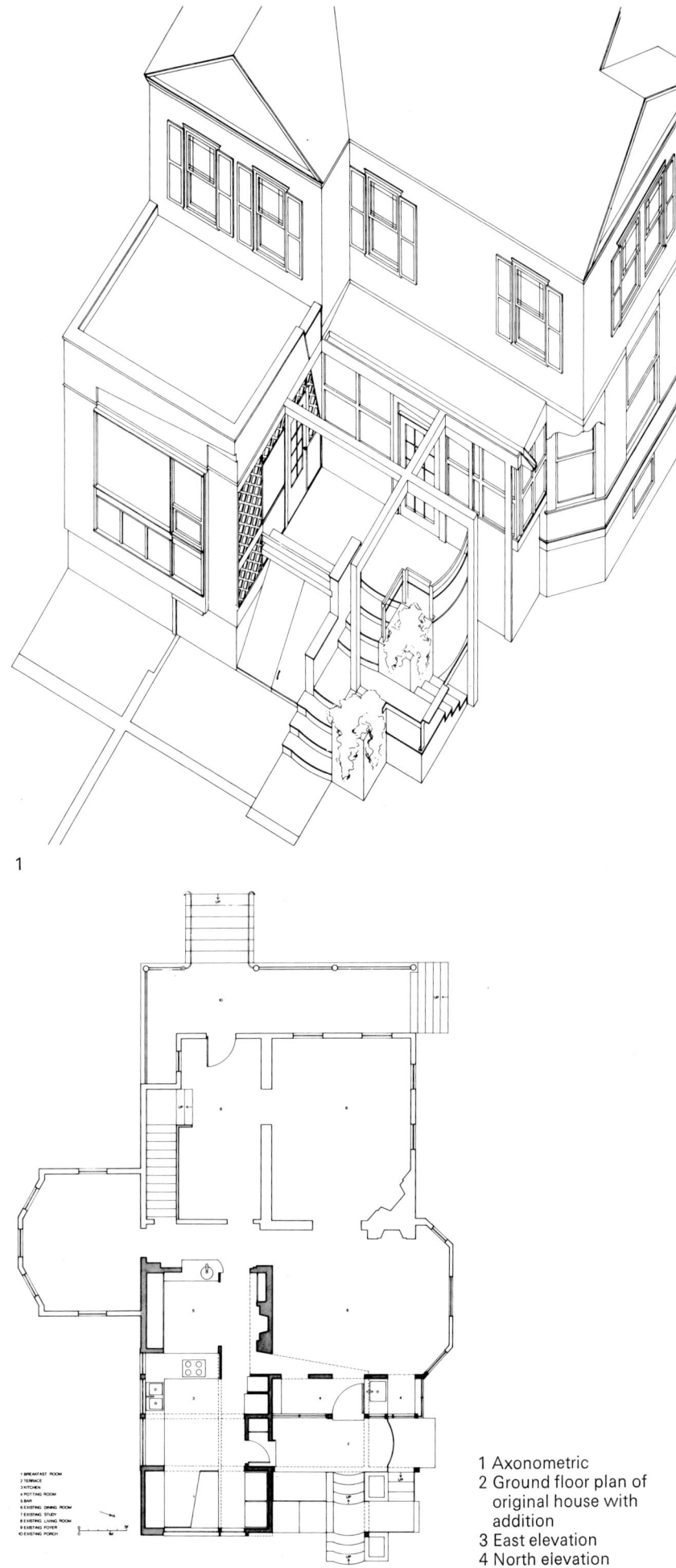

1 Axonometric
2 Ground floor plan of original house with addition
3 East elevation
4 North elevation

CLAGHORN HOUSE

CLAGHORN HOUSE

5

6

CLAGHORN HOUSE

5 Exterior view
6 Detail, porch
7 Detail, porch
8 Interior, kitchen
  Photograph: Norman
  McGrath
9 Detail, kitchen façade

Housing for the Elderly Competition
1975
Trenton, New Jersey

The programme for this competition, sponsored by the New Jersey Society of Architects, included 120 one-bedroom apartments to be rented to the elderly as well as communal social spaces, outdoor recreation spaces and short and long-term parking.

The specified density of site coverage required the building to be larger than the three and four-storey frame dwellings in the surrounding neighbourhood. The institutional image often associated with a high-rise block is diminished here by breaking down the scale of the façades and by making an irregular curve of the primary entrance façade. The windows within windows on this façade mask the thirteen-storey bulk and develop a scalar relationship with the surrounding neighbourhood. The housing is oriented to the park-like setting of the area and its major parking is placed off the site on a nearby street. The building is thus not separated from its surrounding and generous natural light and a good view are assured for each unit. The free-form curve of the façade establishes a relationship with the landscape and elaborates the zone of transition from landscape to building.

In the building, communal activities are located on the ground floor near the entrance to maximise social contact and to maintain the privacy of the individual dwellings above.

HOUSING FOR THE ELDERLY

1 Lobby sketch
2 Typical floor plan
3 Site and ground floor plan
4 West elevation
5 Model, showing west façade and entrance gate

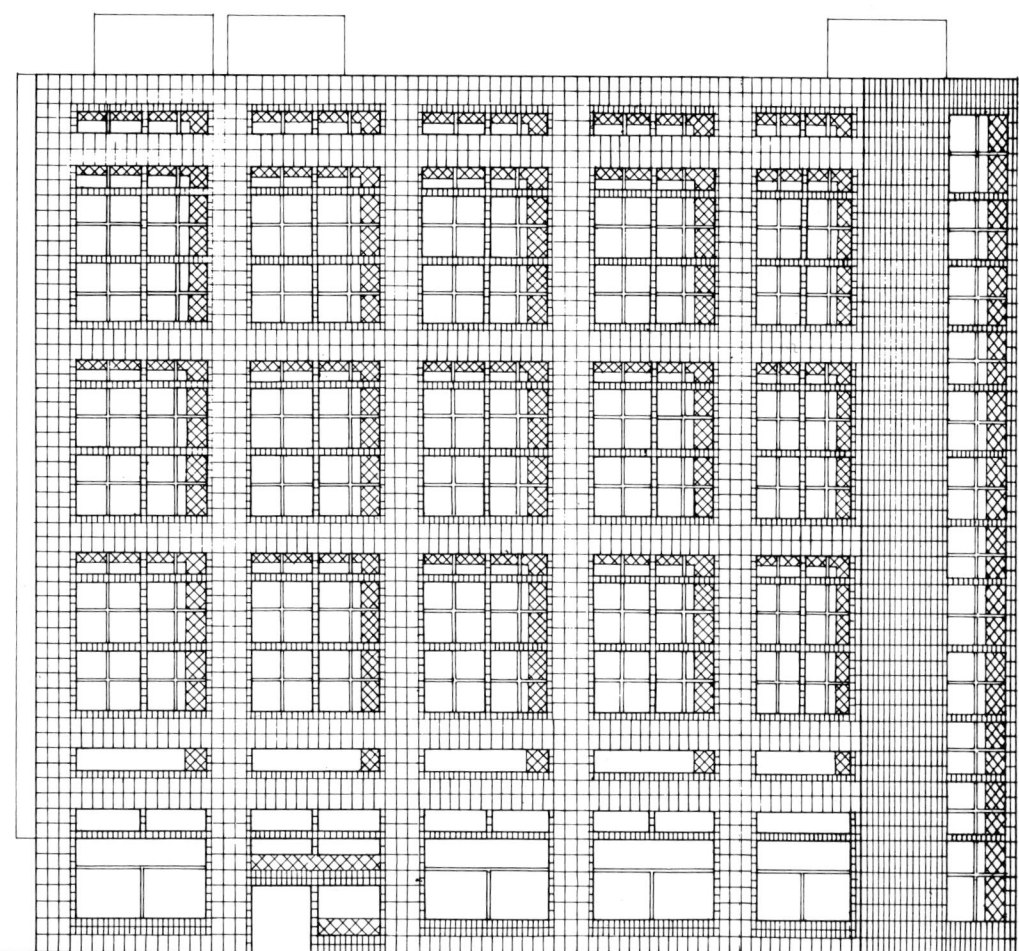

57

Warehouse Conversion: Private Residence 1977
Princeton, New Jersey

The warehouse is located on a quarter-acre lot adjoining a public park with access from an established residential street. The building was built in 1926 of hollow clay tile, surfaced with brick and stucco. It is a two-storey L-shaped structure which, in its original state, was divided into small storage cells along a central corridor in each wing. The renovation provides living accommodation for a family of two adults and four children.

An attempt was made in the design to comment on the ambiance of the existing structure which was built by Italian masons in a Tuscan vernacular manner. The existing openings (truck docks) were used as the primary entrances to the building in an effort to preserve the surface value of the façades. To identify the primary entrance and to gain light in the depth of the building without greatly altering the exterior walls, a courtyard excision was made into the structure. Elements of the new construction were thus established inside the body of the building. The overall simplicity of the existing interior and exterior surfaces was left intact; however, the new surfaces have been elaborated with figural elements in order to allow a closer identification with classical and anthropomorphic sources.

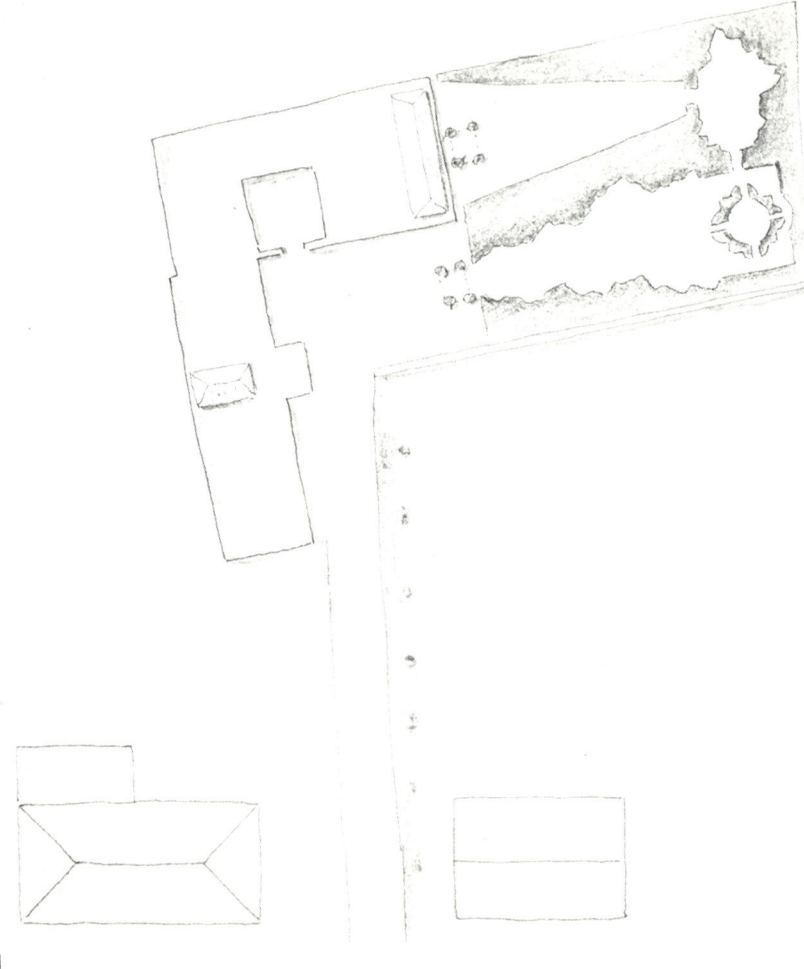

1 Site plan
2 Garden sketches
3 Section through west wing hall
4 Solarium west

WAREHOUSE CONVERSION

3

4

WAREHOUSE CONVERSION

5 Section through west wing and south elevation
6 Solarium east
7 Ground floor plan
8 Upper floor plan
9 East elevation
10 Section through west wing
11 Section through west wing hall
12 West wing stair landing, west elevation
13 West wing stair landing, east elevation

5

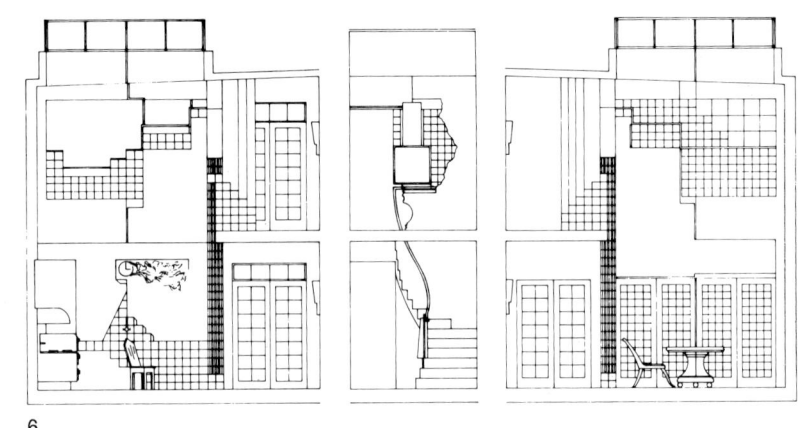
6

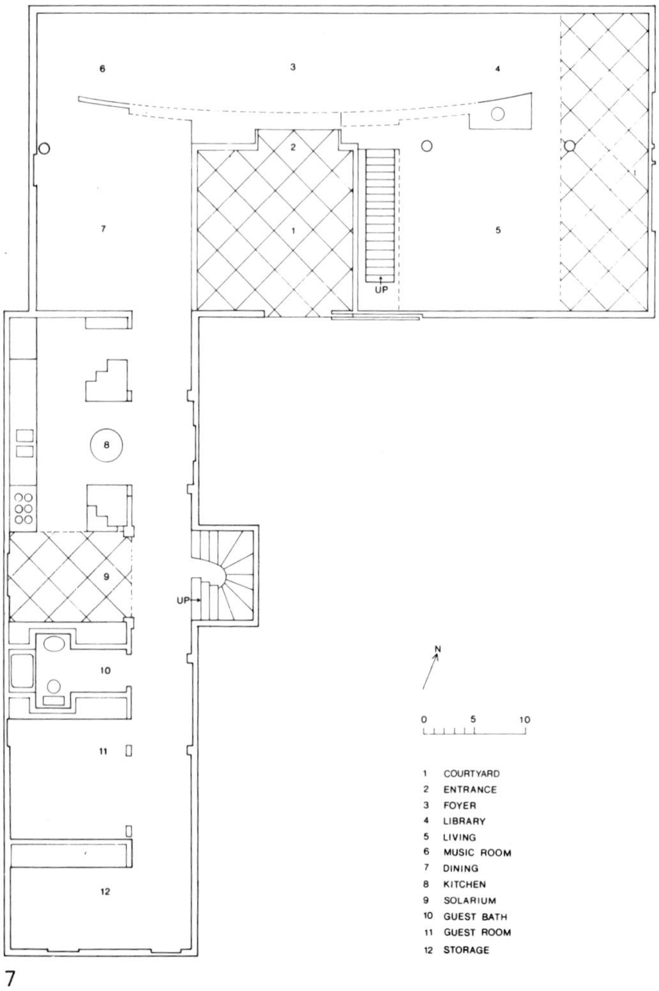

7

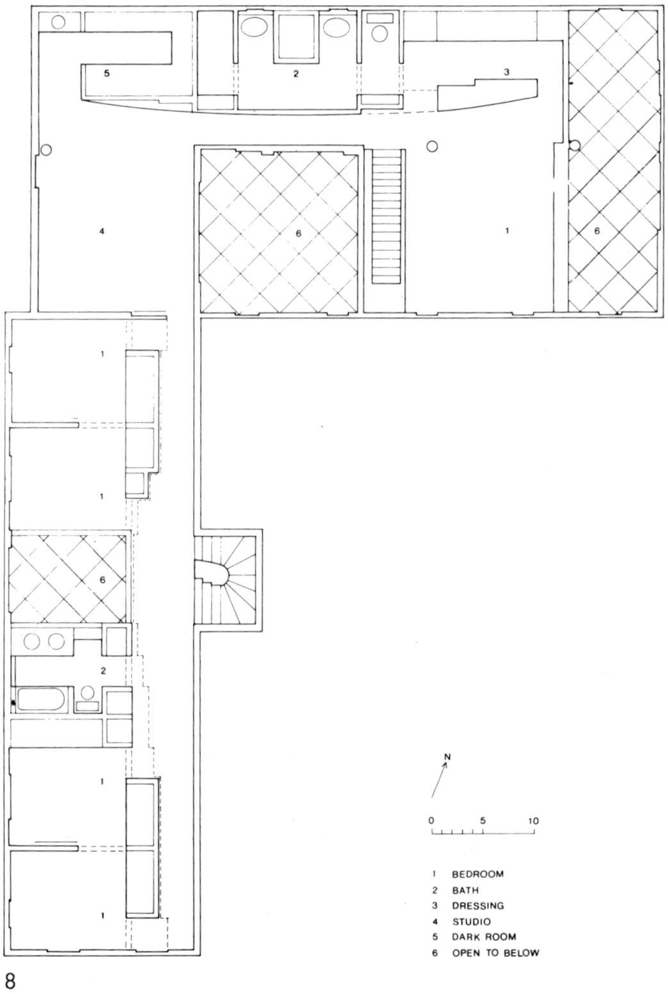

1 COURTYARD
2 ENTRANCE
3 FOYER
4 LIBRARY
5 LIVING
6 MUSIC ROOM
7 DINING
8 KITCHEN
9 SOLARIUM
10 GUEST BATH
11 GUEST ROOM
12 STORAGE

8

1 BEDROOM
2 BATH
3 DRESSING
4 STUDIO
5 DARK ROOM
6 OPEN TO BELOW

WAREHOUSE CONVERSION

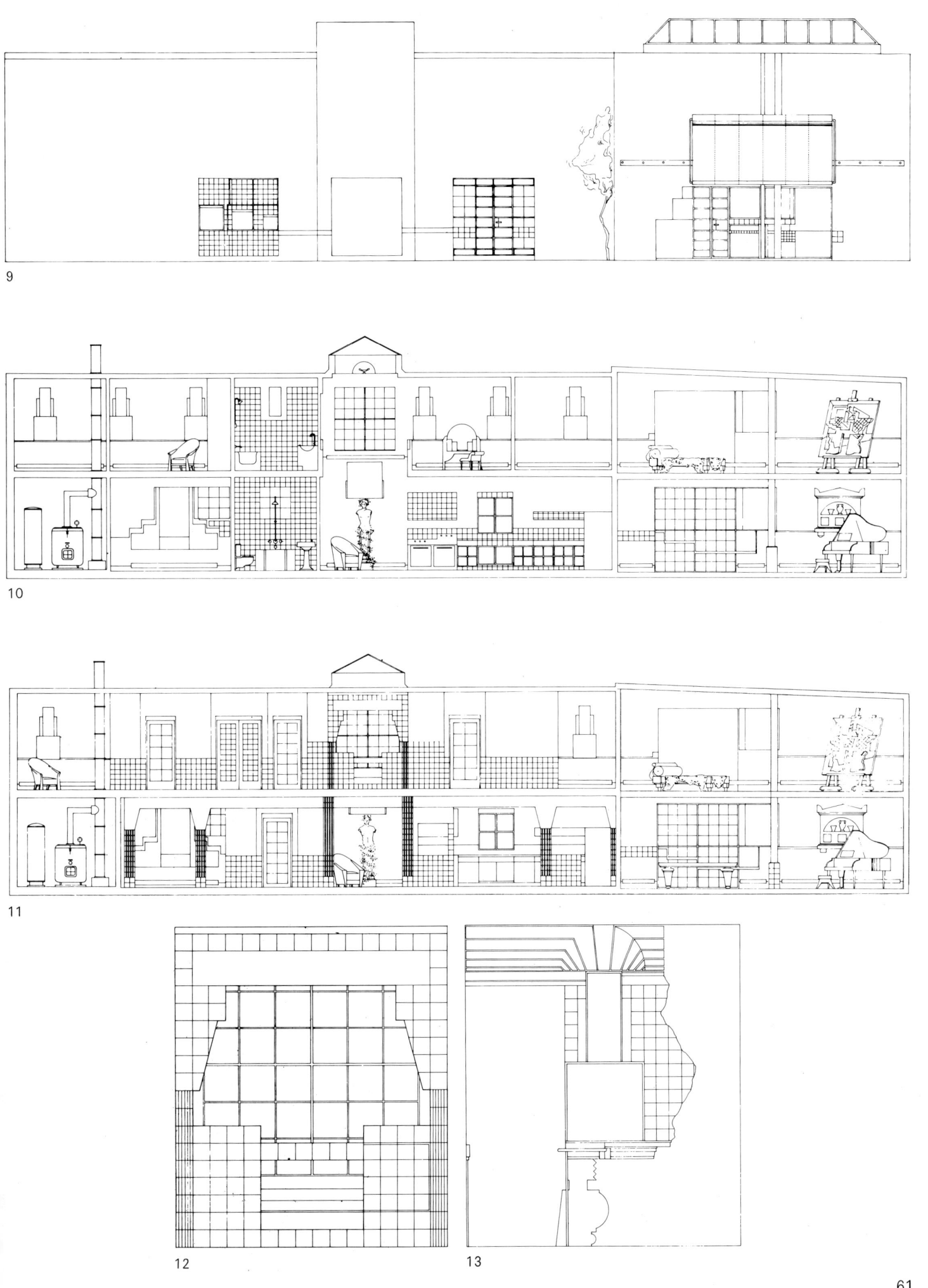

WAREHOUSE CONVERSION

14 Courtyard entrance triptych
15 Guest room window
16 Kitchen door

14

15

16

WAREHOUSE CONVERSION

17 Garden façade study
18 Detail of south façade
19 Guest bedroom
20 Warehouse garden gate

17

18

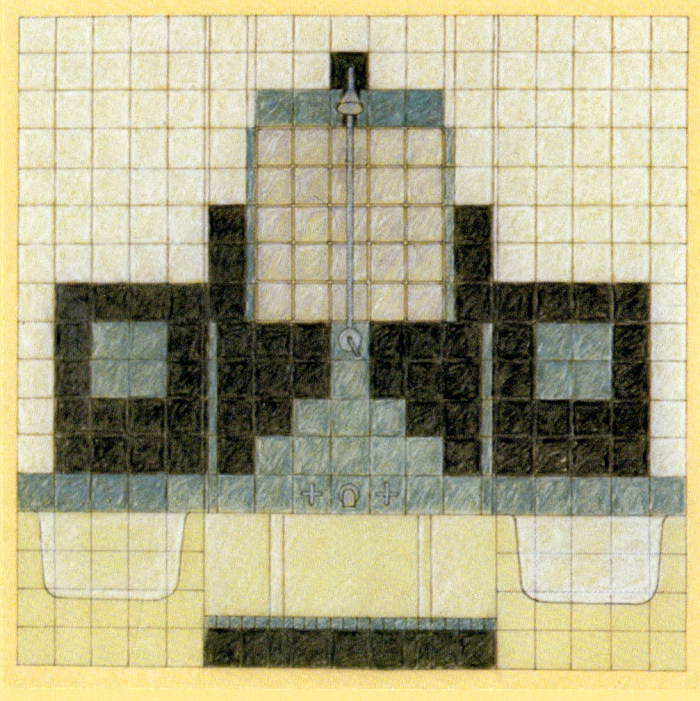

19

20

Crooks House
1976
Fort Wayne, Indiana

The site for the Crooks House is a three-quarter-acre lot in a wooded suburban subdivision in the midst of a series of development houses. The typical suburban solution to the problem of privacy, as evident in the surrounding houses, is to locate the building as an isolated object in the approximate centre of the site, thereby leaving the landscape as residue. While privacy is accomplished by isolation in in the surrounding tract houses, the Crooks House derives its privacy by treating the major formal gestures as fragments of a larger organisation, thereby setting up a dependence of object and landscape. Rather than a single centre, a succession of centres is produced both in the building and in the landscape. These centres are linked and can be understood as a spatial continuum. While the Crooks House is very small, providing accommodation for a family of two adults and one child, it extends its sphere of influence by the fragmentation of both building and landscape. In this way, the residual character of the adjoining sites is diminished and a spatial continuity that provides for necessary levels of public and private domain is established.

Facing the street are the kitchen and garage walls, connected by a screen wall with an opening for the driveway. The drive ends in a court formed by the house, garage and garden. From the court, one enters the house on an axis of light provided by three skylights within a double-height volume crossed by bridges at an upper level. On the left, past a glass block partition, is the living room which receives most of its natural light from a large skylight above the fireplace. On the back side of the fireplace is the sitting room which, like the living room, has windows only in the wall facing the garden. The wall is pulled out at an angle from the house's volume. Upstairs, a terrace off the master bedroom occupies this space between the wall and the cubiform volume of the house. On the second floor, there are two bedrooms and a study which can be converted into a third bedroom in the future.

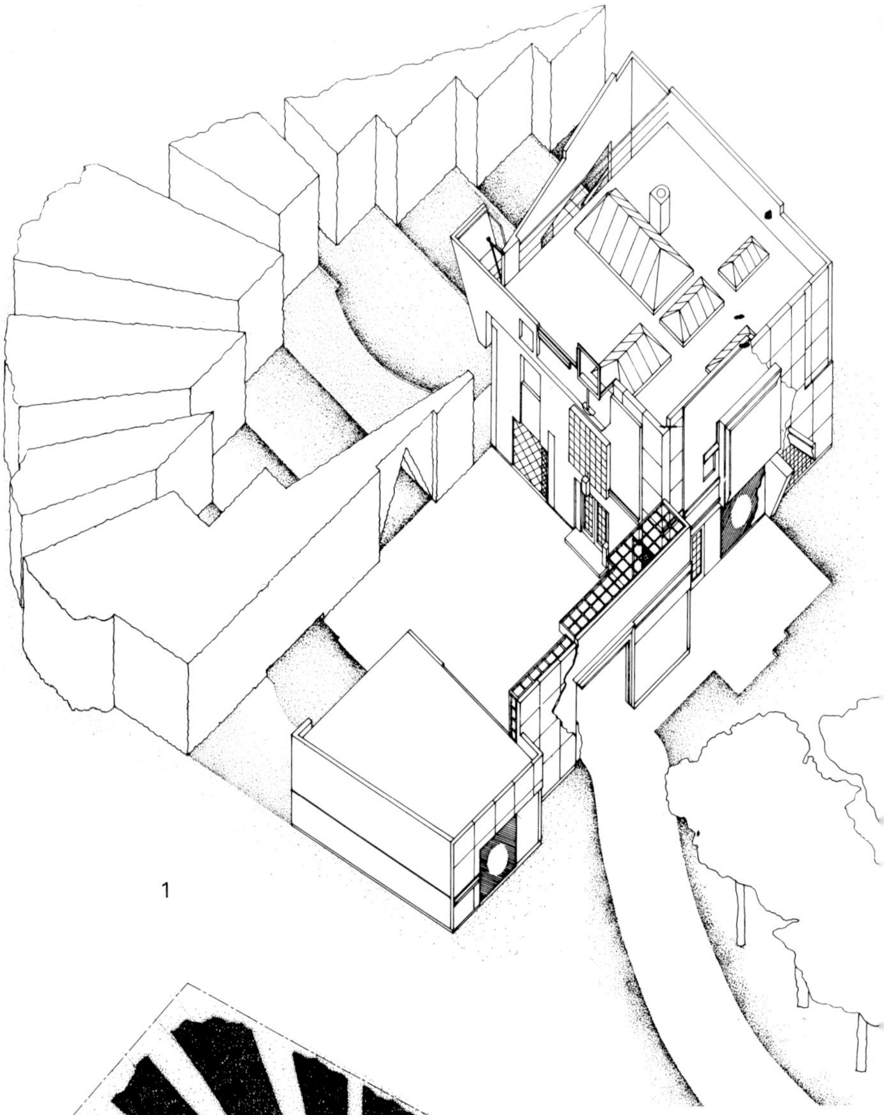

1 Axonometric
2 Site plan
3 Sketchbook, façade projection
4 Model, street façade
5 Ground floor plan
6 Upper floor plan
7 Section through entrance and hall
8 Section through dining and kitchen
9 Section through living and kitchen

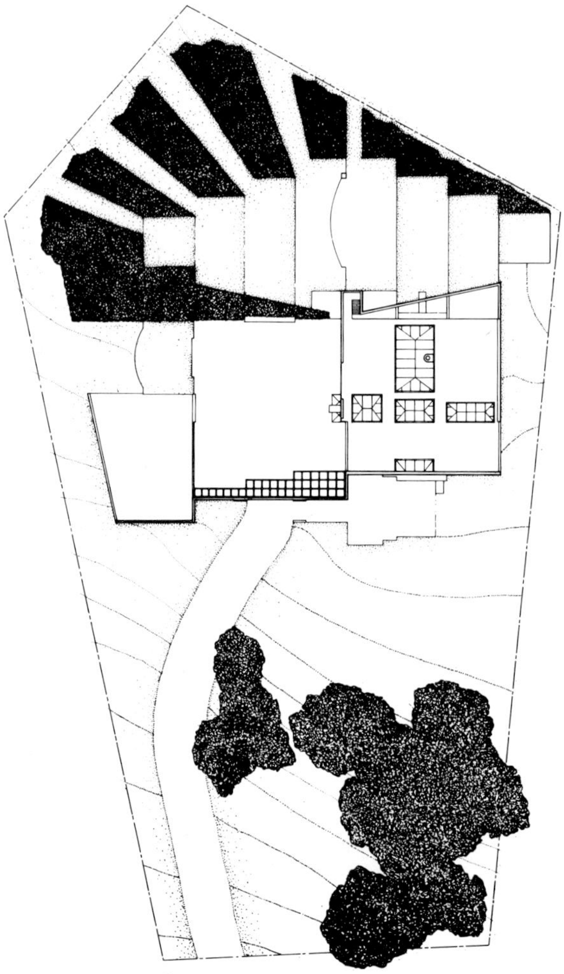

CROOKS HOUSE

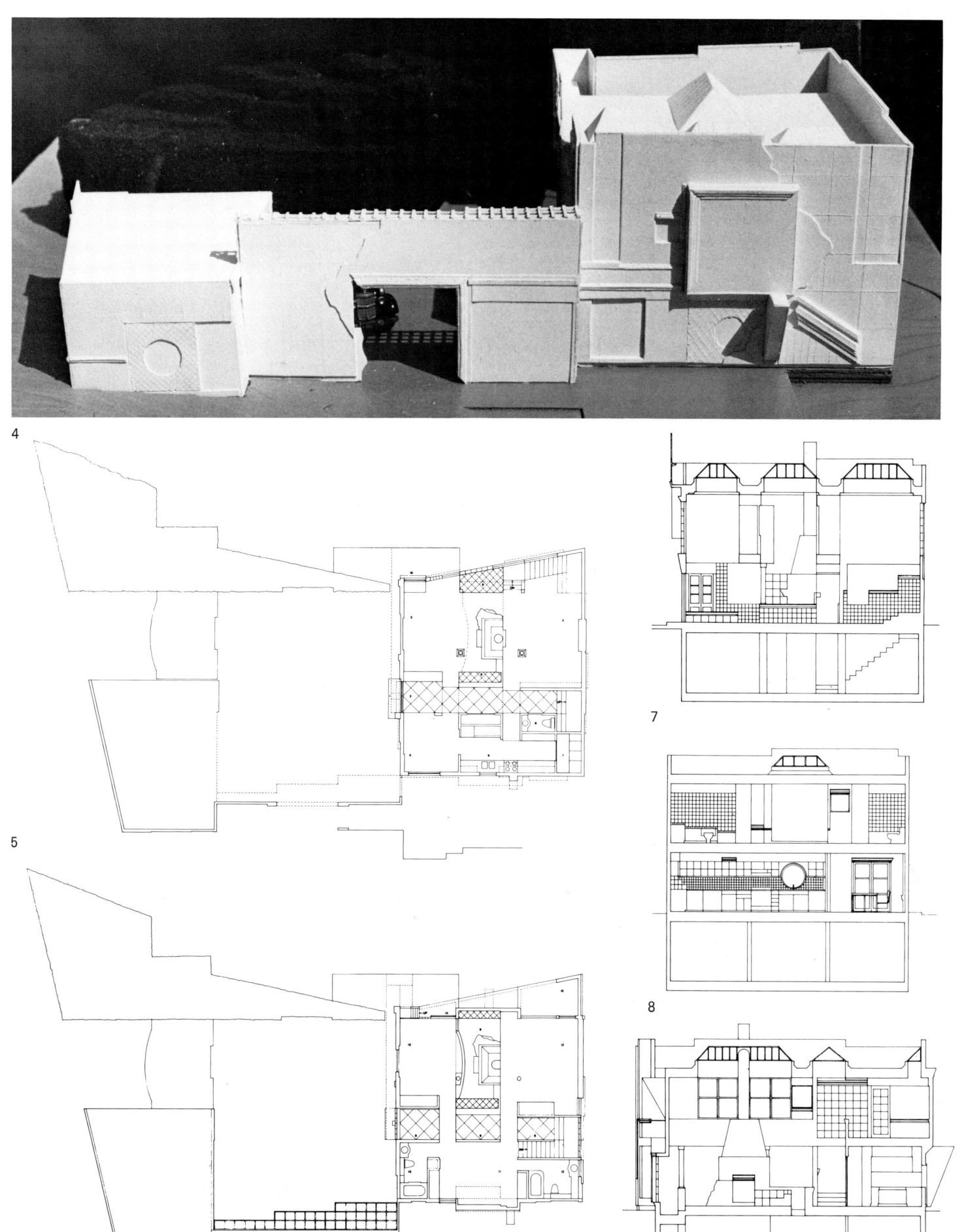

CROOKS HOUSE

10

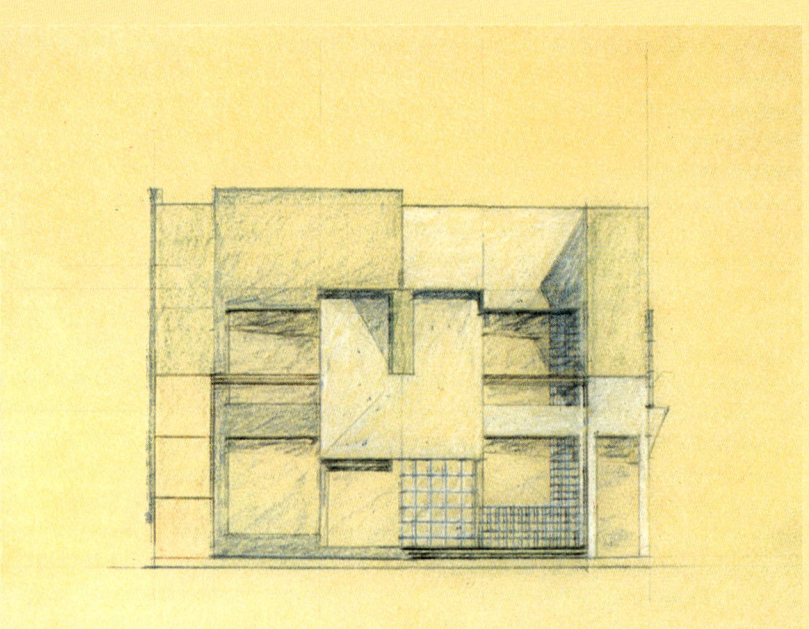

11

10 Final street elevation
11 Final garden elevation
12 Final court elevation

12

CROOKS HOUSE

13

14

13 Final north-west elevation
14 Study for north-west elevation
15 Model

15

67

Furniture, Lamp and Sconce Sketches

These furniture, lamp and sconce designs have been compiled from the architect's sketchbooks over the past five years.

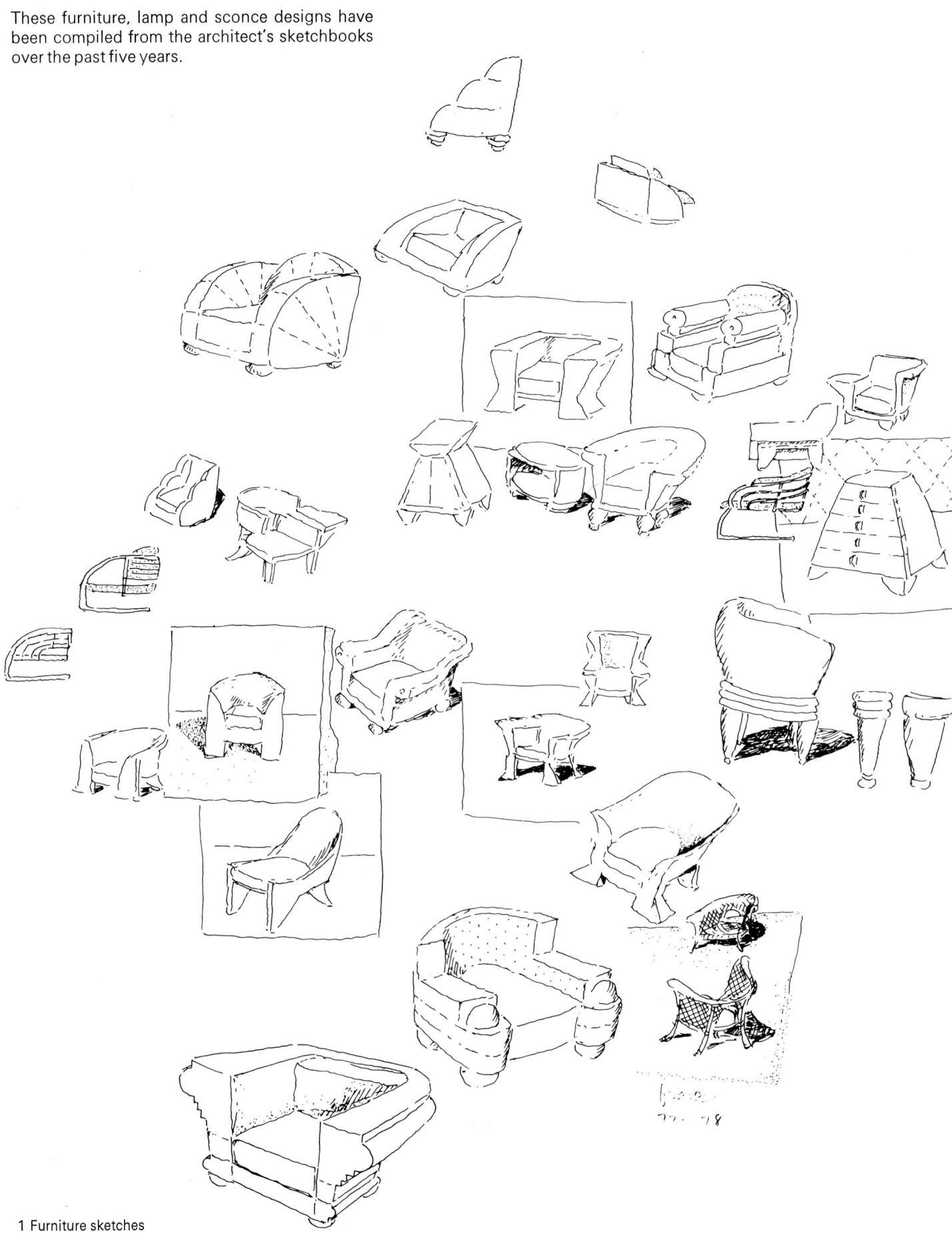

1 Furniture sketches

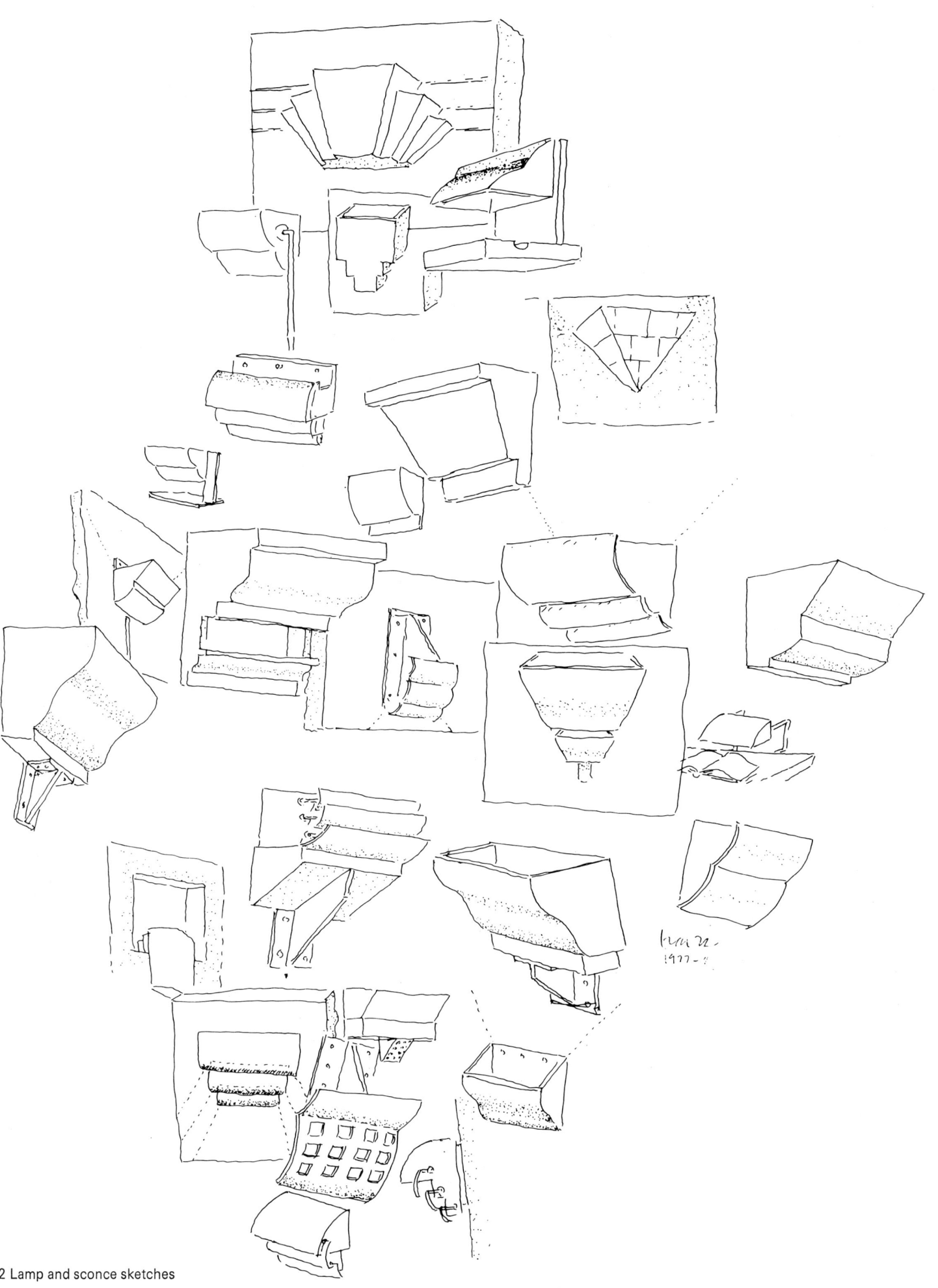

2 Lamp and sconce sketches

The Newark Museum Carriage House Renovation 1975
Newark, New Jersey

This 1890s Victorian carriage house is located on the edge of the property occupied by the Newark Museum. The programme call for its conversion into a museum for modern painting and sculpture. The building is separated from the existing museum complex by an open space to be developed into a small amphitheatre for noontime concerts. The enclosive gesture of the amphitheatre and its hedge wall is carried into the building as a spine which organises the various exhibits according to their requirements for natural light. The artifacts that are to be exhibited outdoors establish formal and ritual themes in the composition, both by their placement in the landscape and by their allegorical or anthropomorphic associations.

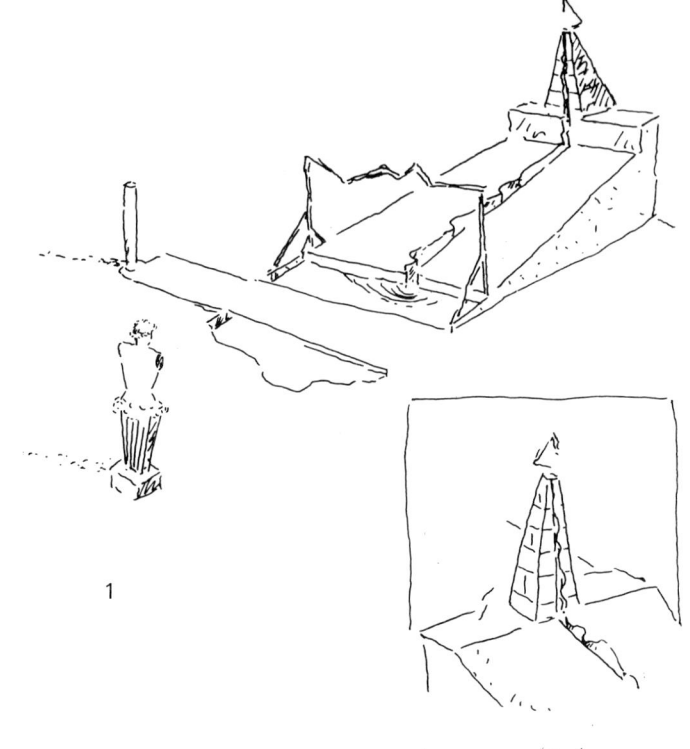

1

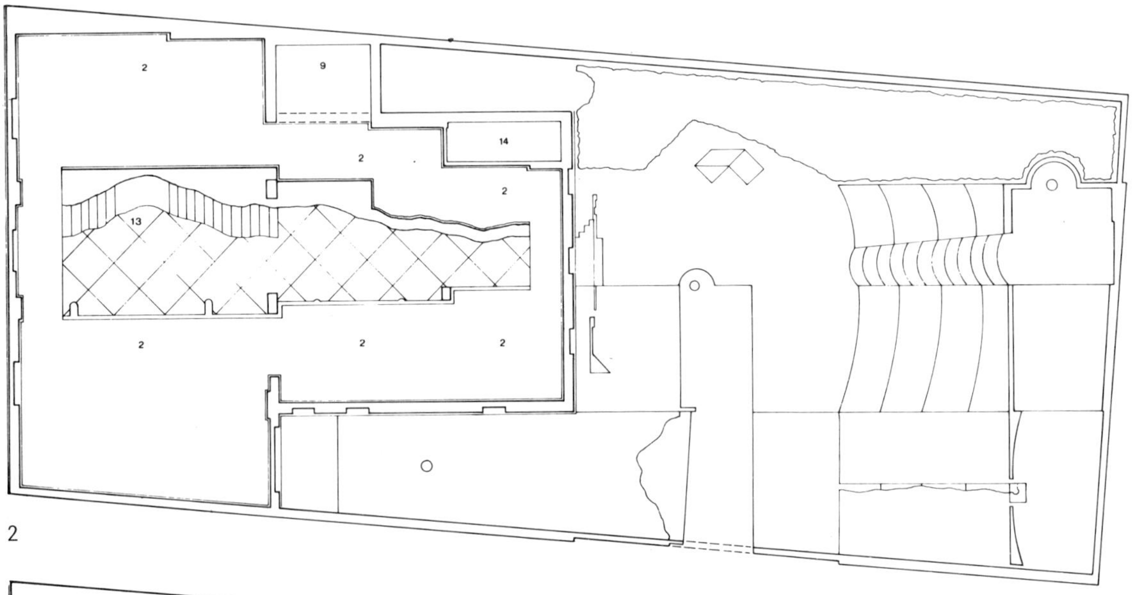

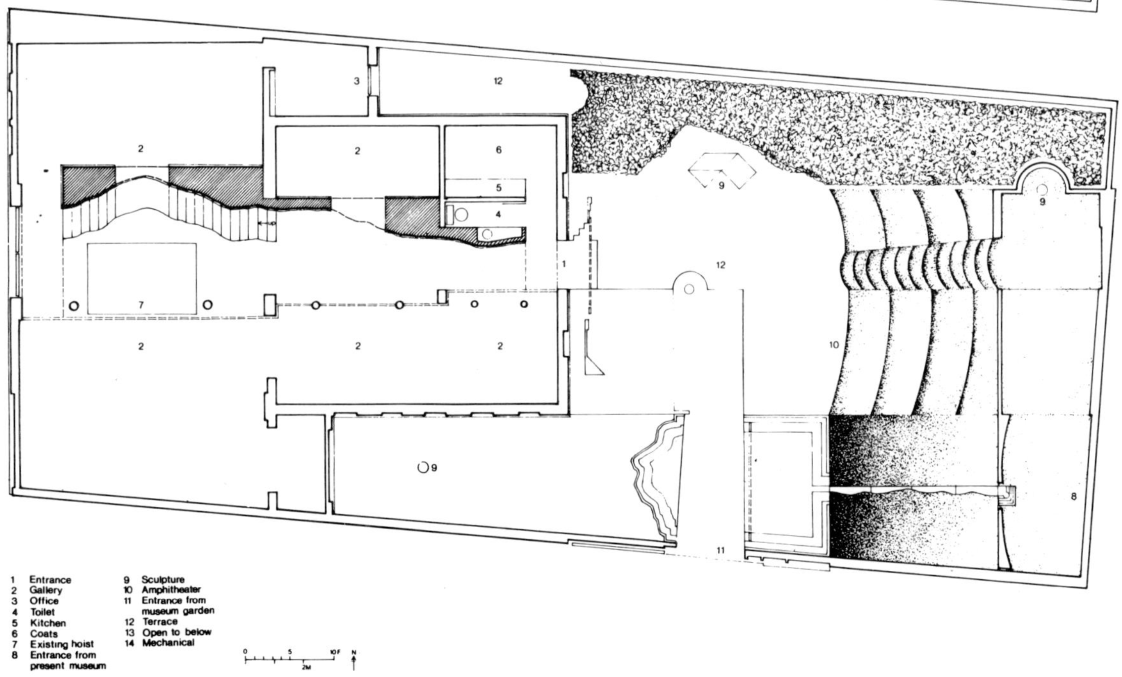

1 Entrance
2 Gallery
3 Office
4 Toilet
5 Kitchen
6 Coats
7 Existing hoist
8 Entrance from present museum
9 Sculpture
10 Amphitheater
11 Entrance from museum garden
12 Terrace
13 Open to below
14 Mechanical

1 Preliminary studies
2 Upper floor plan
3 Ground floor plan

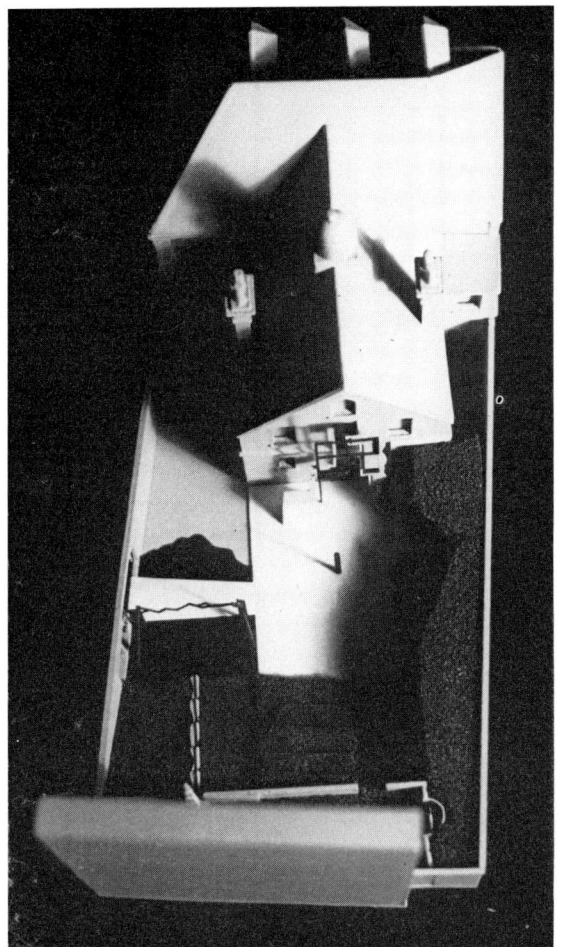

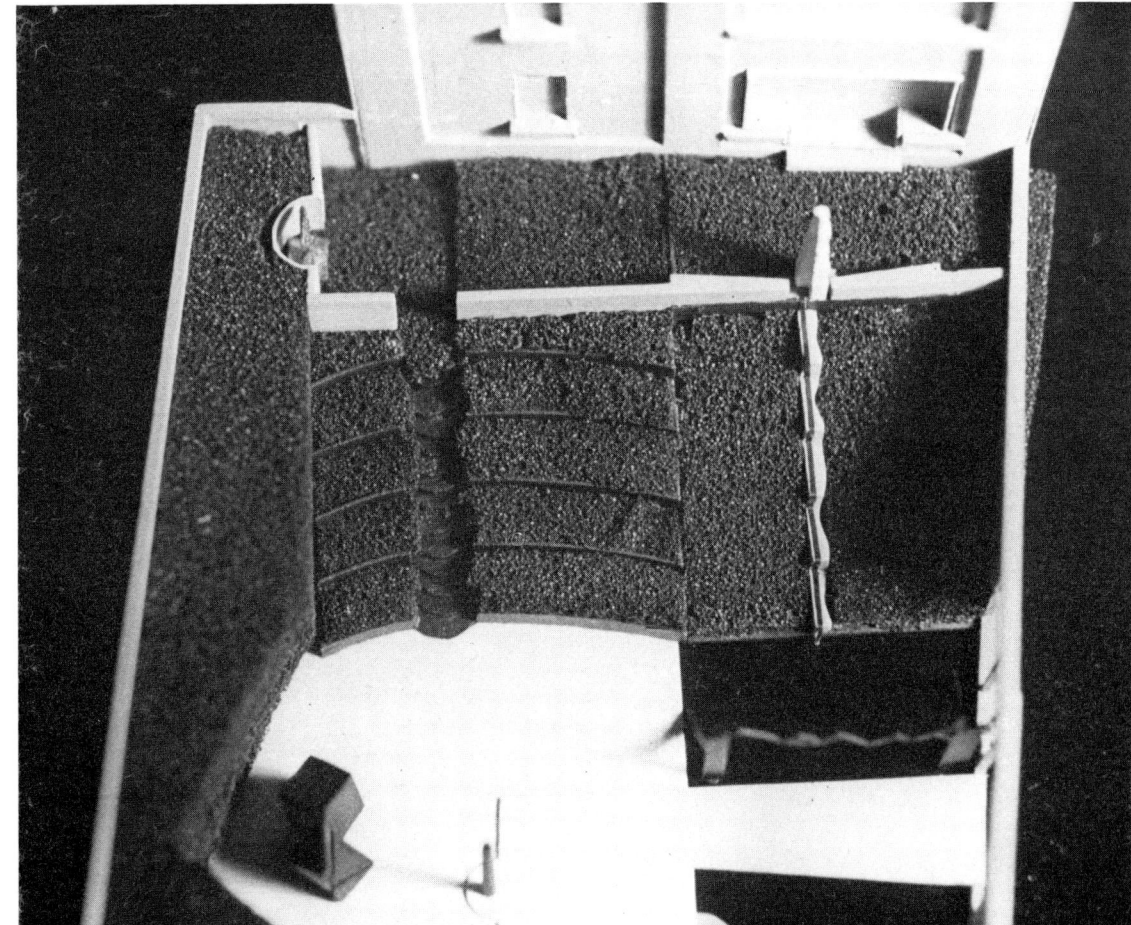

4 Model: view from above
5 Model: entrance
6 Model: garden

Schulman House
1976
Princeton, New Jersey

In this project, a new living room and garden wall have been added to a two-storey suburban house. The three elements of the composition are discrete in plan but are linked serially in the street elevation by their progressively decreasing size and the repetition of similar formal elements. As each segment steps forward in plan, the dimensions of the lapped siding increase in the elevation, thereby setting up a false perspective which accentuates the new entry in the street façade. On the garden side, a new centre is made by a screened porch which connects the living room addition with a former garage, now used for storage. The centre is reinforced by the symmetrical relationship of the fenestration on the living room wall and the gridded frame applied to the garage wall.

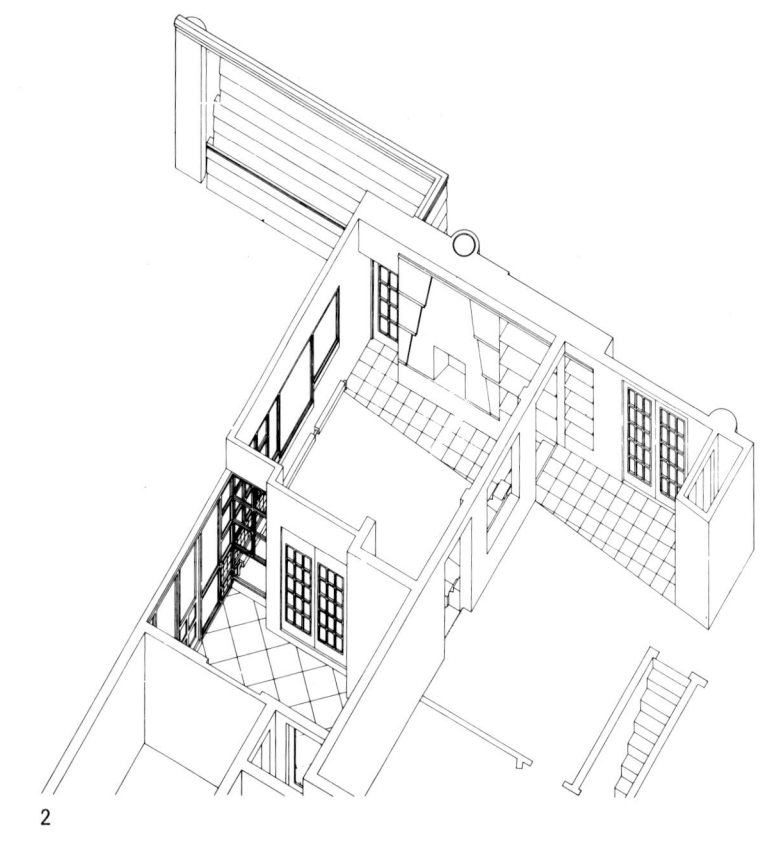

2

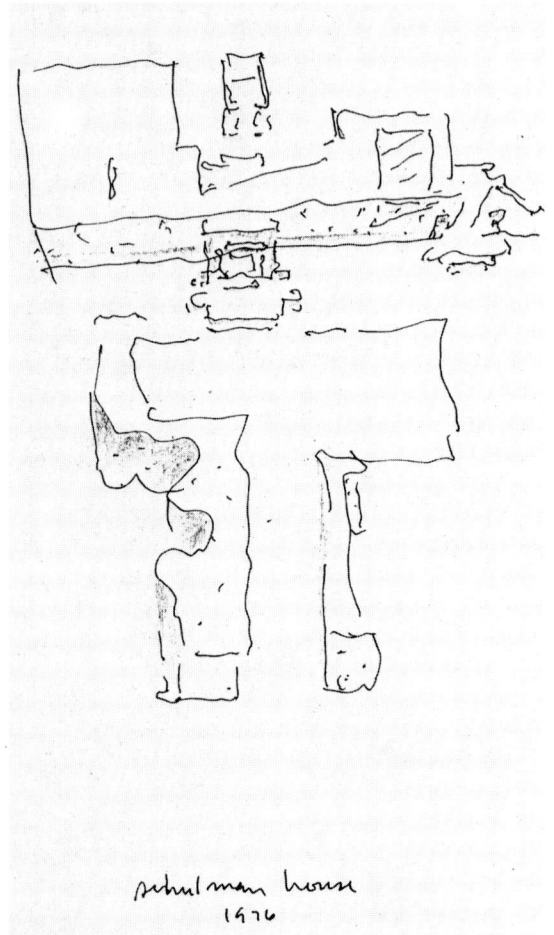

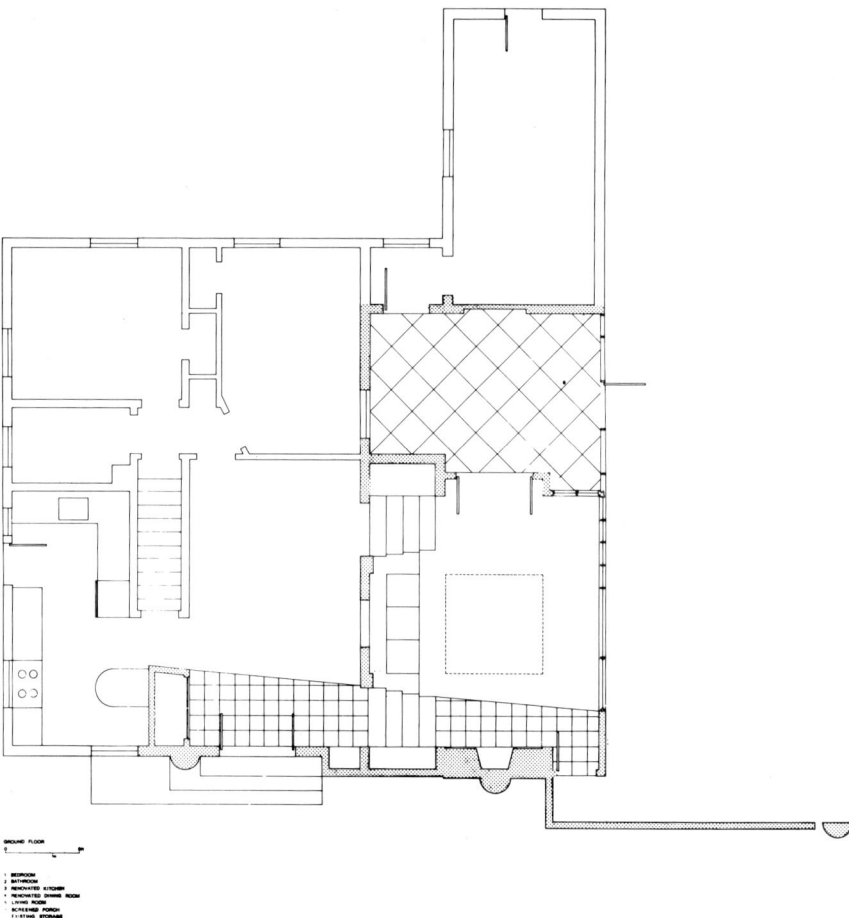

1 3

4

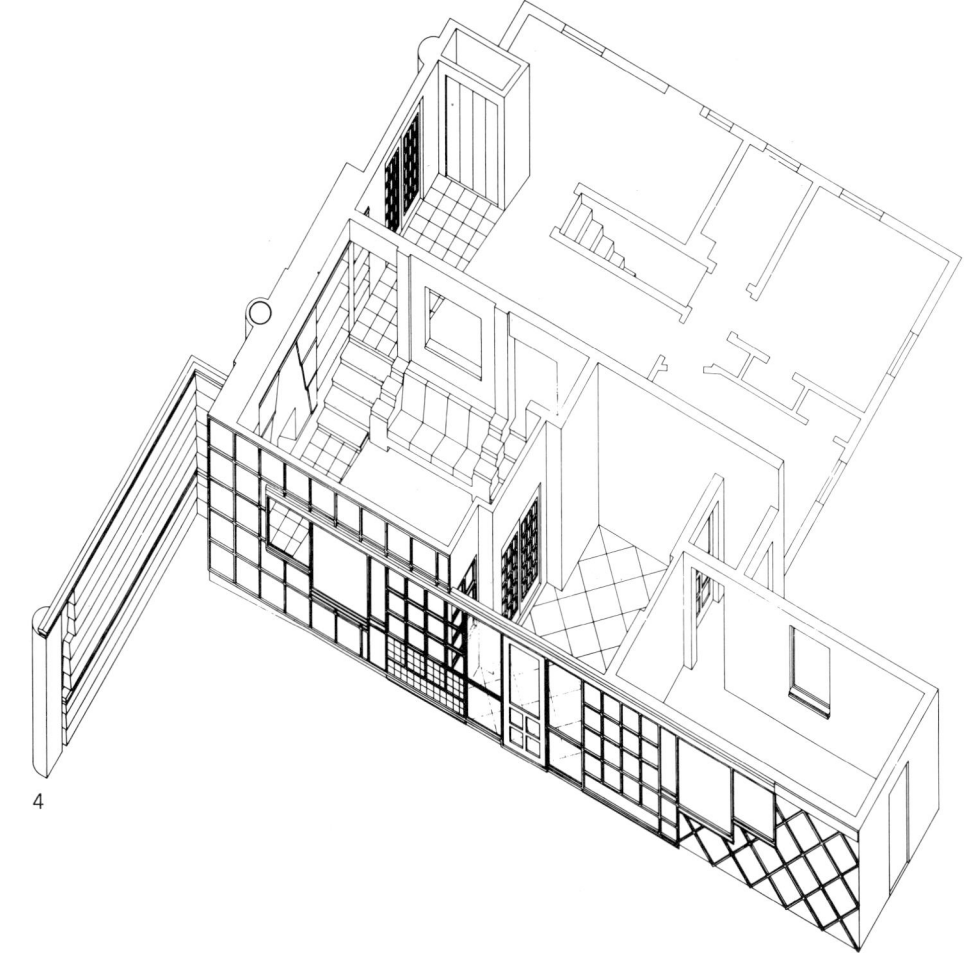

1 Conceptual sketch
2 Axonometric
3 Ground floor plan
4 Axonometric from garden
5 Living room

5

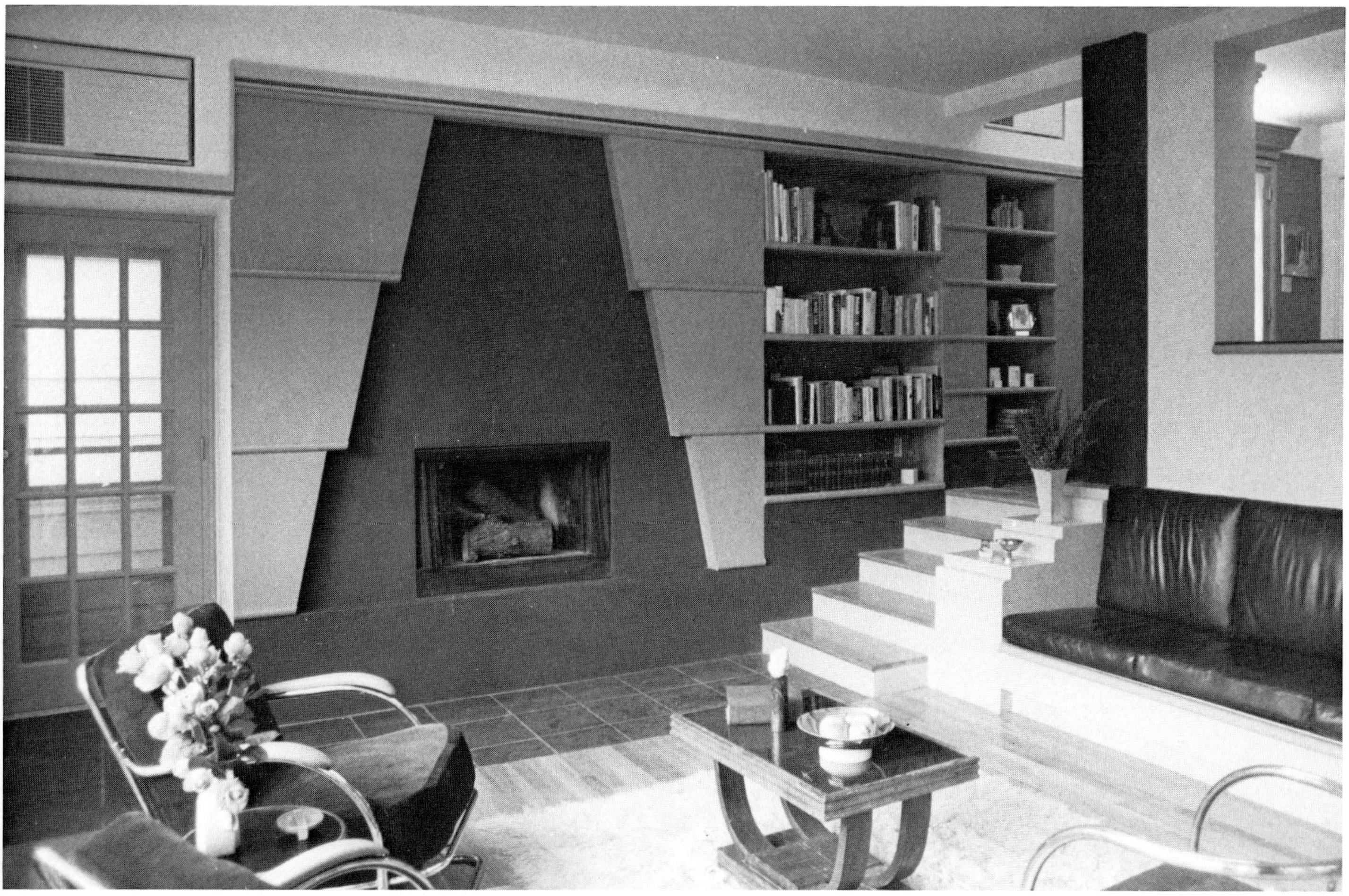

SCHULMAN HOUSE

6 Preliminary sketch scheme
7 Fireplace sketch
8 Garden façade
9 Street façade of completed building
   Photograph: Norman McGrath
10 Street façade

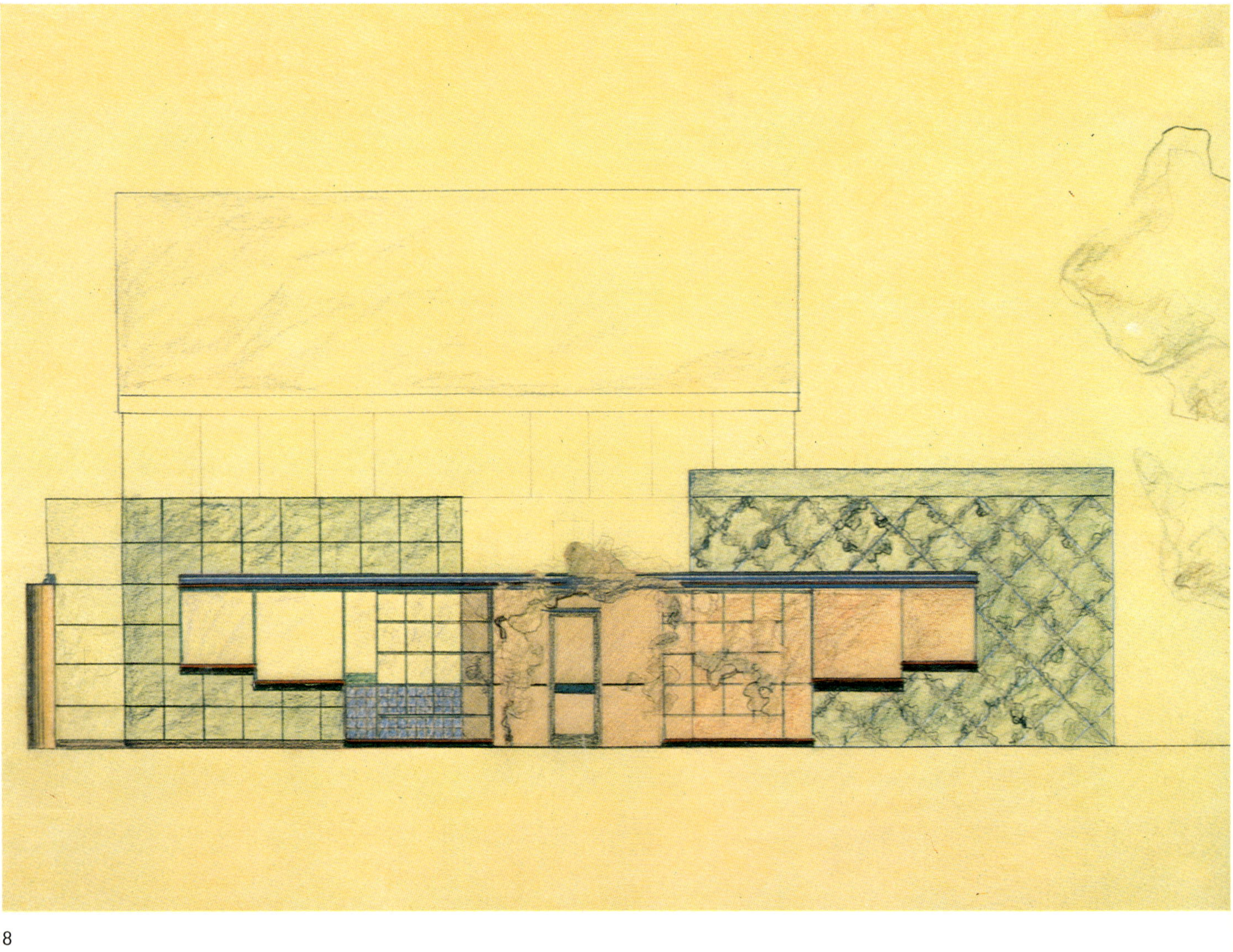

SCHULMAN HOUSE

Chem-Fleur Factory Addition and Renovation 1977
Newark, New Jersey

The client, a Newark-based research and processing company, required that new employee facilities, administrative offices and a warehouse be added to the existing plant. Also, the laboratory space in the plant was to be renovated.

The office wing and warehouse are joined to the existing factory forming a three-part organisation that reflects the programmatic distribution of functions on the site and their relationship to the street. The central circulation spine in the existing building is extended through the addition, binding the three parts of the plan. The common room terminates this axis, in keeping with the primacy of this space in the internal organisation of the factory. The street entrance leads through a foyer to the reception area which, with the common room, forms a system of interlocking centres, thereby connecting the two principal axes.

The inter-relationship among the three primary activities of the expanded facility, seen in plan, is also reflected in the west façade, where the old and new are superimposed. Further, this joint is resolved volumetrically by a skylit void between the existing laboratory and the new warehouse.

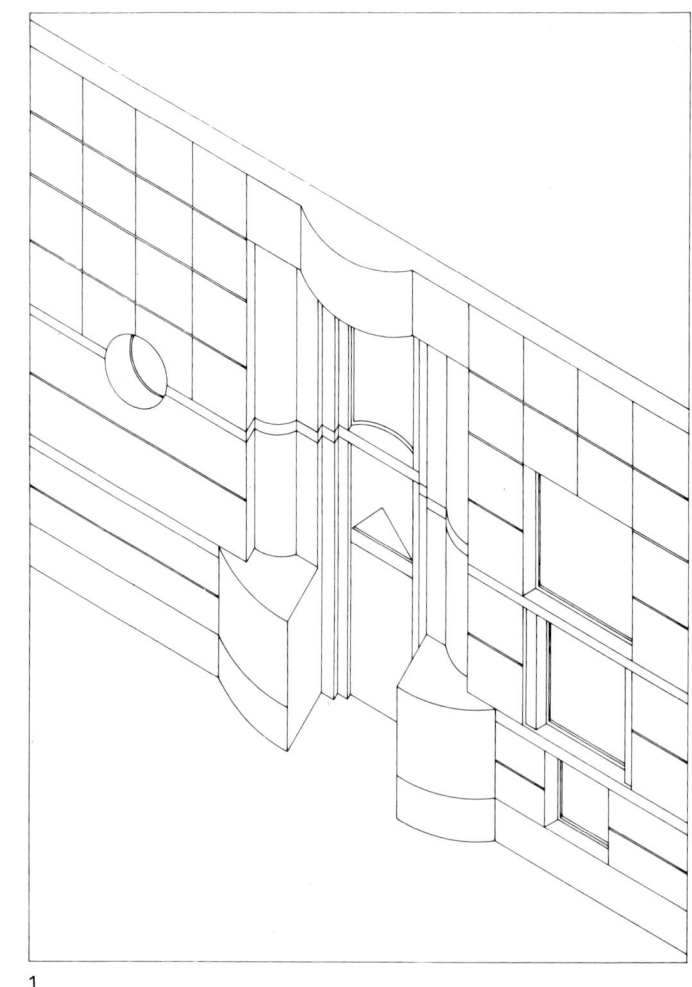
1

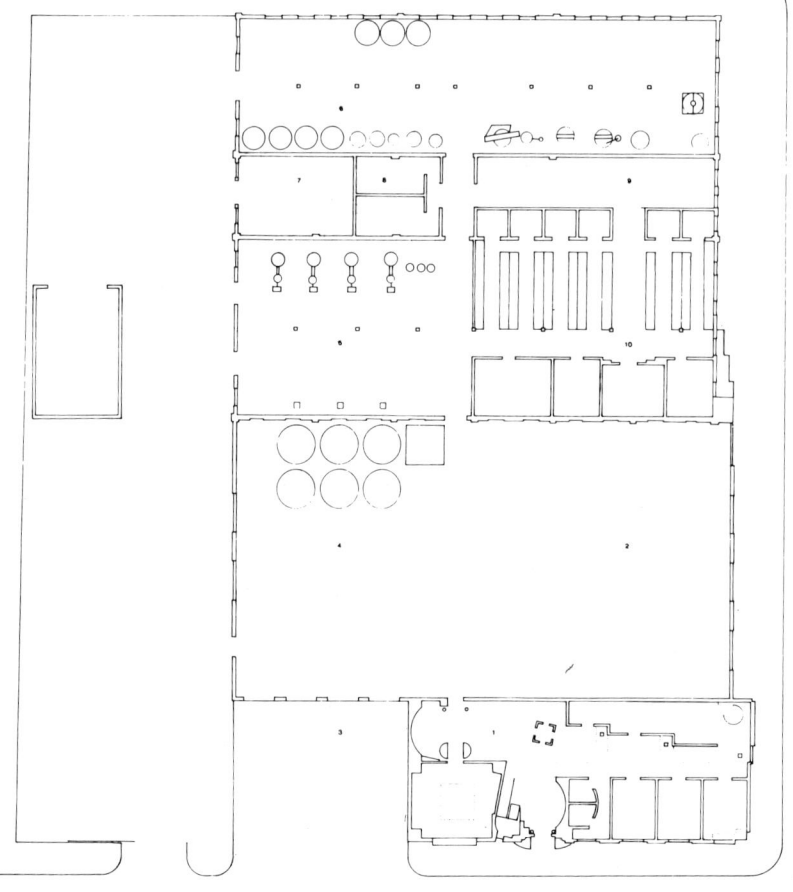
2

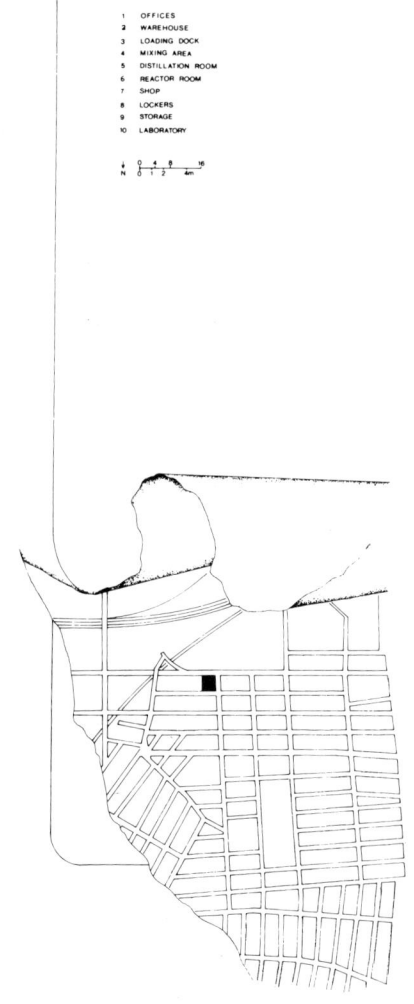

1. OFFICES
2. WAREHOUSE
3. LOADING DOCK
4. MIXING AREA
5. DISTILLATION ROOM
6. REACTOR ROOM
7. SHOP
8. LOCKERS
9. STORAGE
10. LABORATORY

CHEM-FLEUR FACTORY

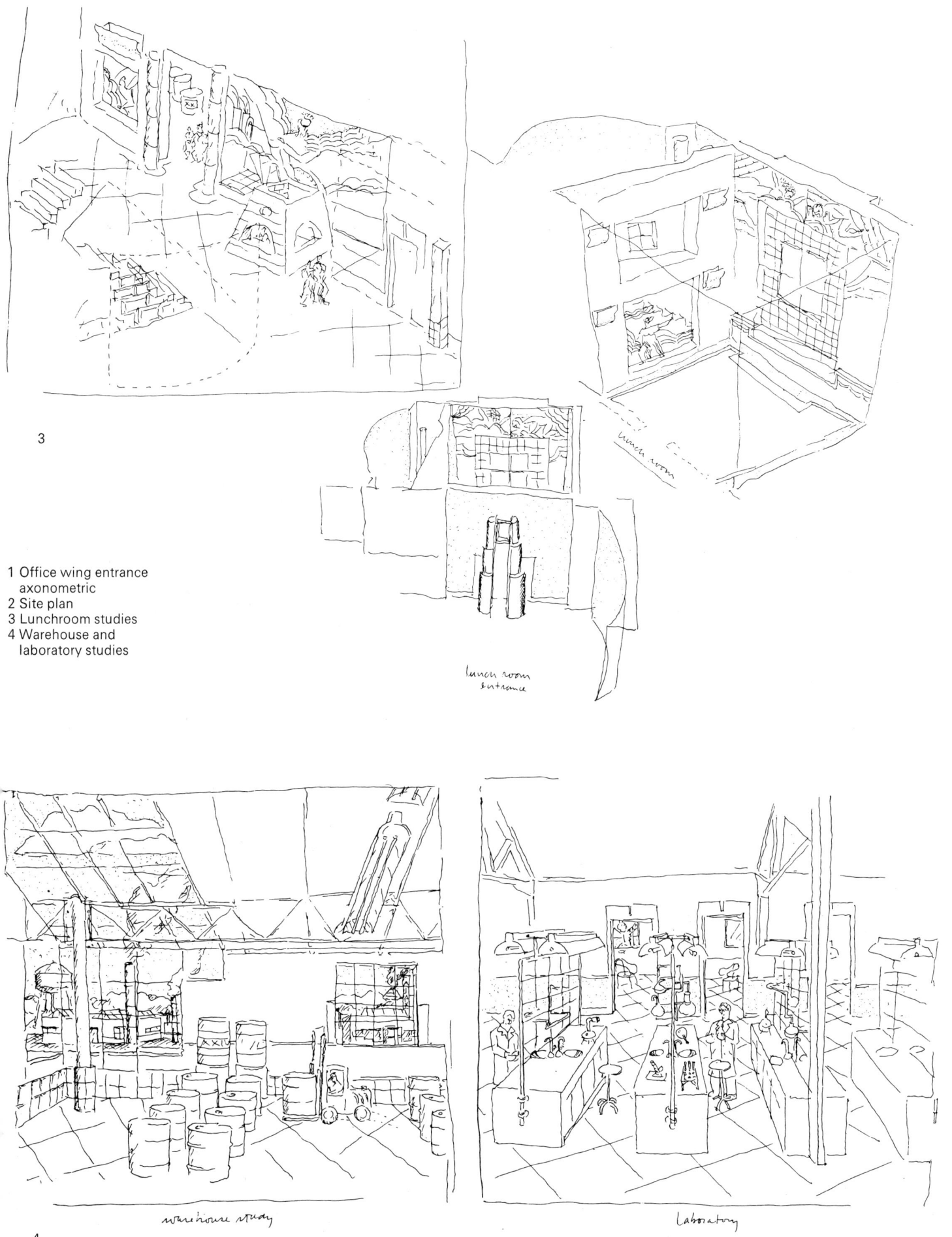

1 Office wing entrance axonometric
2 Site plan
3 Lunchroom studies
4 Warehouse and laboratory studies

CHEM-FLEUR FACTORY

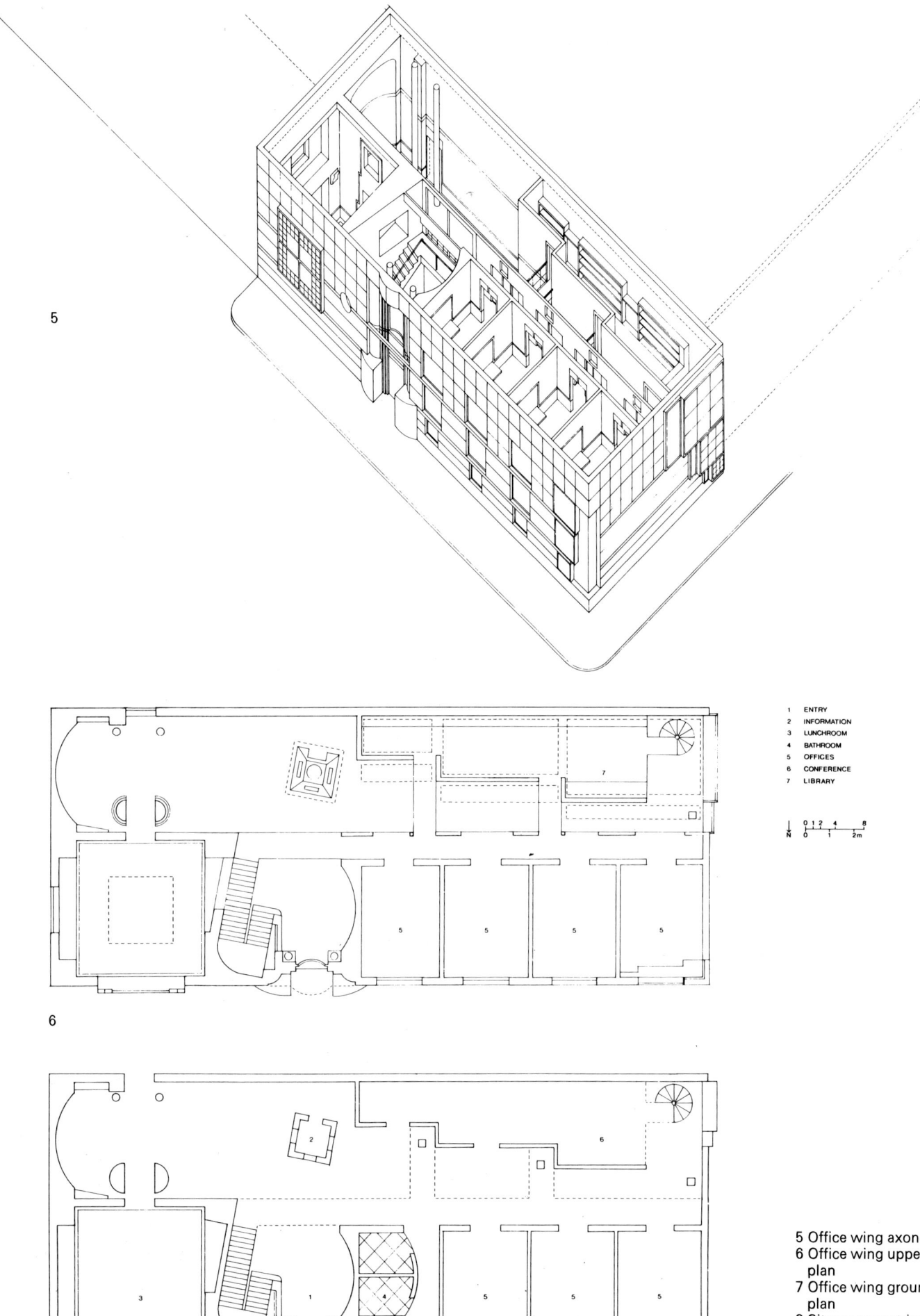

1	ENTRY
2	INFORMATION
3	LUNCHROOM
4	BATHROOM
5	OFFICES
6	CONFERENCE
7	LIBRARY

5 Office wing axonometric
6 Office wing upper floor plan
7 Office wing ground floor plan
8 Site axonometric
9 Section looking east
10 West elevation

CHEM-FLEUR FACTORY

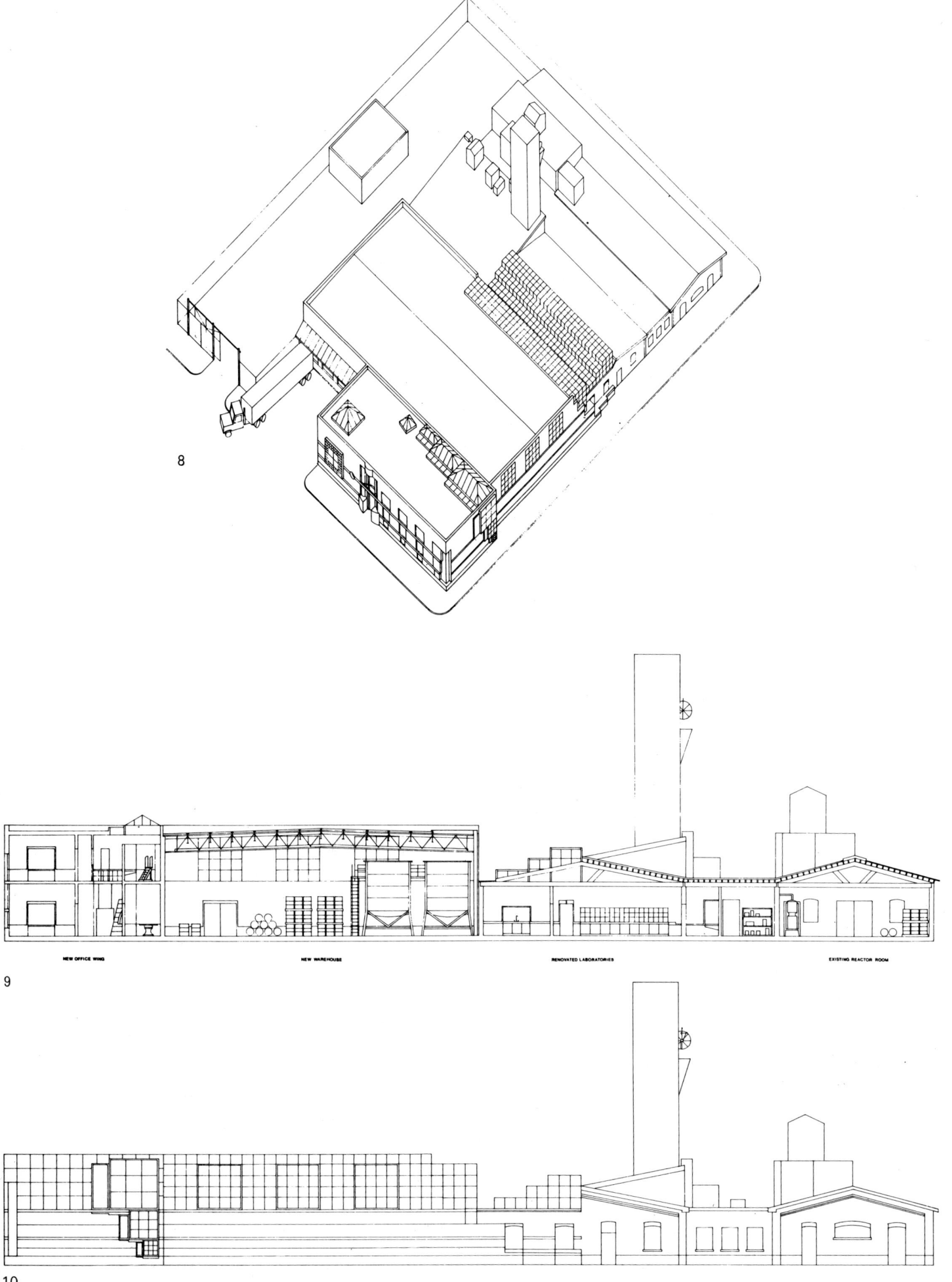

Kalko House
1978
Green Brook, New Jersey

The Kalko House is located in the clearing of a densely wooded site which slopes steeply to the back and side, offering a dramatic view toward New York City. The programme called for a swimming pool and a multi-car garage for the owners' automobile collection. These project as wings from the central portion of the house in order to engage the positive qualities of the landscape. Procession through the site begins at the entrance gate formed by a small garage pavilion and the main garage. These flank the automobile forecourt which provides a degree of enclosure and privacy for entrance to the house at the centre of the composition. The rear wing with its pergola and swimming pool projects to one side of the garden, reinforcing the privacy of the site while opening toward the sun and view.

1 Preliminary sketch
2 Ground floor plan
3 Upper floor plan
4 Street façade (preliminary)
5 Street façade
6 Garden façade

1

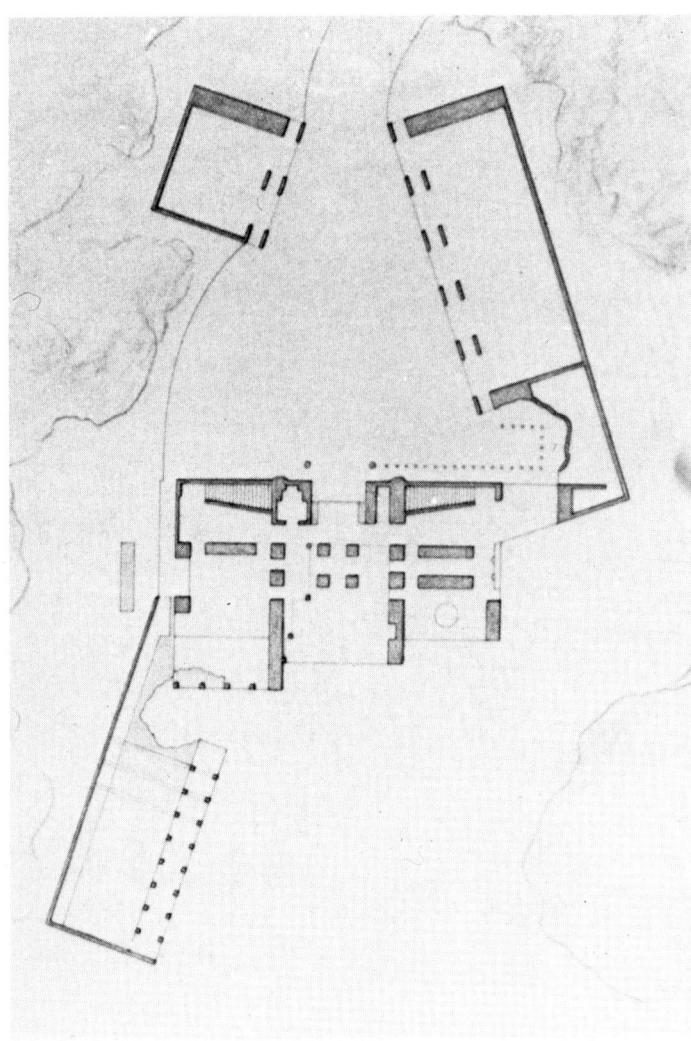

2

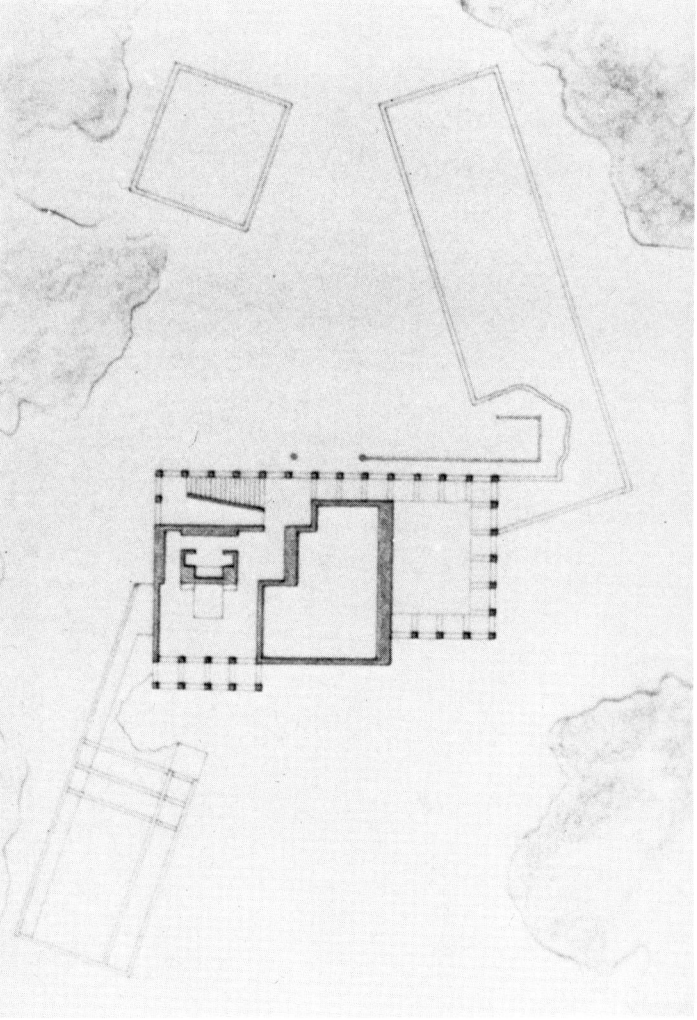

3

KALKO HOUSE

4

5

6

Plocek House
'Keystone House'
1977
Warren Township, New Jersey

The Plocek House, or 'Keystone House', is situated on a wooded hillside in Warren Township, New Jersey. The three stories of the house are restricted in the street façade whose articulation recalls the classical tripartite division of basement, *piano nobile* and attic. One enters the house through this façade at the lower level and also through the east façade at the main level, adjacent to the parking court. The intersection of these two entry axes is marked by the stair column with its base at the lower entry level, its shaft on the main living level, and its capital in the upper storey providing light from above.

In the composition, house and landscape are made formally interdependent. Along the primary entrance axis, a gate relating to the basement storey is pulled away from the front façade while the study pavilion in the garden is seen as the keystone removed from the mass of the upper portion of the house. The relationship of the house to the site is clarified by the understanding that these elements have been displaced and are located along the processional axis of the house.

In addition, the secondary axis at the main level is paired with a parallel axis through the terraces in the garden and is linked to it along the primary axis of the building. The stepped walls of the garden mirror the rear of the house; the garden is thereby read as a figure, allowing the house to be understood as a residual element in the composition as a whole.

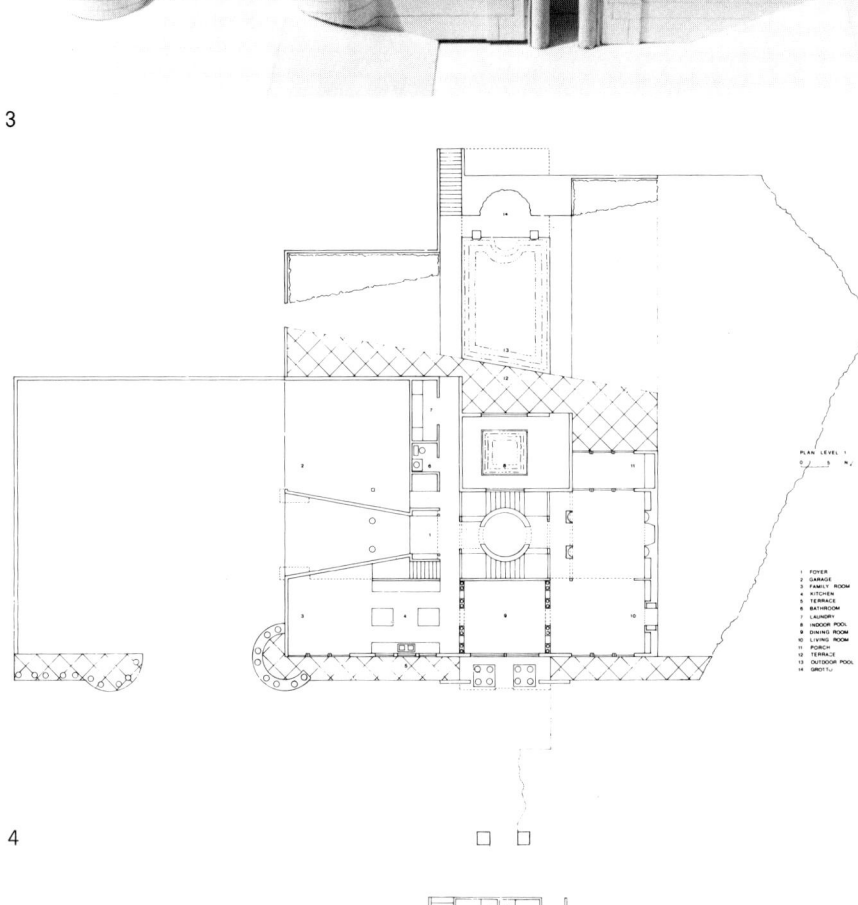

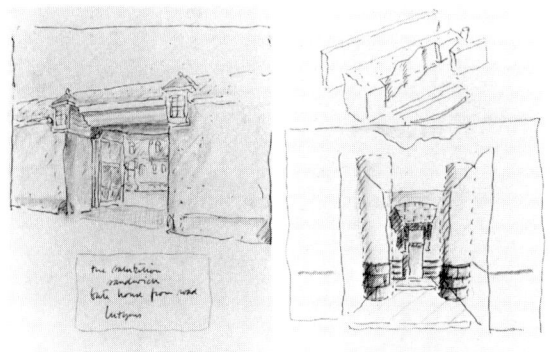

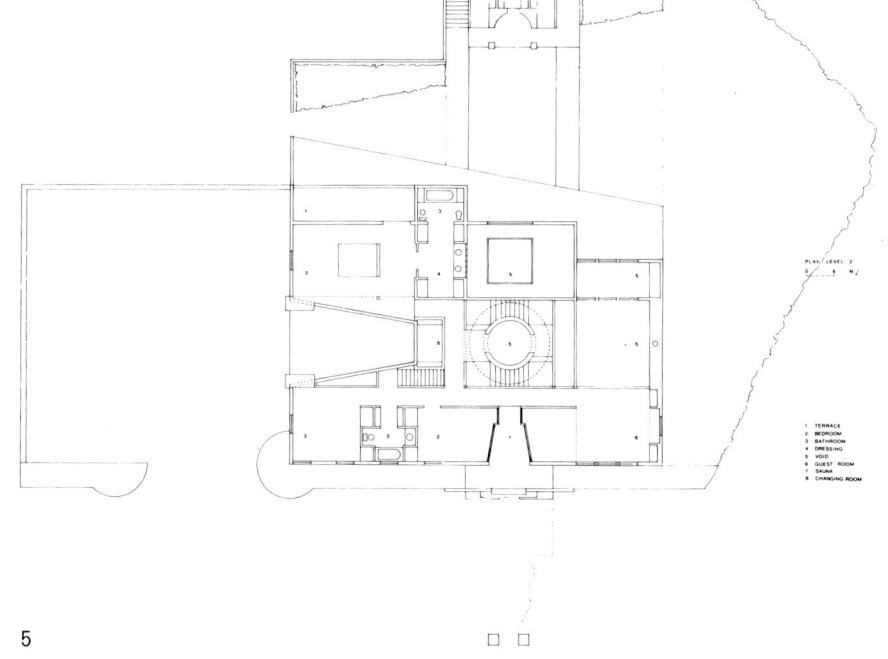

1 Referential sketch, 'The Salutation Sandwich, Gatehouse from the road, Lutyens'
2 Plocek court entrance sketch
3 Model
4 Plan level 1
5 Plan level 2
6 *Parti* sketch
7 *Parti* sketch
8 Preliminary plan
9 Plan studies
10 Plan study
11 Preliminary main floor plan

PLOCEK HOUSE

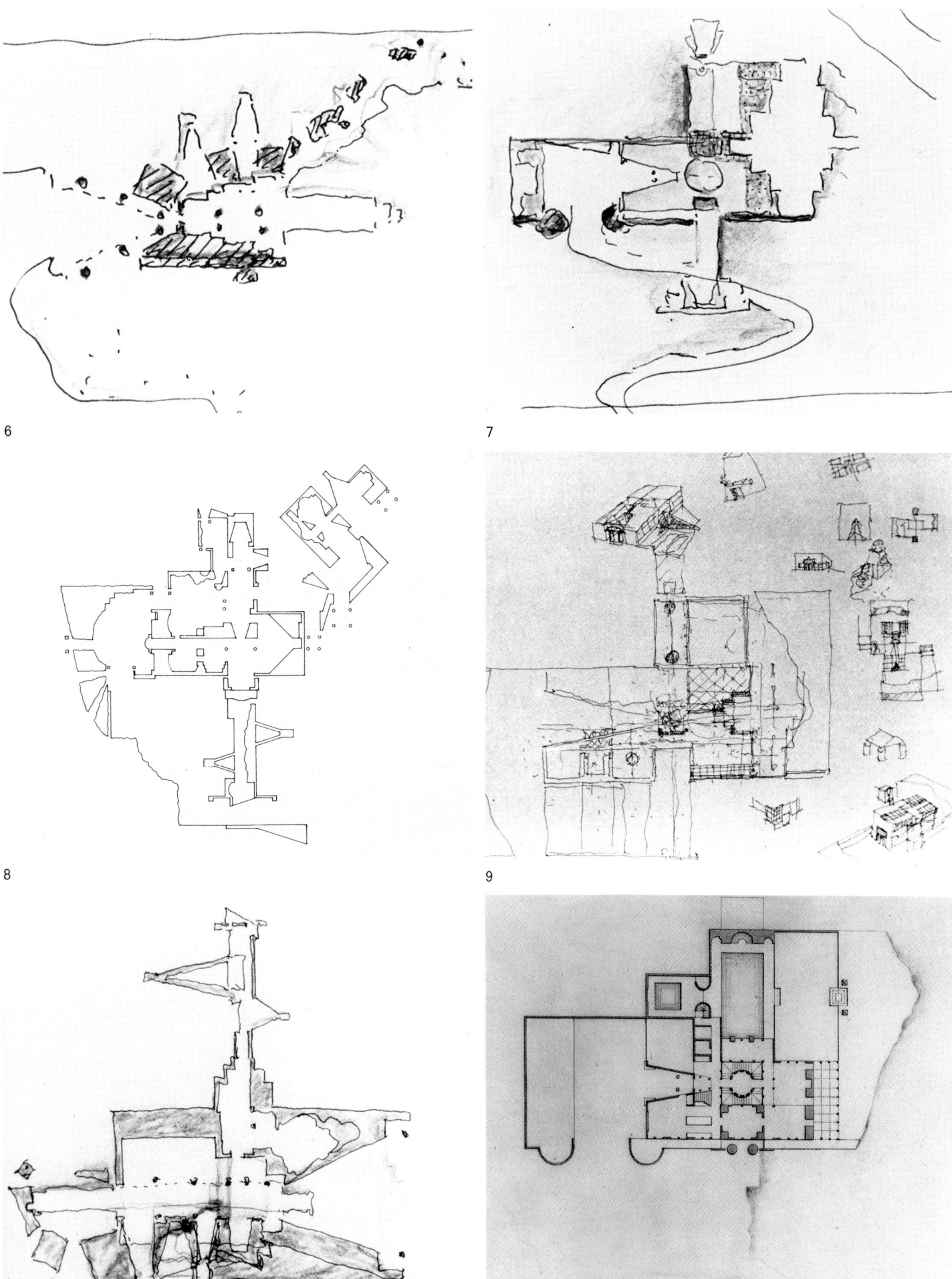

PLOCEK HOUSE

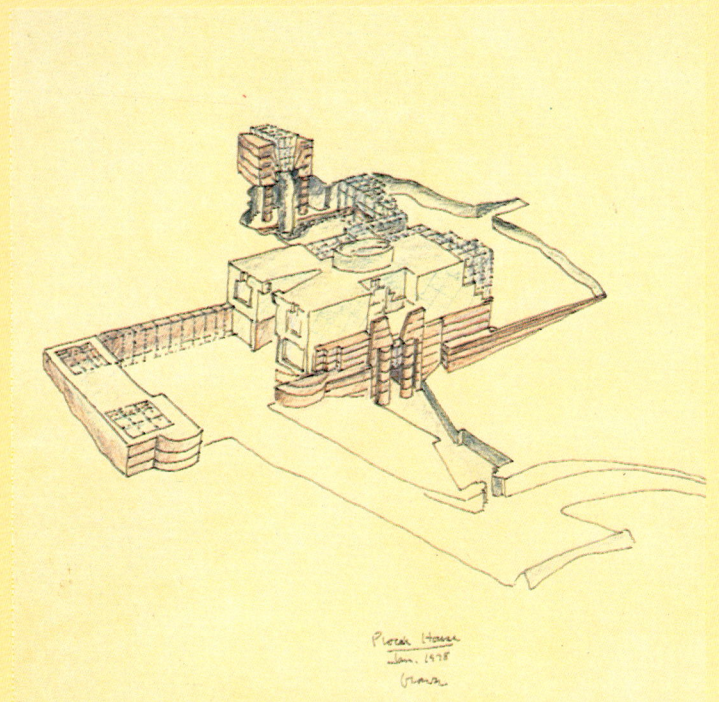

12

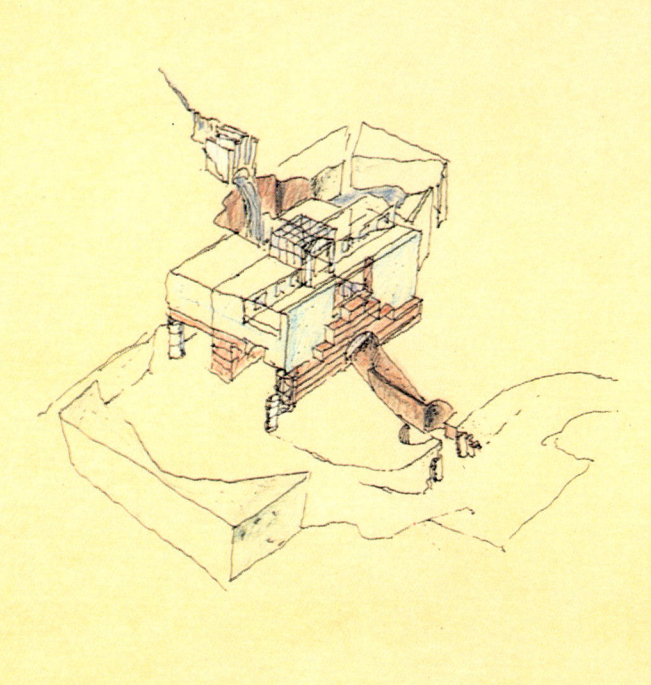

13

12 Axonometric
13 Axonometric
14 Preliminary studies

15 Street façade
16 Court façade

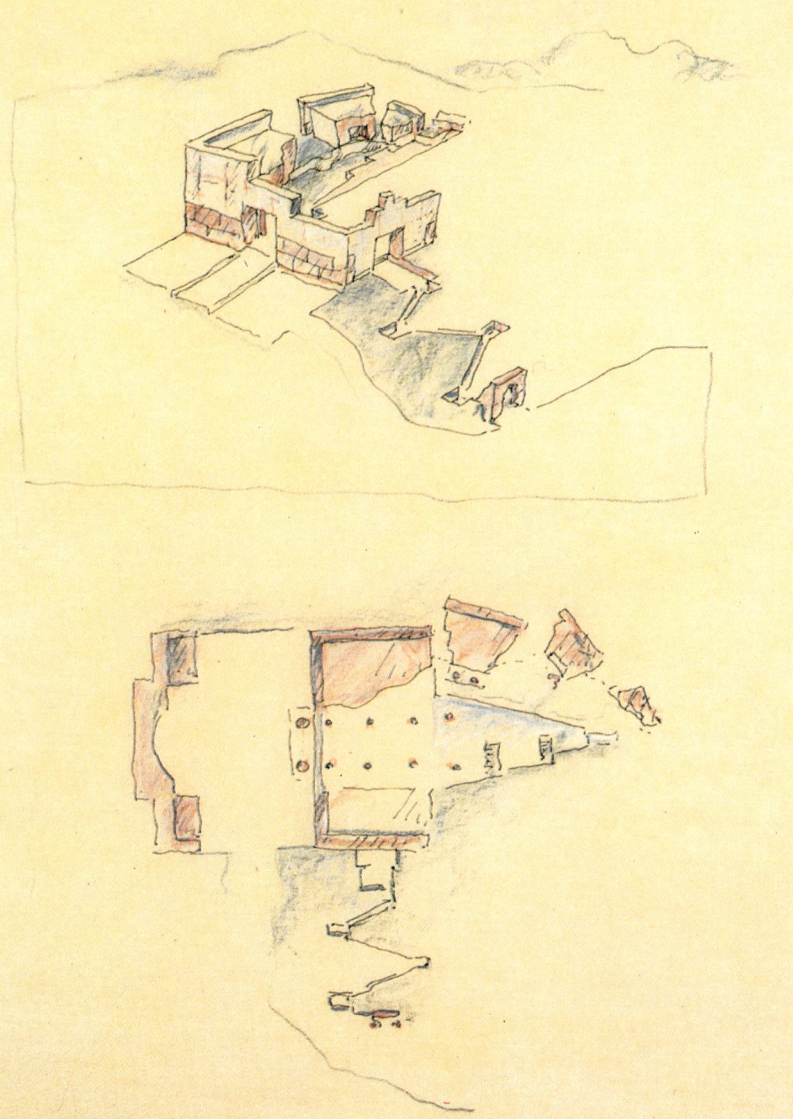

14

84

PLOCEK HOUSE

15

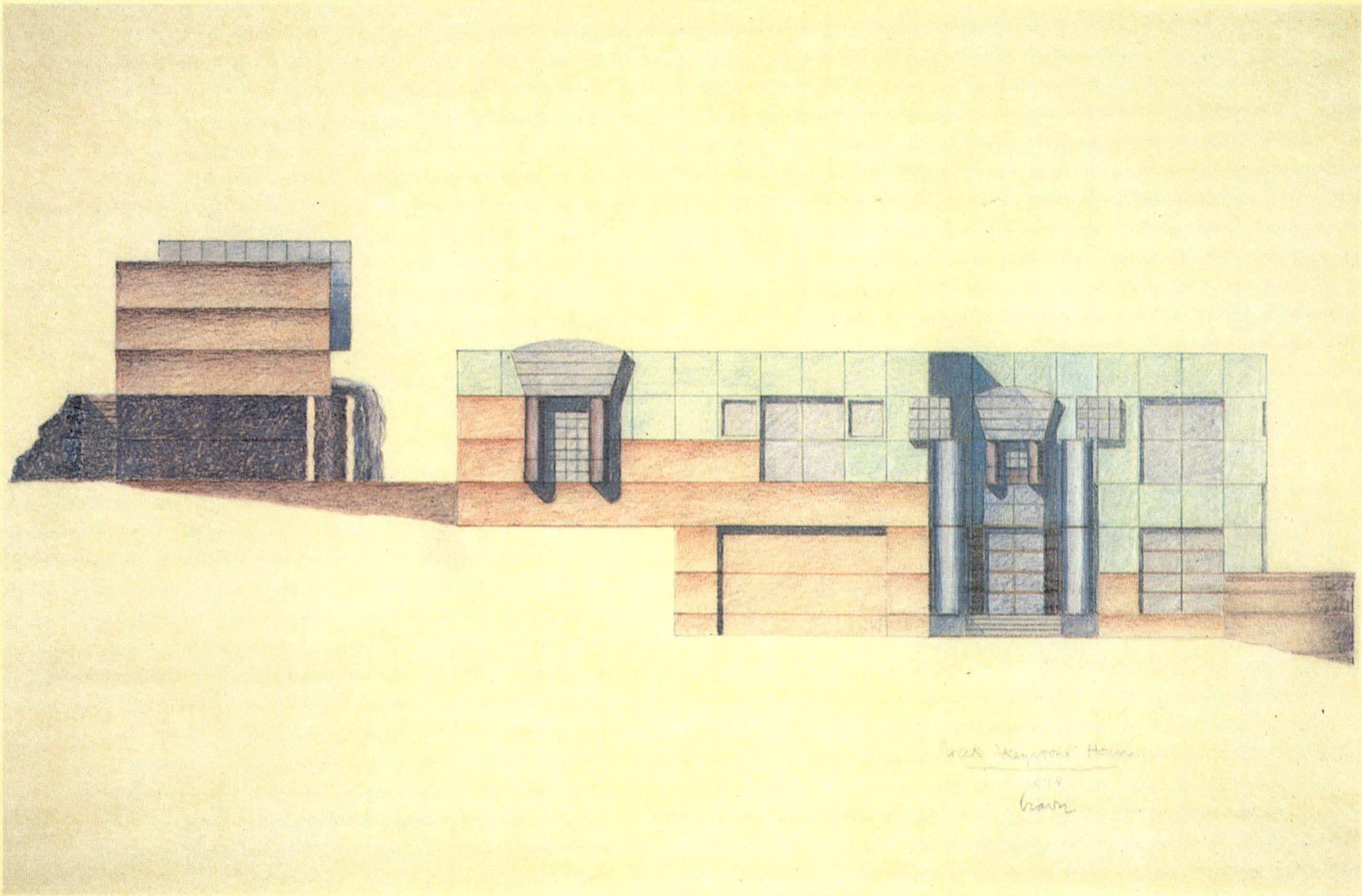

16

85

Fargo-Moorhead Cultural Center 1977-78
Fargo, North Dakota and Moorhead, Minnesota

Fargo and Moorhead are twin cities in the adjacent states of North Dakota and Minnesota, separated by the Red River. In conjunction with the replacement of a vehicular bridge, a cultural centre is planned which would physically and symbolically link the two communities. An art museum spans the bridge and connects a concert hall and public radio and television stations on one side with a history museum on the other.

The concert hall and radio and televisions station complex incorporates the Case Building, an existing three-storey structure, and uses its key position on the site as a significant element in the composition. This building, which is to be remodelled, will accommodate radio and television and provide support spaces for the concert hall. The double entry to this complex was required because of local traffic conditions and the location of public parking facilities. The concert hall is located between these two portals and a common lobby, also to be used for exhibitions, gives access to the art museum on the bridge.

A common lobby is also developed at the entrance to the history museum whose lecture hall and temporary exhibition space will be shared. Exhibitions are arranged in a loop around the central lecture hall and extend out into the landscape along the banks of the river. The building's greenhouse-like enclosure on the river side and the picturesque quality of its configuration reinforce the connection to the outside and attempt to draw a parallel between the artifacts exhibited and their derivation from the land.

The art museum is located on the north side of the bridge above pedestrian and vehicular circulation. The public corridor through the building is developed as a linear gallery. On the south side of the bridge, a large outdoor porch overlooks the river and the amphitheatre outside the concert hall.

In the composition, a vertical unity is attempted by employing the river itself as the basement storey, the vehicular access and the first level bridge as piano nobile, and the art museum above the bridge as attic. The horizontal linking members, which are covered aerial walkways connecting the three cultural facilities, are seen as the cornice line of a continuous building, allowing for compositional completeness.

In its façades, the bridge employs enlarged symbolic elements of architecture such as keystones which have been made void as windows, bringing together the two cities by providing a focus on the river and establishing it as centre. The voided keystone is also seen as a scupper which collects the sky and replenishes the river below through a waterfall which issues from its base. The water is pumped from the river by a windmill which is part of the history museum and reflects the agrarian base of the communities. In this way, the individual elements of the composition are seen as parts of a larger narrative.

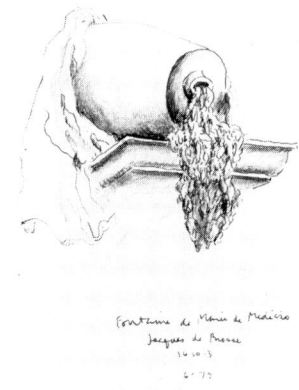

1

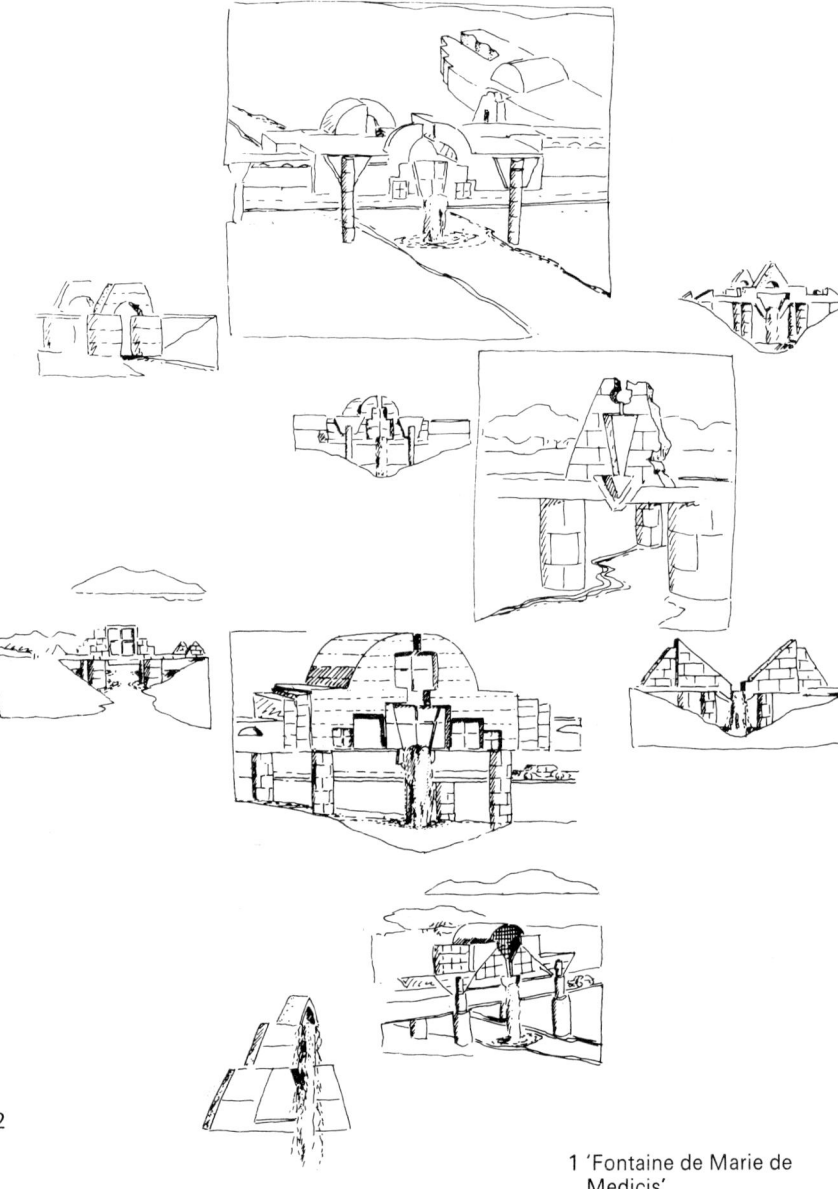

2

1 'Fontaine de Marie de Medicis'
2 Site plan
3 Preliminary studies for bridge

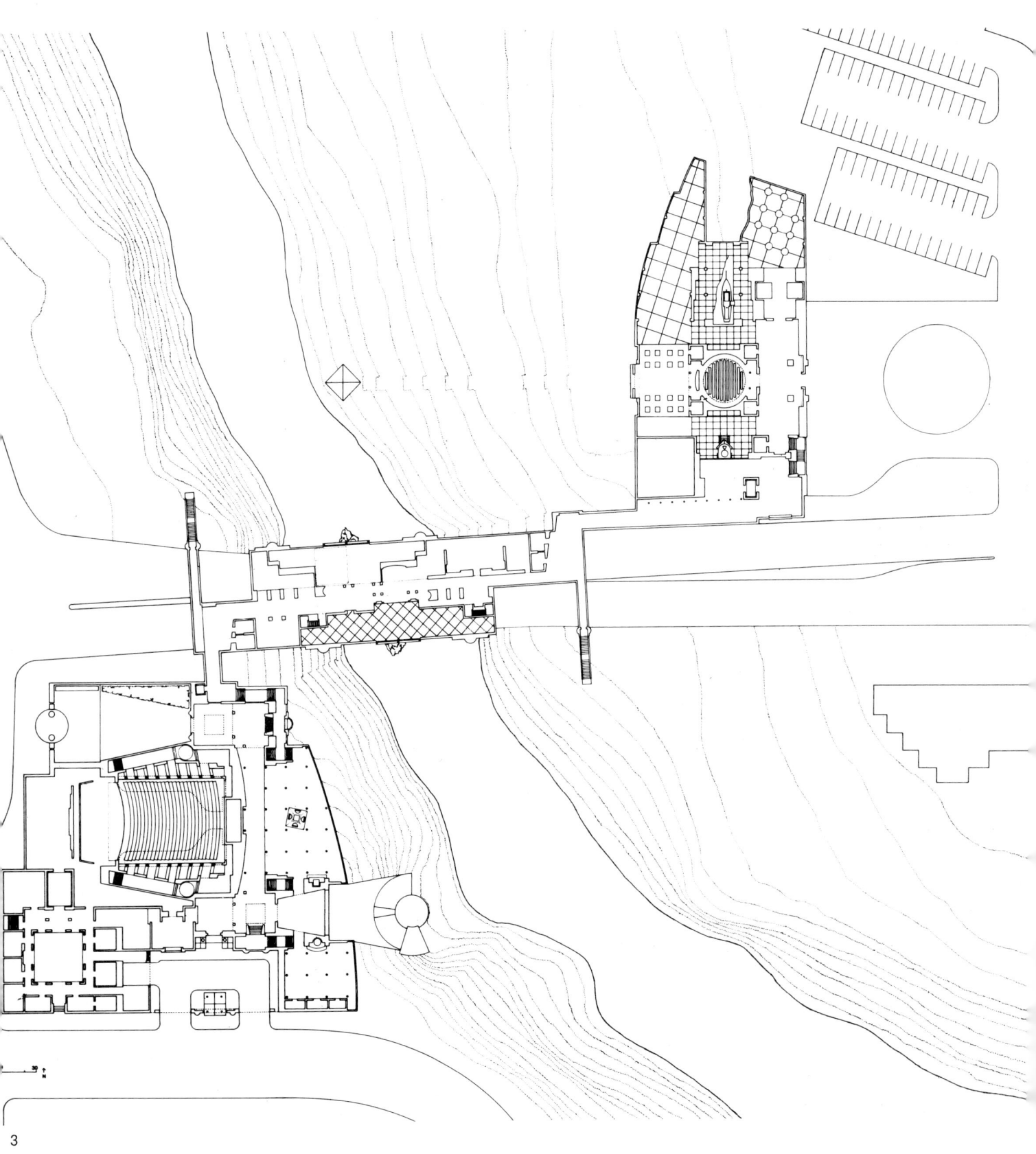

FARGO-MOORHEAD

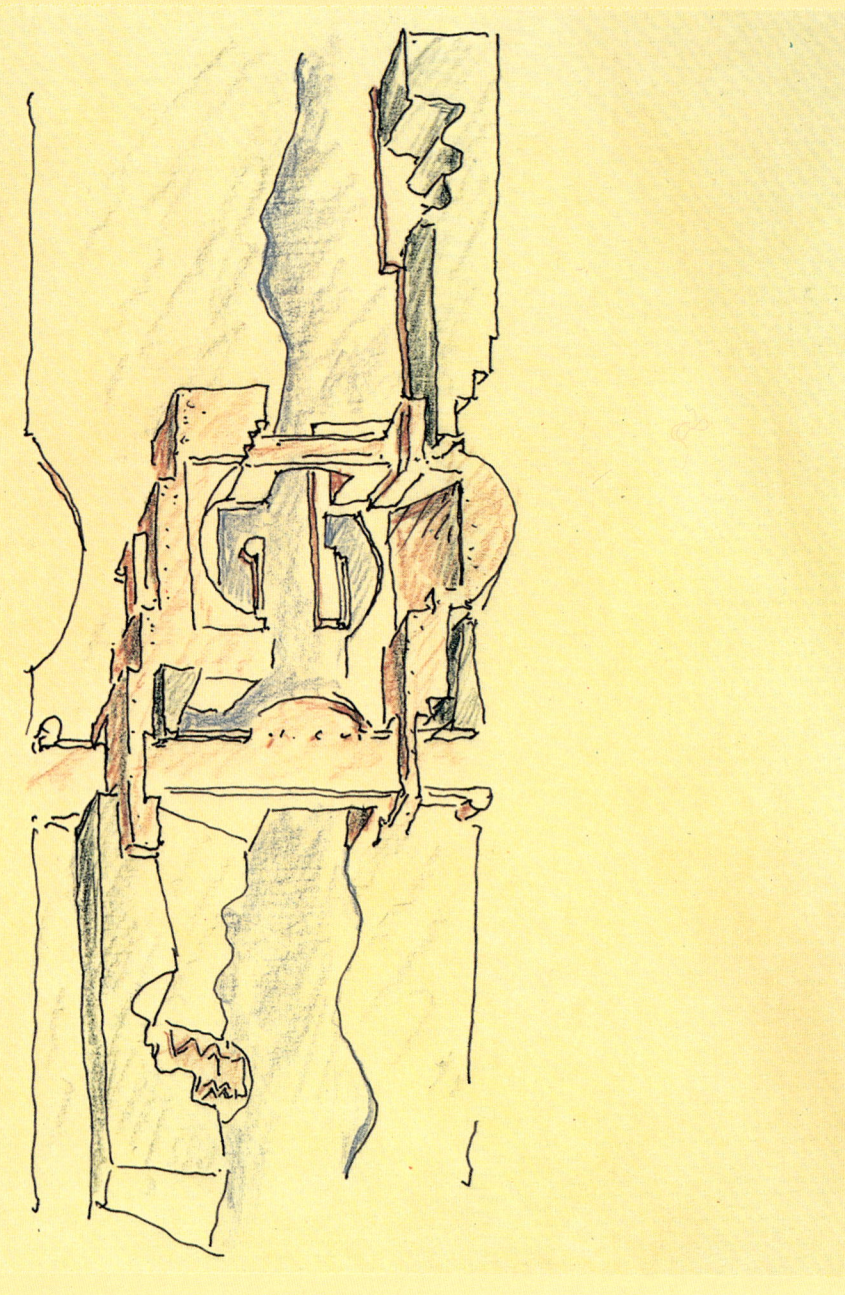

4 Preliminary site plan study
5 South elevation
6 Preliminary south elevation
7 Preliminary west elevation

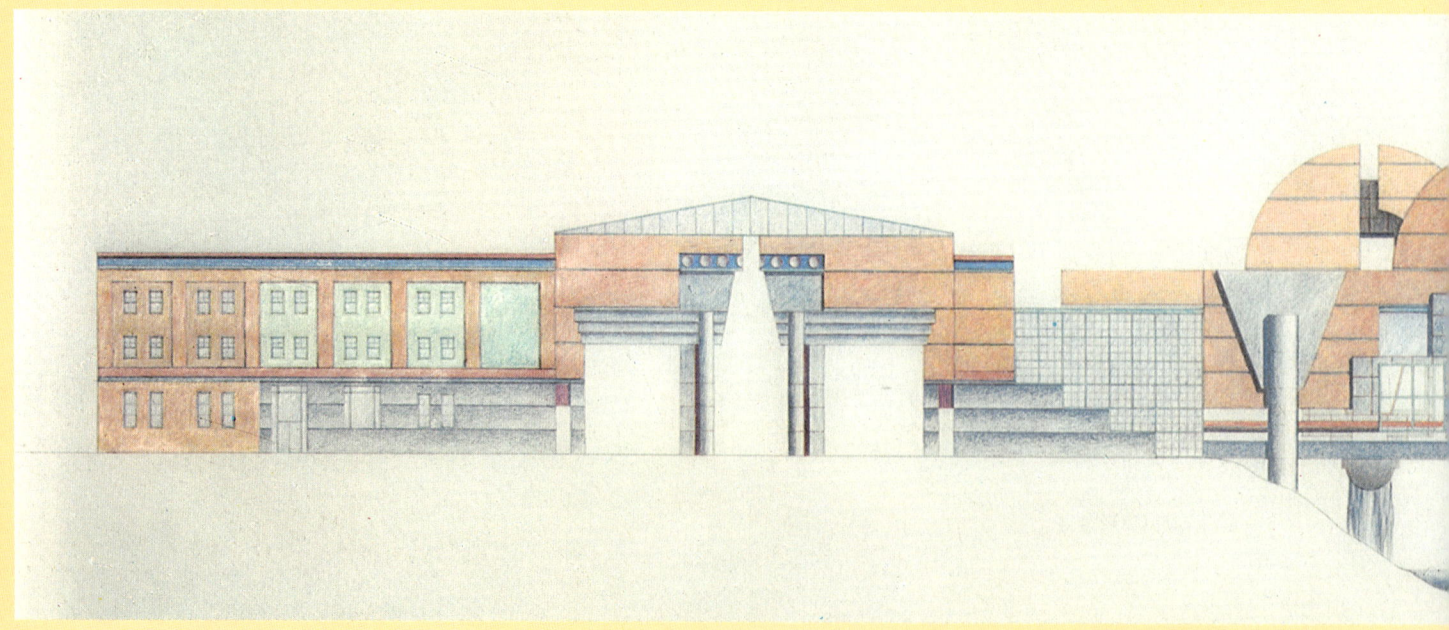

6

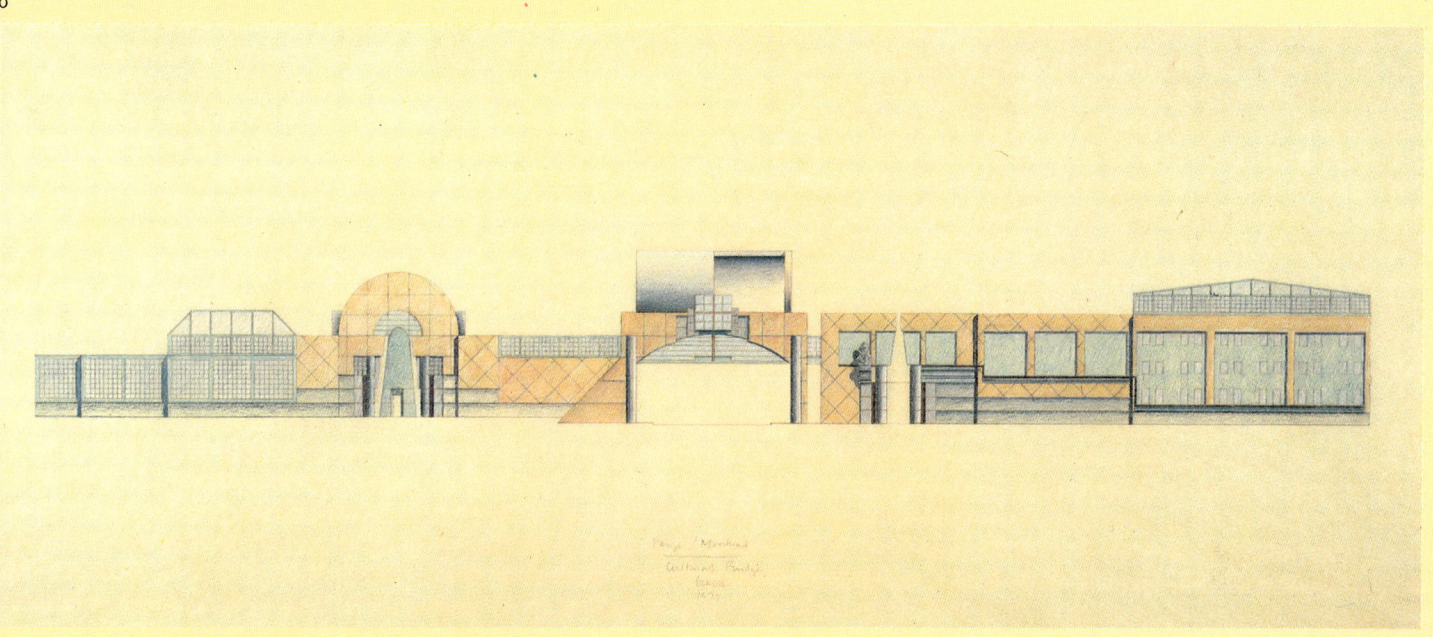

7

Abrahams Dance Studio
1977
Princeton, New Jersey

A private dance studio, new master bedroom and study were to be added to an existing four-bedroom surburban house built in the 1950s. The existing building, with its butterfly roof and cedar siding, is drawn into the composition; articulation of the siding provides a plinth-like base for the new pavilion. The upper portion of the addition, housing the master bedroom and the study, is treated as a light, garden-like structure, similar to a gazebo. The outside window of the study identifies the central aspect of the house both for the interior rooms and for the garden beyond.

1

1 Preliminary studies
2 Ground floor plan
3 Upper floor plan

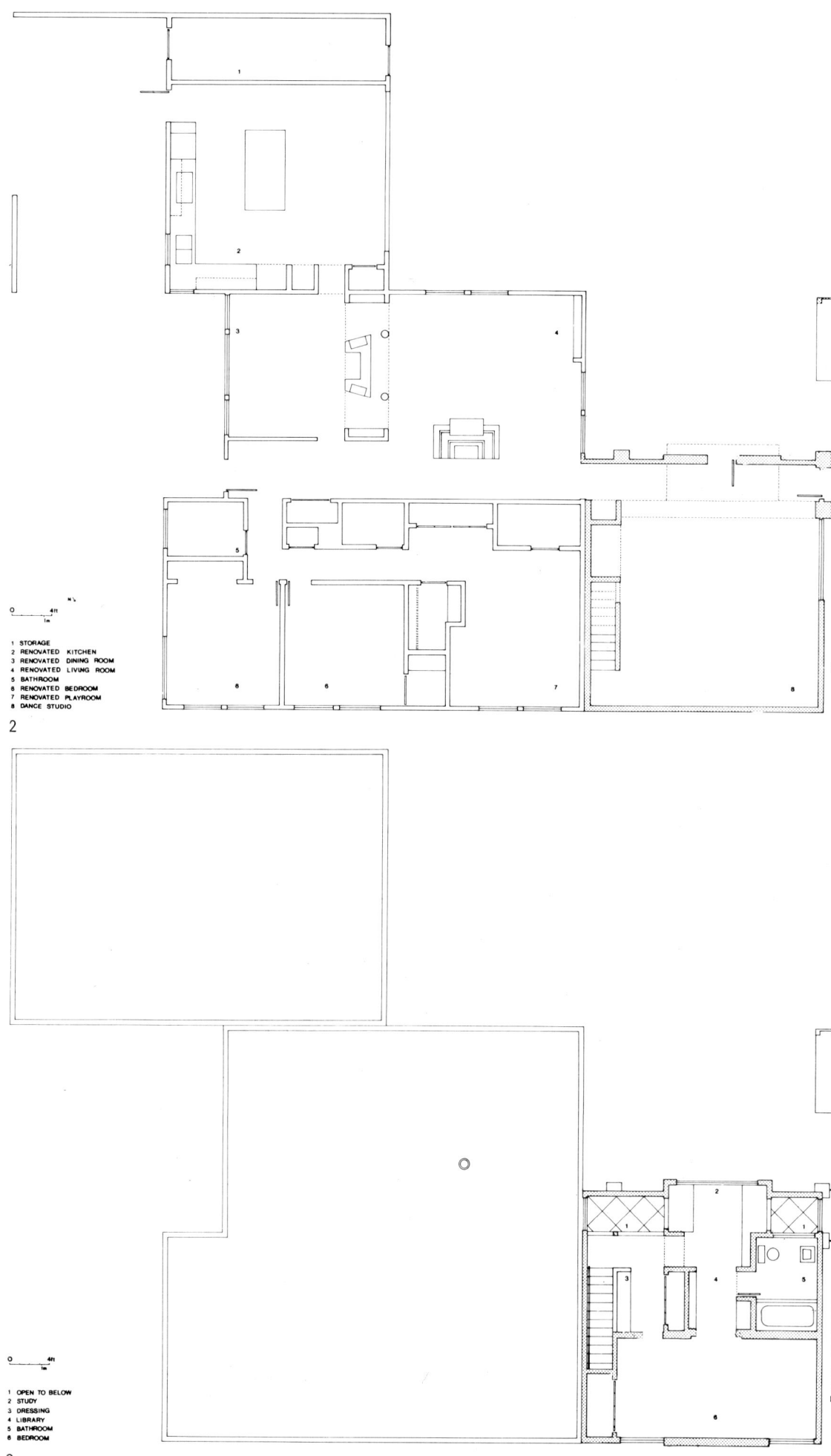

1 STORAGE
2 RENOVATED KITCHEN
3 RENOVATED DINING ROOM
4 RENOVATED LIVING ROOM
5 BATHROOM
6 RENOVATED BEDROOM
7 RENOVATED PLAYROOM
8 DANCE STUDIO

1 OPEN TO BELOW
2 STUDY
3 DRESSING
4 LIBRARY
5 BATHROOM
6 BEDROOM

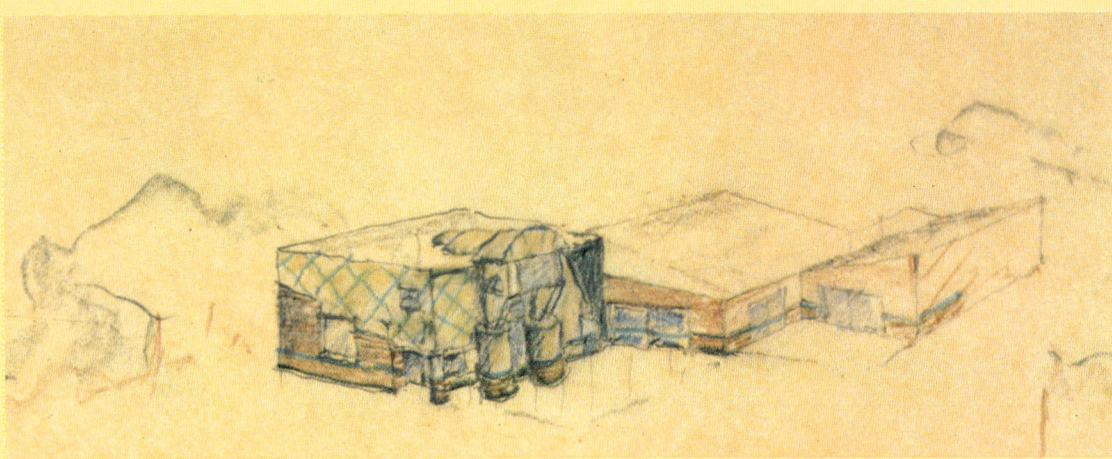

4 Preliminary sketch
5 Preliminary west elevation
6 Garden façade
7 Rear façade
8 Side façade

4

5

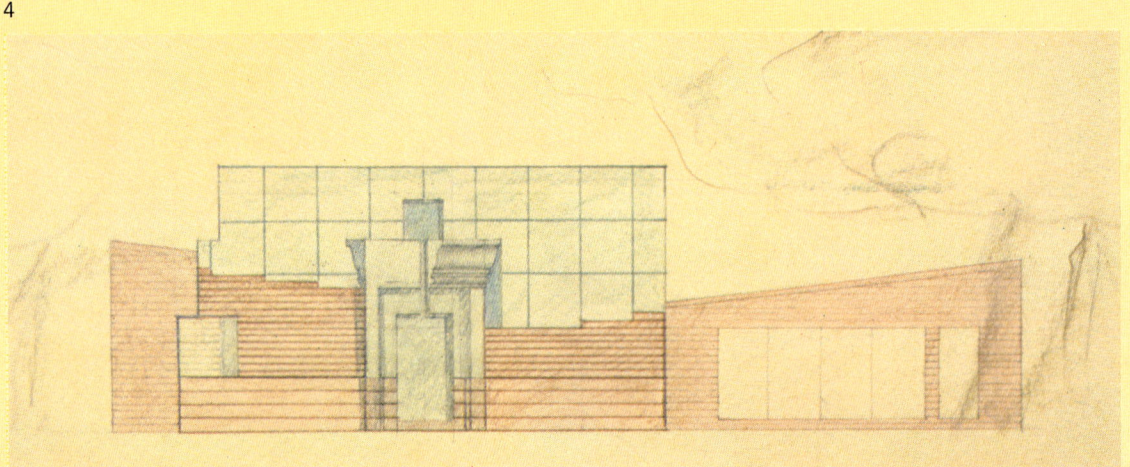

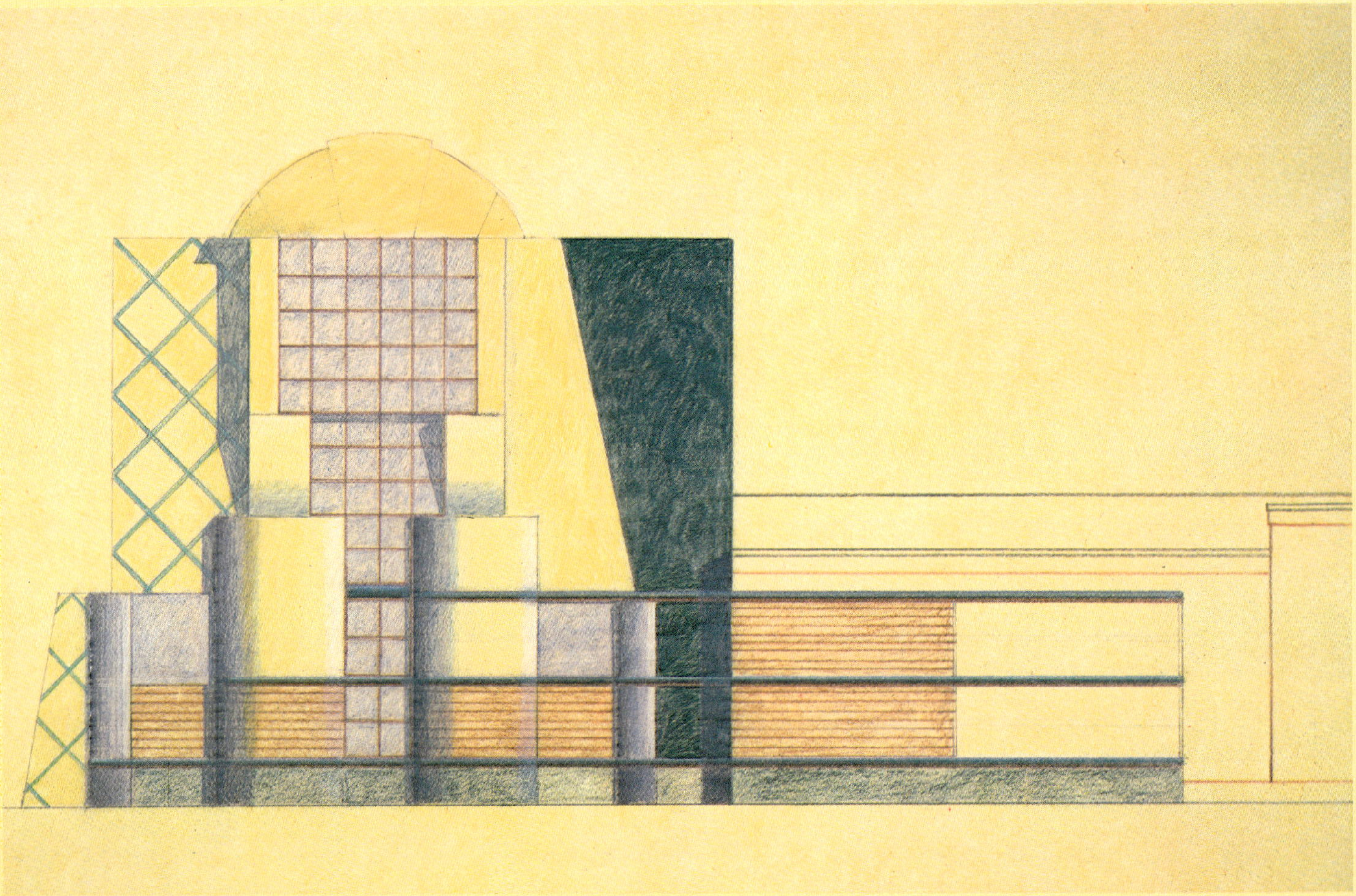

6

'Roma Interrotta' Exhibition 1978
Rome, Italy

'Roma Interrotta', an exhibition sponsored by the Italian Ministry of Transportation, is based on the map of Rome made by Gianbattista Nolli in 1748. The original map was divided into twelve segments to facilitate the printing of the original plates. For the exhibition, twelve internationally known architects were each assigned a section and asked to use it as a base for 'interventions'. The title of the exhibition, 'Roma Interrotta', or 'Rome Interrupted', signifies the intention of making urban assumptions from Nolli's base plan. No requirements for specific activities were given, so the participants could specify those activities deemed appropriate to their sectors.

This scheme for the Porta Maggiore section of Rome uses fragments of significant aspects of Roman city-building in order to take advantage of the figural conditions of object and/or space. In selecting figurative fragments, such as the keystone garden, an attempt was made to use elements of an architectural language not only in their orthodox location but also through their understood potential as symbolic analogies. The keystone garden is surrounded by an assemblage of models of buildings and urban types taken from the local context, together with newly designed elements and reinstated ancient fragments from the site, incorporating housing, cultural and commercial activities.

1 Ancient map: 'Porta Maggiore Section'
2 Modern map: 'Porta Maggiore Section'
3 Sketch: 'Bosco di Pietra' (Woods of Stone)
4 Sketch: 'Passegiata a Minerva Medica' (Passage to Minerva Medica)
5 Sketch: 'Giardino di Chiava di Volta' (Keystone Garden)
6 Porta Maggiore Section, 1748 map by Giambattista Nolli
7 Scheme for Porta Maggiore Section

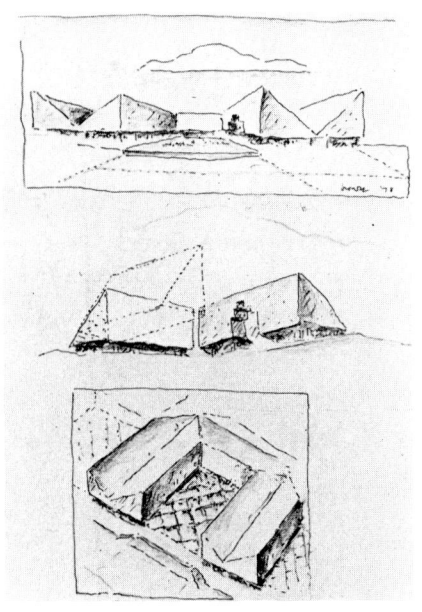

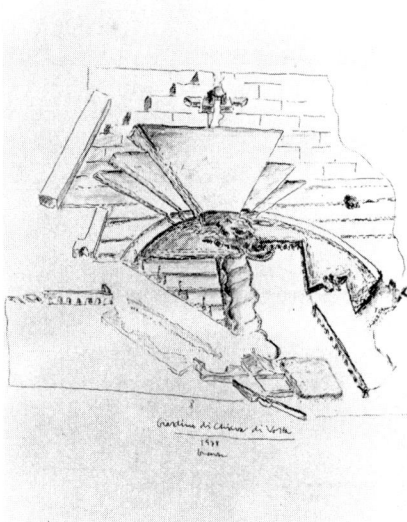

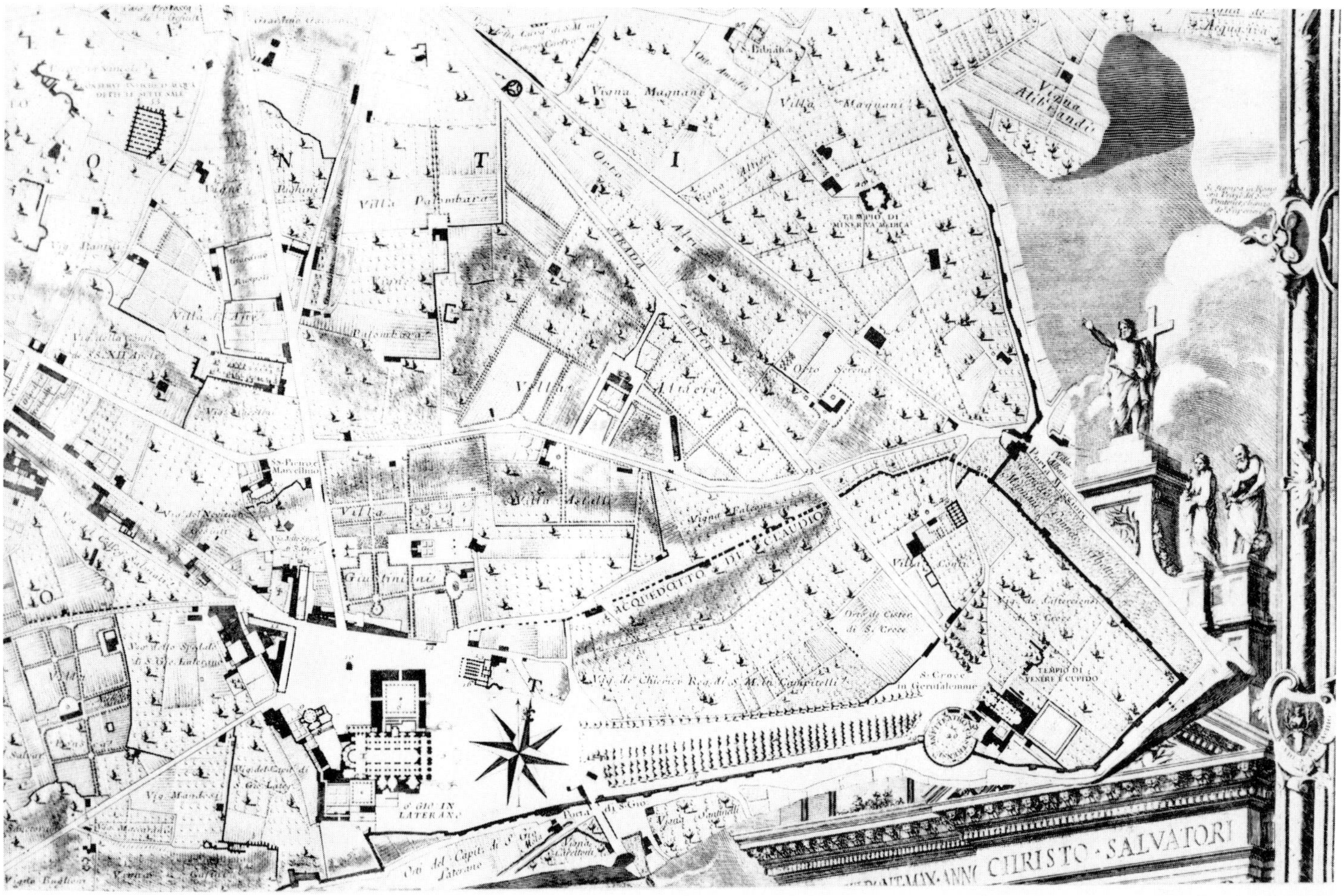

ROMA INTERROTTA

95

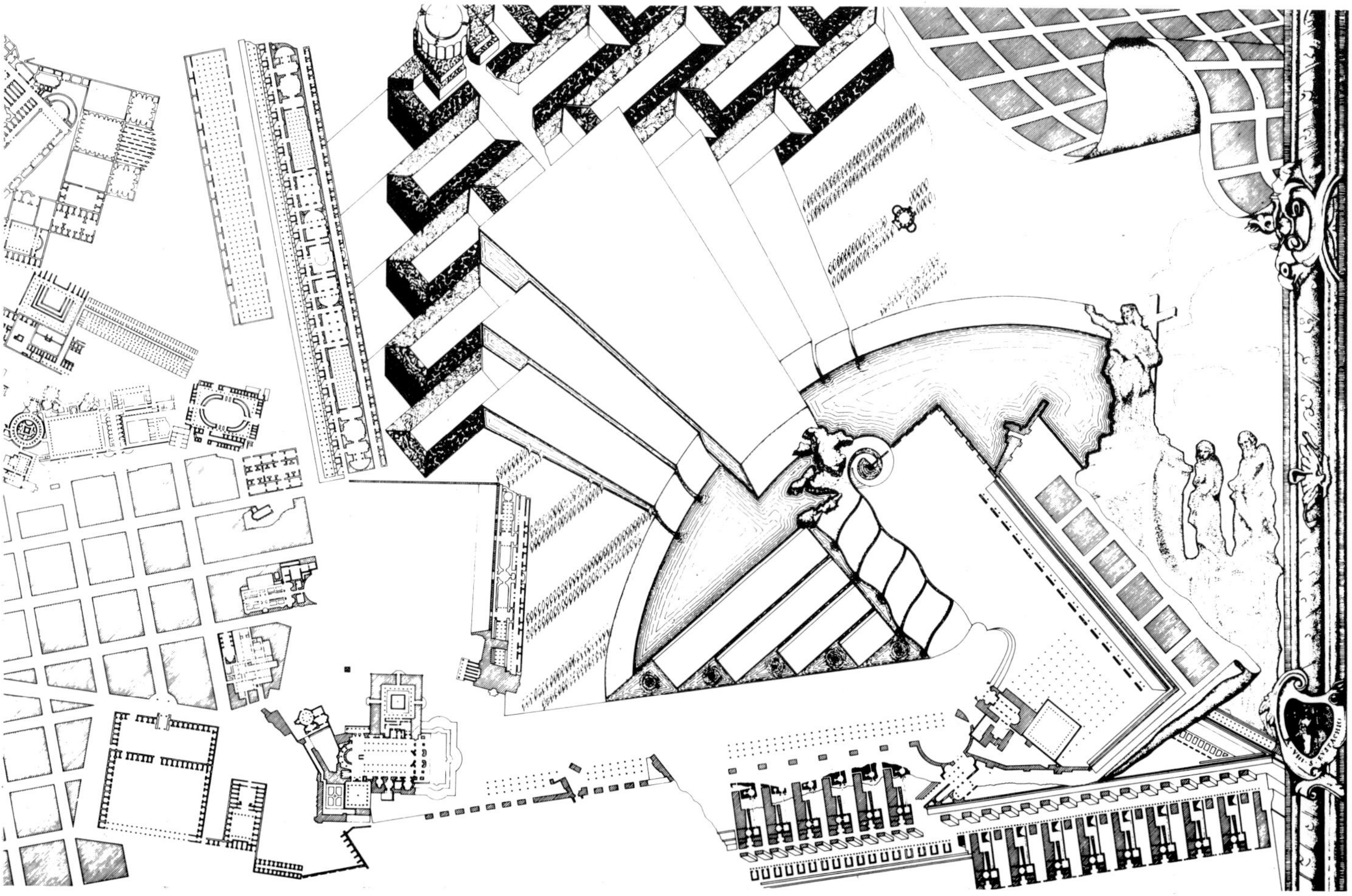

Freud and Russell at the Wherehouse
Peter Carl

'Don Quixote *is a negative of the Renaissance world; writing has ceased to be the prose of the world; resemblance and signs have dissolved their former alliance; similitudes have become deceptive and verge upon the visionary or madness; things still remain stubbornly within their ironic identity: they are no longer anything but what they are; words wander off on their own, without content, without resemblance to fill their emptiness; they are no longer the marks of things... The madman... the man of primitive resemblances... is the man who is alienated in analogy. He is the disordered player of the Same and the Other... At the other end of the cultural area, but brought close by symmetry, the poet is he who, beneath the named, constantly expected differences, rediscovers the buried kinships between things, their scattered resemblances... The poet brings similitude to the signs that speak it, whereas the madman loads all signs with a resemblance that ultimately erases them...*'[1]

There is, in this form of madness, a dilemma of correspondence between the realm of names and the realm of things such that a larger dilemma of identity emerges for Quixote, in which the domain of knowing has forsaken him. He and his battlefield of windmills are a singularity: the alienation in analogy is, in essence, a disordered relationship between the Same and the Other as it has become subject and object. Where the imagination of the poet finds wholeness in the unity of this duality, that of the madman dissolves progressively into an ironic otherness testifying to its disunity. The poet and madman appear dual aspects of the same vocation by virtue of the specific means of representation that they share.

In an incomplete early study — 'A Psychoanalysis of the Place of Arrival'[2] — I explored the extent to which architecture itself might be seen as a matter of naming, of specifying a particular place in terms of contexts which conditioned that naming. It is the game of the Same and the Other played as object/context, but which, for the essential actor in this drama, the inhabitant, is in fact the dialectic between subject and object. The distinction between poesy and madness pertains as much in this case to the architect with whom is lodged the agency of making, as to the inhabitant, who deliberates in terms of his *own* conditionality, not that of the landscape. The fundamental assumption on the part of the inhabitant, that the landscape is present to him in the form which he sees it, is precisely the focus of the architect's doubt. The critic's test for poesy involves re-enacting the drama of inhabitation. As the drama tends toward poesy, there will seem to prevail the celebration of the unity of subject and object, and as toward madness, there will appear the territory of scattered resemblances, of dwelling as alienation.

Presumably those of us who are neither poet nor madman reside on, or to one side or the other, of Foucault's axis of symmetry. His book suggests the degree to which this axis is one of knowledge and offers a history of its vicissitudes. Foucault's model of culture is bounded by the poet and madman who gaze at each other across Freud and Russell[3], or Foucault himself, on the centre-line. I would make a topographical transformation whereby the poets, Freud, and Russell occupy the centre of a region whose periphery is populated by madmen. In this manner a general domain of knowing is produced, which is furthermore congruent with the form of the place of arrival, itself embodying the archetype of centre. The journey of inhabitation, as a narrative of interpretation, is then seen to transpire in a larger landscape: that of the culture; and the architect is engaged in the elaboration and refinement of a vision of Being as inhabitation in the landscape. Thus it is possible that dwelling as alienation be the result of a transformation in the culture itself — as with a Gothic church outside the context of Christianity. Indeed the synchronicity of the moment of proposal has its immediate consequence in the diachronic character of the culture. The vision of Being is the communality in the tripartite (architect, inhabitant, critic) interpretive event recognising that what for the critic and architect is hypothetical and unique is for the inhabitant actual and enduring.

The apparently extreme critical category poesy/madness (and therefore, to sustain the reference to Foucault, between Velázquez and Don Quixote) seems appropriate given the structure of the means of representation itself, and given the breadth of polemic that characterises architectural discourse at this time (consequent to the disintegration of architecture from a movement to a plurality of architectures).

The Early Work
It appears an essential characteristic of the place of arrival that while the architecture conspires to effect a chamber of repose in enclosure, the decoration (which may include the architecture) will display a contrary intention: that of elaborating the space beyond its explicit boundaries. The architectural surround provides an orientation, even the occasion, for seeing beyond, for speculations of a transcendent nature. A second characteristic of the place of arrival is that it appears to demand that a continuity be maintained along the duration of the path of arrival (the journey of inhabitation), such that the journey be foreground and the space shade off to privacy in the *poché*. The full argument is summarised in a baroque church such as Borromini's San Carlo alle Quattro Fontane. The space of the dome draws into a single but ambivalent chamber the tripartite iconographic arrangement of the plan[4] and the journey of passage established by the façade, culminating in a dialectic between the secular/horizontal and the celestial/vertical (visible in the parent of all such schemes, the Pantheon). The urban equivalent of the place of arrival might best be summarised in the *Civitas Veri* (City of Truth) of B. Delbene, 1609. Two attributes make this city preferable to other 'ideal' cities — the conflation of city and body (the five gates are the five senses, etc.), and the vision of the entire landscape as a topography of knowing. Indeed imagining the *Civitas Veri* and San Carlino as a singularity with the inhabitant provides a reasonable approximation of the intended sense of 'place of arrival'.

Graves' early work replicates the arrangement of San Carlino as a simultaneity rather than as a sequence — the former singular frontal irruption of

Opposite:
Crooks House 1975
Fireplace detail

the façade has become a series of regressive frontalities distributed through the place of arrival. The transaction between the two realms is a matter of co-ordinating their fragmentary junctions with a generating grid oriented to the axis of arrival.[5] The tradition that the place of arrival be as well the place of reference beyond one's immediate circumstance is fulfilled, in Graves' early buildings, through the agency of the mural. It will be observed in these works that the journey of frontal encounter, which co-ordinates seeing with inhabiting, culminates in a terminal wall that is in fact the mural wall. The polychromy of the architecture (with form the basis of the metaphoric readings) re-emerges as part of the general thematic synthesis that takes place in the plane of imagination that is the mural. The role played by frontal encounter in these works as the basis of inhabiting, of understanding, is the same as that played by the promise of enclosure in the traditional form of the place of arrival. This is so particularly in that the conception of vista is consistent in each case: in the traditional form originating in the theatricality of Albertian perspective[6], in the later form originating in the shallow frontality of cubist painting. On the other hand, it must be recognised that the substitution of an implicit for an explicit surround carries with it — because of the peculiar structure of cubist space — the threat of the place of arrival becoming a region of analytic dispersion. It is possible that Graves intends this (we will see its reappearance in a different form). But the illusive realm of the original sustains the coherence of the drama of orientation, of understanding; the allusive realm of the new case precipitates a radical inversion of that experience. If the wholeness of perspective vision (revelation associated with axially aligned or linked voids) is replaced by the field, and if colour, mass, enclosure, etc. emerge as subjects in their own right, it would appear that the entire discourse were carried on at the two extremes of the conscious (grid) and the unconscious (effects of the plastic). The medium of exchange in this arrangement is that notion of the 'abstract' that usually signifies non-figural; indeed in painting the procedure characteristicallly involves working back from these extremes toward the figural, that is, man.

Thus the interchange between painting and architecture as it was practised in the Italian Renaissance emerges as the antetype for which Le Corbusier's mural on the inside of the rubble wall in the Pavillon Suisse (though painted against his wishes) becomes the prototype[7]. The transformation of knowing with respect to architecture effected by this procedure emerges as an attempted reconciliation of the ideal with the picturesque, but ultimately of *'the nineteenth century's double advance on the one hand towards formalism in thought and on the other towards the discovery of the unconscious — towards Russell and Freud'*[8].

At least since Goya, our conception of painting sees completed works as mediating the space of the painter's internal psychological landscape with that of his experience, which is given, synthesised in the making necessary for representation. As a result the work exists as a counter-form to its author[9], specific to its moment of completion — indeed the work attains to its highest aspiration as an interpretive stasis distributed within the picture-plane. As this situation applies to the making of architectural drawings, the site is analogous to a canvas (in the case of some of Graves' drawings, literally and intentionally so) in its role as a theatre of revelation in personal and direct interaction with the painter. The result is successful as the mysteries of the site (one's canvas is never blank) are accounted for in the imagination of the architect. As the architectural drawings and the murals tend towards congruency, the latter acquire an autobiographical aspect whereby the edifice recapitulates its origins. The narrative of creation has been made to refer to the narrative of inhabitation. At this point it is possible to see that 'simultaneity' has come to stand for 'totality' — that the architecture has indeed become a counter-form for its author. This raises the subtle but fundamental distinction for the inhabitant between the tyranny of living in another's poetry and the freedom of dwelling in a realm that promotes reveries of inhabitation (*vis*. Bachelard).

The combined effect of the escalation into architectural design strategy of the totality of the painter's drama and the extension on the part of Le Corbusier and then Graves of these particular paintings towards the general condition of space, of orientation, can only be opposite to its intention. The constitutive reveries of Bachelard become open-ended sequences of configurational or psycho-analytic analysis. The efforts on the part of Graves to cause these analytic sequences to reconverge upon the excluded middle of the case, man, through the exploitation of redundancy, metaphor, and multiple reference actually serves to increase the density of *possible* meanings and therefore the interpretive load altogether as the price of closure. The value of the strategy — that it could sustain an extraordinarily dense array of meanings — emerges as a compensation for the fact that, at its core, it is devoid of all simple meanings.

The Intermediate Work
What became the focus of the effort in the last of these early projects, the investigations into the properties of metaphor, symbol, and allusion, eventually provoked their liberation from the scheme of representation for which they had been necessary. Two transitional works, the Crooks House and the renovation of the Newark Museum Carriage House, are essential to the chronology of the shift.

The long primary façade of the Crooks House establishes entry into an arrangement of exterior and interior spaces that relate one to another across their literal boundaries (a strategy transferred from works as old as the Hanselmann House). In general, the narrative of the site involves a reconciliation of the hearth with the landscape. There is a major garden sequence in which the space of the house participates as follows: the garden itself progresses in three spatial stages, from open on the street side through striated to radial in the private garden; the house proper occupies the striated region and is divided into a primary NE/solid, SW/void pair. The figure in this field is the hearth. If the field appears to recall the phenomenal transparencies of the early work, the characteristics of the façade, while respecting it, go a long way to unload its dominance. The four façades participate their own serial system, causing the hearth/landscape dialectic to transpire actually as part of a three-part exchange involving the system of façades as intermediary. This clearly represents a step away from the earlier assumption of spatial homogeneity.

The three-part exchange between landscape, façade, and hearth begins to converge upon a closed argument as one recognises that, a) with respect to the garden series, the thickened SW façade/hedge (essentially wall) acquires conceptual parity with the garage/NE living zone (essentially space); b) with respect to the façades, the pictorial incidents serve to 'restore' gravity and processional entry (by references to the apparatus of Renaissance palace façades) and to fulfill as well the expectation of an exterior discourse upon the interior (for example, the stair-rail/frame moulding on the street elevation); and c) with respect to the figural independence of the hearth, one observes that the interior elevation of the NW wall has become, in part, a projected fireplace elevation.

Where, in the early work, the façade was primarily the initial break in a sequence of regressive frontalities, and therefore the opening curtain in a drama of interpretive removal, these façades begin at the opposite end of that chain of meanings; their ambiguities arise from their initial clarity as nameable entities — façade, opening, spatial box, etc. In general, the same could be said for the entire edifice — what could be more American than a home organised about the hearth?

The Newark Museum Carriage House renovation pursues this new objectivity differently. At the most literal level the scheme appears to be objects distributed about a contained interior/exterior field through which paths have been worked. The most striking aspect of the plan is that circulation seems to have been liberated from revelation, in apparent violation of the basic assumption underlying the place of arrival; in fact its restoration at a higher poetic level is the key to the scheme. Parallelism and the logic of the place of arrival demand a suitable agreement between the four-part circulation grid (pinned by axially aligned sculptures) and movement itself, which deviates across the back of the site. It is achieved through allegory, where cascade=stair, and pool=piazza of intersection. The palpability of the allegory is enhanced by placing across one axis an Anthony Caro portal-like sculpture (which when reflected in the pool becomes, from that entry, a window to the bather), and by placing a Tony Smith (as a black, faceted crystal, an icon for objectness) in the niche aligned with, but beyond the reach of, cross circulation, thereby establishing these two axes as primary.

The portal to the Carriage House, which includes in its imagery the obelisk and cascade, is a free-standing object as well. In fact it constitutes one end of a diagonal arm whose other end is the obelisk and which intersects at the central feature the other diagonal established by the bather and term, the whole forming a giant 'X' on the site. The effect of the overlay upon the circulation of this geometry-by-constellation is to bring to the foreground of one's attention a general topology of object and arrangement that includes the original façades of the two buildings, the chimneys and cupola in the roofs of the Carriage House (thus confronting the romanticism of that structure), and, most important of all, one's own existence and journey of intention in this relativistic landscape.

The transcendent, poetic reality of the cascade's descent to the sky reflected in the pool — across which the lower circulation must bridge — ultimately fulfills the implication of the initial axial promise: particularly insofar as it corresponds to the most significant level of the expression 'I see'.

With respect to the early work, the scheme of meanings has been turned inside out. The strategy at this point appears to involve the careful working of objects and the potentialities of their arrangement. There is no longer the question of where reality leaves off: there is no longer the *gestalt* of the systematic whole, of the interconnectivity of everything; meaning is no longer seen as a unified substance originating in poetic will. Rather the aim is to participate in the uniform discontinuity of empirical reality on its own terms. If, in the early works, the tendency was to conceive of meaning essentially from above (the seventeenth-century French Garden), the tendency now is to make a clearing in it (the eighteenth-century English Garden).

The Warehouse

If the Crooks House may be seen as the reconciliation of the hearth with the landscape in terms of the façades, the Warehouse (which is Graves' home) may be seen to have substituted for the hearth Graves' personal collection of furniture, dishes, utensils and objects. This collection dates from the 1930s, and concentrates upon that portion of Art Deco characterised by straightforward but subtle geometries. What initially appears to be a conflict between the exigencies of production (favouring extreme geometries) and those of the rituals of everyday life (favouring intimacy and personal nuance) is resolved in primitiveness (and indeed wit[10]). The pieces become as it were the cult objects of those rituals. They are all *objets-trouvés* enjoying an afterlife or rebirth, as is the building itself, built by immigrant Tuscan craftsmen using Italian construction procedures and materials. It is the interaction of two themes — a) a pictorial unity of objects and architecture, and b) the rebirth in reuse as the basis of that unity — which suggests a resemblance between the sections for the Warehouse and those for Sir John Soane's house. However, there is the important difference that Soane's house suggests a house of knowledge, where a didactic intent is fulfilled in a dramatic context, reminiscent of the theatre of memory[11]; Graves' building, on the other hand, refers inward, as a reverie upon inhabitation.

The building before renovation gave an impression of blankness, of a field of too-small windows arranged in a broad, high wall — all of which was of course consistent with the Tuscan farmhouse as a type. This provoked, particularly with respect to the early work, a fear of blindness, of eyes too small and too few, and of darkness. The building is furthermore withdrawn to the very corner of the site — its west and north elevations are buried in the neighbours' trees: it cannot therefore be understood as a whole from without — all that is apparent is the foreground, the south and east façades, and the interior. In response, a thematic of opening has been engendered, and the dependency of window upon wall becomes a more equal exchange. But one intends all senses of 'opening' — a breach in a wall, a dilation in plan opening to the sky, and finally an opening to understanding that transcends the given circumstance in particular and dwelling-as-alienation in general. Thus the double-height spaces open to the sky become 'expansions' of the house as wall towards the enclosive interior chambers of the imagination that characterise the place of arrival. These openings are in each case affiliated with entry; the solarium and courtyard are further associated with a bath and stair, the full narrative of circulation being thereby revealed in their presence. The murals of the courtyard reflect a transformation concerning subject-matter, which remains within that already established for the interior walls; indeed the courtyard is an overture prefiguring the entire essay on the materiality of wall/window, the thematic of opening.

The degree to which these chambers are actually independent events on the site is exemplified by the solarium, the most interior of the three. The great window in the west wall frames a neighbouring tree, whose foliage overhangs the solarium skylight. Reaching up to meet it, at the east face of the solarium, are two 'trunks' of a green-tiled arboreal column line (Laugier's hut, one presumes). The sketches for the garden indicate that the west wing is part of a garden zone, which endows the north wing with a new spatiality as the fulfilment of the journey of inhabitation, as the place of arrival. Closer inspection of the solarium reveals that it possesses a special complexity. The 'missing window' of the west wall series can be found reconstituted pictorially in the east wall; it is supported by a negative of the tile grid, emerging from a rent in, or a ruin of, a classical wall. The 'missing' (blank) central window of that same east wall can be found as the great west window. The term, a forest figure, is undoubtedly performing his expected function at the termination of a journey at the impassable west wall; but his role as telamon for the west window suggests a larger reading, whereby he becomes a pivot of space reaching from the observer to the tree, the central figure in a clearing whose light falls upon a transcendent, pictorial reality. If that is the case, I see no difficulty with taking the obvious parallelisms between the courtyard and the solarium for what they suggest: that the painted tri-partite portal tower in the courtyard (reminiscent of the Carriage House portal) is meant to refer to the extended west elevation in the solarium. Entry through the portal is then the initiation of a narrative whose end is marked by the term. The world of objects aspires to self-portrait in that confrontation in the enchanted realm of the garden.

The Latest Works
With regard to the interaction of building and landscape, it will be remembered that the L of the Warehouse, withdrawn to the corner of the site, acted — initially at least — as a frame to the foreground. That the two actual corner walls were inaccessible, and were therefore no more than interior faces, enhanced this reading. In other words, the dominance of figure (building) over field (landscape) had been reversed.

Subsequent works of Graves seem to have capitalised upon this discovery. The aim is to discover a *gestalt* for the building such that it will retain its own coherence and yet cause the site to act as figure; in his *Roma Interrotta* exhibit, Graves offered the example of the Villa Madama in its current, unfinished state. A building fulfilling these conditions is thus attempting to be simultaneously centre — with an experienced place of arrival — and wall — and therefore backplane for the various stage-spaces on the site generated by the intervention. The effect is to make the landscape itself open to manipulation from within, as it were, and to make the places of intensity direct participants in it. Interpretation of the site is more a matter of induction from a number of implicit orders than of deduction from a single order. Thus with regard to occupation of the site the prototype lies more in Hadrian's Villa than in great baroque palaces such as Versailles or Blenheim.[12]

One of the principal aims of the modified fields of the early work was to develop such an interaction of several orders. The point of origin, however, lay in the assumption of the essential dissimilarity between edifice and landscape. The power of this dialectic was first realised in modern architecture at Savoie; and the subtlety and profundity of which it is capable is apparent to anyone who has visited La Tourette. The first strategy of reconciliation employed by Graves, that of metaphor and allusion in a pictorial framework, became, as we have said, the basis for transformation of his architecture generally. The second strategy was the establishment of a middle-ground where landscape became architecture, and building became landscape. In particular, this meant the carving of ground and verdure on one hand, and on the other displacement from the primary mass of independent pieces connected by circulation. The extent to which the middle-ground still retains potency for Graves is visible in his curious Plocek House. This building began life as an essay in middle-ground, ascending a hill; the current scheme has collapsed the argument to one essential, but ambivalent, structure that is Villa Capra in plan and elevation and Villa Aldobrandini in section.

These two (i.e. regarding the primacy of figure and field) *parti* strategies are of course actually dual aspects of a single involvement with the landscape as a configurational argument concerning, or symbolising, architecture/garden = man/nature = rational/irrational, etc. The domain of possible manifestations of these themes is immense, and includes at least the Great Wall of China and the Spiral Jetty, highway architecture and vacant lots, Central Park and botanical gardens, the so-called Festhaus at Assur and the city of Pergamon on its hill, ecology and the Babylonian creation myth, Milton's 'Paradise Lost' and Goethe's vision of Italy[13]. The rendering of meaning in such a circumstance is hardly a matter of the given themes; it is only as significance outside that framework is attained, as the density and specificity of argument are increased, that anything other than a field of clues testifying to a vast absence of meaning is achieved. It is on this basis that one accounts for the effort of Graves to insinuate the thematic of opening, in the Warehouse, into a chain of associations that converge upon a higher, poetic reality. Characteristically Graves works this theme back through the landscape of illusion to Italian Renaissance gardens. It is a vision of landscape as a function of the theatricality of vista and of its causality: *'The antinomy freedom-necessity is transformed into a correlation. For the common characteristic joining the world of pure knowledge to that of artistic creation is that both are dominated, in different ways, by a moment of genuine intellectual genera-*

tion. In Kantian language, they go beyond any "copy" view of the given; they must become an "architectonic" construction of the cosmos.'[14]

In this context, a comment upon Graves' prolonged interest in the linking device between self and landscape is appropriate. Within Graves' work, the portal is a theme of apparently inexhaustible richness — we have seen its transformation from the place of simultaneity as building in the early work to a general thematic of opening in later work.

The portal signifies the whole building and is, as a fact of the imagination, a proto-building. It is not, however, the building; it is entirely anticipatory to inhabitation. The term 'portal' derives from the break in the continuity of the *pomerium* for the city gates produced by the lifting (*porta*) of the brazen plow during the founding ceremony of the Roman town. The sacro-political meanings behind the *pomerium* have been retained at a metaphorical level by Graves — it has been transformed into a philosophy of boundary, which is in essence (once the building has become its inhabitant) a philosophy of wilderness. Whether it is the wilderness of the garden or of the city — the term 'landscape' will provisionally do for both — a dilemma is provoked concerning the reconciliation of the self with the landscape. If it is really the building that provides reconciliation in orientation — the augur situated in a landscape immanently significant — the portal is then testimony to an in-between realm that is both. It is the place which alludes always to the otherness of the within or the without to which it opens. Thus, from within, the portal is a proto-wilderness, the irony (and truth) of which lies in the interaction between the particular and the general. The frame as the conditioning factor in an understanding of landscape through vista is the inevitable consequence of a drama of interpretation grounded in the dialectic between subjectivity/will and object/being-in-itself.

It is with some surprise that one finds the portal emerging from its inferential and subtle role in the early work to a rather singular monumentality. It is as if all the energy that had hitherto been distributed throughout the building in one way or another had returned to its source, causing it to swell out of proportion. It is a story told to the landscape on its own terms, perhaps provoked by the transformation in *parti*-type discussed above. In the Plocek House, for example, the portal with its displaced keystone becomes the full journey of inhabitation. The house is the intermediate space, organised about its own centralised geometry. If one is meant to read the semi-circular bastions to the left of entry (for automobile access) as something concerning civic fortifications[15], and the displacement of the keystone to its present position as water-source (presumably related to the work of the studio taking place within it) as being an elaboration upon the theme of ruin we observed in the Warehouse, then perhaps we have a project akin to the inventions of Clerisseau.[16] Such a scenario accounts for its appearance as a rather plausible transformation in pictorial intent; however, like other projects of this period, there remains the gigantism of the portal. And this particular pictorial intent surely confirms an impression that the work has become dominated by the possibilities of working with the landscape as figure — which, in the absence of ritual support, runs the risk of committing an ozymandian *hybris*.

At the top of my notes for this building are 'Ledoux-Art Deco-Hawksmoor'. The likelihood of the resolution of these three sources in the rest of the building would seem to depend upon the capacity for the architecture to fulfill the promise of the main façade. To some extent this may already have been started, as the two great columns of the portal foreshadow a columnar stair space at the heart of the building. However, the tension between the drama of the stone portal (Freud) and the refined thinness of what appears to be metal panels and windows (Russell) seems as great an issue of resolution, but in a different thematic sphere, as that of the sources.

There is of course no *a priori* basis of preference for an architecture of continuity; the work examined so far has led us to expect that it is this assumption which is under investigation. It is perhaps a logical consequence of the shift from the plastic unity of the early work to a unity of narrative in the transitional period, that the next stage would involve an explicit disunity, or at least the displacement of the doubt concerning unity to the foreground of the enterprise. The re-emergence of the place of arrival as dispersive, however, suggests that the vision expectant of understanding and the interrogatory search of the path in the wilderness have become the same glance. The architecture has become the always allusive realm of the portal. Indeed this would seem to constitute the *invention* of a proto-wilderness: the affiliations of objects with history and the categories of difference in space which have heretofore acted as cultural fixes now seem to participate in a pervasive contingency in which doubt and knowing are simply two aspects of the same vocation. In any event, the displacement of the structurally most essential element of the portal to a temporal and spatial 'beyond' as a garden *fabrique*, may indicate that this renovation of our cultural model were intended.

A number of our hypotheses concerning unity advanced in the preceding discussion seem to find a more radical expression in the Fargo-Moorhead Cultural Center. The proposition involves the linking of twin cities, one in North Dakota and the other in Minnesota, by a cultural bridge across the river that divides them. The first scheme provided a space for this 'bridging' centred about the river. The current scheme has folded across the landscape, making the bridge one of three virtually independent elements. Furthermore, the bridge, a museum, allows a slip along its longitudinal axis; thus another reading of the site sees two L-shaped entities shearing along this face.

In apparent confirmation of our thesis, the argument of portal that animates the Plocek site is summarised in the façade of the bridge itself. The glass keystone-window has been reinstated in the central position (with its cascade), as if the bridge were a lintel. The two columns of the Plocek entry have been displaced to the edges; the lintel seems to have slipped, however — perhaps reflecting the displacement in plan — and the columns now sustain the sky on their brackets. The central stair cylinder of the Plocek House appears here as an arcuated pediment. And though the gridded wall is present, the role of fenestration is quite different — it enjoys a figural prominence that seems to be a focus of the narrative of the site. The association through shape between the keystone window and brackets would suggest that a third column and bracket, the sculpted water, were part of the discourse (the term supporting the window in the Warehouse solarium suggests a prototype). This 'column' rises not from the ground but rather falls to the water. It is probable that this column is part of the iconographic scheme of the Plocek House – the Chem-Fleur Factory (conceptually) and the *Roma Interrotta* plan (actually) provide confirmation – and that a myth is being invoked with which I am not familiar. It is tempting to find a consistency with the remarks concerning the place of arrival: this column of water is connected to a keystone missing from the primary portal and is therefore illogical at every level. This is not, however, the distortion of dreams, which would permit rebirth in a surrealist architecture; rather I feel it represents the sign's dissolution to a resemblance that ultimately erases.

The other buildings of the Cultural Center share with the Plocek House the laconic, enigmatic walls in which the essential points of focus are the portals. Of particular interest here is the concert hall automobile entrance in that it has influenced the others. Wall and portal have been so thoroughly bound to the void inside them (or between them, since the void goes all the way to the cornice) that it seems to be the dominant continuity. As the walls expand to the corners in echelons of one sort or another, one cannot help but feel that the incorporation of their rustication and mouldings in the mysteries of the portal are the walls' lease on stability. However, the portal as division tends to suggest that in fact the corners are the centres of walls which terminate at the portals. And so even the portals have been deconstituted, becoming equivalent to the passage between two buildings.

To the left of the pedestrian entrance to the concert hall is mounted a bust of what I will take to be a choice between Mozart and a local musician. He slips easily into the structural arrangement prevailing at this portal, even acquiring parity with it. He appears to be at the apex of an echelon, whereupon he initiates the wall narrative – or concludes it. In that role, he becomes literally a figure interacting with the field of the wall. One would expect to find a place for him as part of a tradition that has the Medici Chapel at one end and the empty rhetoricism of some late nineteenth-century civic sculpture at the other, with Le Corbusier's attempts to impose depth (both pictorial and iconographic) upon blank walls with such figures in between. However, Mozart remains outside this tradition – ultimately, like a reverse Pygmalion, imprisoned within the architecture. Acknowledgement of the bust precipitates the chain of disengagement of the architecture to its allusive self-sufficiency, and the inhabitant finds himself in something like a museum space: alienated by studious gaze within the categorised detritus of culture and the neutral chamber of its exhibition.

One wonders when a dispersive topography sustaining broad cultural reference simply merges with the archetype it seeks to articulate – the city, as the landscape that is first of all artifact. For, at bottom, this dilemma possesses an eschatological dimension that comes to rest with the city. The balance between the timeless ideal that we have associated with Russell and the timeful inner consciousness that we have associated with Freud was negotiated in the early works largely by remaining within a metaphoric world of the plastic, of the material. One had the sense of reference 'out', as it were, of a desire to reconcile the present with the distant, the particular with the general, in sum, of that present subsuming a past for the unconditioned future. The recent works seem to have remained within this material drama, but have attempted to turn its geometry inside out (and therefore that of the place of arrival as well). The question then is whether this topographic transformation can really have its desired effect, that of eluding Stephen Dedalus' nightmare of history, and if so, whether the basis of argument does not similarly need to transform. The consequence of a failure in this regard is the undifferentiated field of clues testifying to an absence of grounded, whole meaning, and therefore to dispersal in its absolute sense.

Landscape and Making
It has been argued that the stasis of arrival was associated with a condition of knowing, of orientation with respect to the landscape, and that the kinesis of the journey of arrival took on the character of a search, with each of course echoing the other. The field for which this event is figure is the landscape. I have been using landscape to mean the play between the full extent of one's present vision and the repository of such visions (and their meanings) in the memory; thus 'interior', 'urban', 'natural', 'psychologic' are all legitimate prefixes for the term 'landscape'. It will be observed that intentionality with respect to the landscape is the animating factor in this definition; Quixote and his field of windmills constitute an indivisibility. Landscape commands the limits and full extent of knowing in this context, and like some ancient geographer's vision of the consequences of passing beyond the edge, at some point shades off to an ultimate Other – as searching displaced to the horizon of any possibility of arriving. In a dilemma reminiscent of that concerning the proximity of poesy to madness in the cultural model, it can be seen that the otherness of the landscape is latent throughout its domain by the very fact of horizon. The aspiration to reconcile the interior landscape with the exterior is then rooted in the intentionality of knowing and the drama of inhabitation transpires in that realm as a theatre of the emergence of identity. Finally, it is perhaps the essential characteristic of the architect in particular that he comprehends the landscape as a function of its susceptibility to manipulation through making. Despite long affiliation of schools of architecture with universities, one can detect a relatively recent shift in the apparent junction of humanistic studies and architectural making, in what is usually called theory. The effect has been the precipitation of a new landscape, one which dwells inside the prevailing landscape but which renders it conditional, at least for the architect.

In general there prevails a tension between learning, which seeks to be encyclopaedic, and producing, which seeks to reduce the amount of effective information. The necessity to distinguish between the interpretation of suspicion (unmasking) and the interpretation of revelation[17] emerges inside this tension in such a manner that the four components begin to cross over upon each other; and, in the case of Graves, for example, Cassirer or Jung can play a dual role of poetic inspiration and justification. A topographical chasm in the philosophical or psychological landscape may find itself part of the uniform plausibility of an architectural one. This is a privilege of poetic authorship of course (and not *so* much a chasm in this instance); and this reconciliation of the endured life with its understanding lies at the heart of the several dualities with which we have been working. But I would think that one risks a crisis of representation: the promise of broadening the realm of discourse becomes identical with the threat of its unintelligibility[18].

It is, at any rate, to this interpretive landscape that Graves' work responds, indeed seeking to make poetic clearings within it[19]. Meditative regard is the underlying experience of dwelling in a Graves building, and therefore it could be said that in his work the journey of search in the landscape returns back upon itself in the place of arrival. Despite what appears to be a pictorial evenness in any particular image of Graves, the density and nature of meanings are quite uneven in their distribution. This is intentional, the general vision embodied in these images is derived from that of the landscape — in appearance uniform and plausible, but when subjected to interrogation unstable and fragmentary, suggestive of animating forces beyond and within. Graves' fluctuant image mirrors this structure: the pictorial uniformity dissolves to an instability that interpretation alone restores to its wholeness. The image has come to require the word for sustenance.

Thus, for example, the romantic and fulsome Warehouse, eliciting memories of the Tuscan countryside, is made to lose its rotundity, and a curious alter-rotundity is inserted within it. Graves' approach is close to that of Peruzzi's at the Castel Bel Caro, where the enclosive, medieval singularity is cased to sustain the full argument of fifteenth-century urban theatricality, its virtual opposite. The specificity of the original is effaced; the work is tuned to such a level of ambiguity that the original must be rediscovered in terms of the whole. The whole in the Warehouse involves an interpretive envelope that renders even the transcendent poetic understanding a component of the intent. In other words, the Warehouse, as a narrative of regeneration, or rather of metempsychosis, proposes to be the palpable manifestation of a two-part dream which trails off in one direction towards the primitivism of rural existence (Freud) and in the other towards pure order (Russell). Arising in a subject/object dialectic involving the inhabitant and the site (the confrontation in the garden), the building seeks to unify both aspects of the dream, in a general reconciliation of image with word, of sensuality with its interpretion (that is, of Being with Understanding), in response perhaps to a more fundamental need to reconcile body with soul.

The Warehouse *parti* of inserting a villa in the interpretive landscape reveals the architecture to be what the later architecture of portals indicates it to be: the metaphoric frame between the object and subject of self. And therefore the shift from the confrontation with the mural, in the place of arrival, to the confrontation with the term resurrected from ancient Rome through neo-classicism, embodying the place of arrival, is not nearly so radical as the shift which exiles Mozart to what is essentially slightly to one side of the horizon of any possibility of arriving.

To the remarks made earlier concerning the totality of the drama of the picture-plane/studio, and concerning the specificity of doubt, I would like to add an examination of the role of drawing in the context of a discussion surrounding image-word. Clearly the drawings represent the domain of image at their most intimate; and one imagines (one has witnessed) the unravelling of thought as a constituent increment of the duration of their making, as the representative role of word. This relationship probably feels whole to its author as a ballet originating in the unity of the basic dilemma.

The extent to which some concern may be manifesting itself for this wholeness may be visible in the curious extremes between very fine draughted lines (Russell) and strong rich colour (Freud) that characterises the later drawings. Insofar as this phenomenon appears to be if anything more prevalent in the drawings for the Fargo-Moorhead Center and for the Plocek House (whose whole existence seems the product of this duality), one might risk the opinion that the interpretive dilemma as it is registered in the architecture is returning to its source — an inversion of the earlier attempt to include drawing in the landscape. It does not seem very difficult that a fascination with the portal (the root of the theme of opening) as a prolonged involvement with the metaphoric frame between being and understanding be seen as a psychological 'projection' of the ritual of drawing (as the realm of its emergence, of its susceptibility to manipulation) — particularly given the sustained focus. If there is a place that is not dual, that is not ambiguous, in Graves' architecture, it is this ritual of drawing. It must be said after all that the events of his architecture are almost universally susceptible to being drawn — they are not, for example, of the order of the affection for a piece of wood, because of its place of origin, in a Japanese tea house, a concept not easily drawn. It would seem possible that the narrative of transformation that we have traced from the totality of the early work to this point could be paralleled by another detailing the progressive absorption of the ritual of drawing into language. And where Gandy saw the future ruins of Soane's Bank of England as some partially recovered Roman town or palace, as a material drama touching the romantic sense of loss and of the passage of history (indeed preferable to its actual fate), we would substitute for Graves the potential breakdown of the wholeness of the relationship between architecture, drawing, and landscape. Thus we are not really confronted with a choice between Velázquez and Quixote, but rather with a dilemma of reconciliation between Velázquez and twentieth-century western culture. The transformation to which we alluded in the beginning of this essay must then involve the full domain of the means of representation.

Marcel Duchamp first liberated art from the nexus of its making (readymades), its utility as a meaningful window to culture (the 'Bride Stripped Bare'), and its endurance as a plastic artifact (the substitution of verbal for retinal readings). In general, the last subsumes the other two; for it represents the transfer to language from space of the fundamental experience of unity in the representational field[20]. The Sumerian Temple of Enki (whose explicit meanings included the painted mud structure it in fact was, an edifice of silver and lapis lazuli with which it was at best decorated, a home for the effigy, a hotel for the god, a mountain, an edifice capable of flying across the depths, a city, and an oracle) is an indication that linguistic unity succeeded spatial: the temple itself is clearly the only realm of experience which could coherently sustain such an array of meanings. This matter of the primacy of the means of representation (or the potential interaction of more than one) must then be the basis of the transformation. To the extent that the journey of search that is making has had as its object the unification of the tripartite interpretive event, and its manifestation in a superimposition of discourse, one sees a parallel to the late stages of the early work, wherein the density and complexity of the presentation compensates for an ambiguous source, and becomes the basis of renewal.

In examining any particular work of Graves, one finds oneself pursuing really brilliant passages to an allusive frontier; it has been the contention of this essay that the history of the work as a whole seeks similarly to include, or be included in, this frontier. In an analysis of the expression 'the nature of things', Hans-Georg Gadamer remarks that '... *the concept of the thing* (Sache) *is marked above all by its counterconcept, the person*'. His aim in this essay is to lay the groundwork for the reconciliation of 'the created soul' with 'created things'. At one point he remarks: '... *the illusion that things precede their manifestation in language conceals the fundamentally linguistic character of the world. In particular, the illusion of the possibility of the universal objectification of everything and anything completely obscures this universality itself.*'[21] The magical intent within language, rooted in animism, displays the origin of this illusion, and testifies to the profundity of the mystery of our otherness in things. It is not accidental, in any case, that Artaud begins his discussion in *The Theatre and its Double* at precisely this point. If for Graves the destiny of this intent has been temporarily fulfilled, it should be expected that it is only in the service of the further elaboration of the mystery.

Notes

1 Michel Foucault, *The Order of Things*, trans. of *Les Mots et les Choses*, 1970, London and New York, pp. 47–48. The manner in which spatiality plays a constituent role in this work is extraordinary, originating of course in the discussion of 'Las Meninas'.
2 Unpublished paper, Princeton 1971.
3 I am making too much of a conceit of Foucault's, which will appear subsequently, for the sake of brevity.
4 Leo Steinberg, *Borromini's San Carlo alle Quattro Fontane. A Study in Multiple Form and Architectural Symbolism.* New York 1977.
5 *Cf.* Colin Rowe and Robert Slutzky, 'Transparency, Literal and Phenomenal' in Rowe: *Mathematics of the Ideal Villa and Other Essays,* London 1977.
6 The predominance of post-Renaissance Italian examples in this context derives from their proximity to Graves' own endeavour. A more general discussion of the model, for example, with respect to iconography, is out of place here. *Cf.* as well Dalibor Vesely's excellent work on perspectivity.
7 The archetype lies in something like the shrines of Catal Hüyük, where the mythic drama and the space of the chamber seem identical — though ceremonies of costumed or painted people would suggest an antetype even to this.
8 Foucault, *op. cit.,* p. 229. The interaction between notative layering and enclosive space in these works embodies this duality.
9 *Cf.* M. Merleau-Ponty, 'Cezanne's Doubt', *Sense and Non-sense,* Chicago 1964.
10 Russell and Freud resolved in primitivism, a solution that reaches from Gaugin through Picasso, Matisse, and Purism to Ronchamp.
11 The memory-theatre of Guilio Camillo, as described by Dame Francis Yates (*The Memory Theatre,* Chicago 1966) is completely exemplary of the place of arrival as a place of knowing. The use here of the memory-theatre with respect to Soane is obviously metaphorical, and connotes a less specific referential relationship in which a place aspires to the detailed embodiment of its cultural context.
12 Although, as usual in Graves' work, it is a bit of both. The urban equivalent of this principle would be the Hôtels of Paris of the seventeenth and eighteenth centuries.
13 The rapture of wilderness, where man confronts the spectacle and process of nature in the absence of his architecture, his civilisation, has its obverse in the biologist, who peers inside his technology, his civilisation, to an artificially illuminated world of liquid matter and electrical impulse. The point is one of representation: for instance they prevail as a simultaneity in Kubrick's *2001*, suggested particularly by the quality of time in that work — a junction of drama (timefulness) and tedium (timelessness).
14 Ernst Cassirer, *The Individual and the Cosmos in Renaissance Philosophy,* in a discussion on the convergence of the theory of science and the theory of art in the Renaissance, and therefore the origin of the duality concerning Russell and Freud; pp. 191 *et seq.*, Philadelphia 1963.
15 *Cf.* for example, E. B. Smith's *Architectural Symbolism of Imperial Rome and the Middle Ages* (Princeton 1956) for a good description of the meaning of many of these elements at the time of their use as part of Imperial Roman iconography, with comments as well upon their origins and subsequent fate. To the extent that one's references, in the twentieth century, recall their history, embodying faithfully their cultural context, they are grounded, and sustain profound meditation. To the extent that they, with Durand, become primarily a compositional instrumentality for producing buildings, they are ungrounded, being merely sophisticated rhetorical display. It is not a question of pedantry: the first permits a wit that is revelatory, the second allows only a nervous, defensive laugh.
16 As a variant upon the *capriccio,* he would invent a Roman ruin and its subsequent medieval inhabitation as a rustic house.
17 *Cf.* Paul Ricoeur, *Freud and Philosophy,* Introduction, Yale 1972.
18 This is not a question of elitism, but one of the inability of the representational effort to attain fulfilment.
19 Or in the case of the early work '... poetic analogues of it'.
20 To the insistence upon grammars, which sees the evidence for language in architecture in something like the uniformity of portals throughout a building (like parts of speech obeying laws of arrangement and even called syntax), I would prefer the essential realm of unity of a means of representation as the basis of architecture's affiliation with language. The comment that follows upon a quotation from Gadamer is pertinent, but more to the point is Merleau Ponty's description of the positioning of oneself in the world of meanings. (*Phenomenology of Perception*, pp. 174 ff., and 402 ff., London 1962).
21 Hans-Georg Gadamer, 'The Nature of Things and the Language of Things', in *Philosophical Hermeneutics,* trans. D. E. Linge, Los Angeles and London 1977, pp. 77–78.

Michael Graves: List of Buildings and Projects

1964-65	Jersey Corridor Project: A Theoretical Study of Linear Urban Planning Applied to the Urban Corridor between New York and Philadelphia. With Peter D. Eisenman and Anthony Eardley
1966-68	Urban Design Proposal, Oyster Bay, New York
1967	Hanselmann House, Fort Wayne, Indiana
1967	Union County Nature and Science Museum, Mountainside, New Jersey
1967	Urban Design Proposal for Upper West Side Manhattan (exhibition), Museum of Modern Art and the City of New York. With Peter D. Eisenman
1967-68	Low-income Housing and Housing for the Elderly, Coatsville, Pennsylvania. Associated Architects: Geddes Brecher Qualls & Cunningham
1967-71	Housing Rehabilitation for N.E.S.T., Trenton, New Jersey
1968	Middle-income Housing (project), Newark, New Jersey
1968	The Newark Museum, Master Plan (project), Newark, New Jersey
1969	Benacerraf House, Princeton, New Jersey
1969	Rockefeller House (project), Pocantico Hills, New York
1970	Drezner House (project), Princeton, New Jersey
1971	Medical Office, Ear, Nose & Throat Associates, Fort Wayne, Indiana
1971-73	Alexander House, Princeton, New Jersey
1972	Investment Office, Gunwyn Ventures, Princeton, New Jersey
1972	Keeley Guest House (project), Princeton, New Jersey
1972	Snyderman House, Fort Wayne, Indiana
1973	Mezzo House (project), Princeton, New Jersey
1973	Sklute House (project), Bucks County, Pennsylvania
1973	Mural, XV Triennale (exhibition), Milan, Italy
1974	Murals (3), Professional Office, Transammonia, Inc., New York, New York
1974	Mural, School of Architecture, University of Texas, Austin, Texas
1974	Claghorn House, Princeton, New Jersey
1974	Wageman House (project), Princeton, New Jersey
1975	Housing for the Elderly (competition), New Jersey Society of Architects, Trenton, New Jersey
1975	The Newark Museum, Carriage House Renovation (project), Newark, New Jersey
1975	The Newark Museum, Art School Renovation, Newark, New Jersey
1976	Crooks House, Fort Wayne, Indiana
1976	Schulman House, Princeton, New Jersey
1977	Factory Addition and Renovation (project), Chem-Fleur, Inc., Newark, New Jersey
1977	Warehouse Conversion: Private Residence, Princeton, New Jersey
1977	Plocek House, Warren Township, New Jersey
1977	Abrahams Dance Studio, Princeton, New Jersey
1977	Fargo-Moorhead Cultural Bridge, Fargo, North Dakota and Moorhead, Minnesota
1978	Railroad Station Conversion and Office Building, Millburn, New Jersey
1978	Mural, John Witherspoon School, Princeton, New Jersey
1978	Porta Maggiore, 'Roma Interrotta' (exhibition), Rome, Italy
1978	Kalko House, Green Brook, New Jersey

Bibliography

Writings by Michael Graves

(with Carol Constant) 'The Swedish Connection', *Journal of Architectural Education*, September 1975
'The Necessity of Drawing: Tangible Speculation', *Architectural Design*, June 1977
'Gwathmey Siegel', in 'Charles Gwathmey and Robert Siegel, Residential Works 1966–1977', Tokyo 1977

Writings by others

Banham, Reyner
'On the Sixth Day'
New Society, October 2, 1975
Beck, Haig
'Letter from London'
Architectural Design, November 1975
Boekraad, Cees
'European Graffiti'
Wohnen – TA/BK, February 1977
Colquhoun, Alan
'New York Five, an English Reply'
Net 2, 1976
Carl, Peter
'Towards a pluralist Architecture'
Progressive Architecture, February 1973
Dean, Yvonne
'The Famous Five, a Literary Exploration'
Net 2, 1976
Ely, Douglas
'Towards reading an Architecture: an Interview with Michael Graves'
Nassau Literary Review, Spring 1978
Gandelsonas, Mario
'On Reading Architecture: an Analysis of Eisenman and Graves'
Progressive Architecture, March 1972
Gregotti, Vittorio
'Fenomena USA'
Domus, March 1974
Hoekema, James
'Drawing Towards Architectural Drawing'
Artforum, December 1977
Huxtable, Ada Louise
'Architectural Drawings as Art'
New York Times, June 12, 1977
LaRiche, William
'Michael Graves: Architecture as the World Again'
Modulus, School of Architecture, University of Virginia 1974 and in *Five Architects*, New York 1972
Maule McKean, John
'The Architect as Intellectual Artist'
Building Design, October 10, 1975
Monroy, Antonio
'Plani e Progetti per Manhattan'
Lotus 7
Murray, Peter
'Only Architecture'
Building Design, July 4, 1975
Papademetriou, Peter
'Architecture?'
Architectural Design, November 1973
Pommer, Richard
'Architecture. Structures for the Imagination'
Art in America, March/April 1978
Portoghesi, Paolo
'Cinque Matite in Cerca di Retorica'
Tempo, April 25, 1976
Raggi, Franco
'Architettura D'Opposizione'
'Templi e Roulottes'
Casabella, February 1974
Pelli, Cesar
'White and Gray'
Architecture + Urbanism, September 1974
Rossi, Aldo
'Mostra Internazione D'Architettura'
Casabella, January 1974
Rykwert, Joseph
'15 Triennale'
Domus, January 1974
Stephens, Suzanne
'Semantic Distinctions'
Progressive Architecture, April 1975
'Living in a Work of Art'
Progressive Architecture, March 1978
Silvetti, Jorge
'The Beauty of Shadows'
Oppositions 9, Summer 1977
Stern, R., Robertson, J., Moore, C., Greenberg, A., Giurgola, R.
'Five on Five'
Architectural Forum, May 1973
Tafuri, Manfredo
'L'Architecture dans le Boudoir'
Oppositions 3, May 1974
'European Graffiti. Five x Five = Twenty Five'
Oppositions 5, Summer 1976
'Les Cendres de Jefferson'
L'Architecture d'Aujourd'hui, August/September 1976
Wild, David
'Idealist Cycles'
Architectural Design, November 1975
Van Zanten, David
'Architectural Ornament: on, in and through the Wall'
Via Ornament, Graduate School of Fine Arts, University of Pennsylvania 1977
Zevi, Bruno
'Piazza Italia e Uno Stivale'
L'Espresso, April 25, 1976

Books

Five Architects, New York 1972
Roma Interrotta, Rome 1978

Résumé en francais

Michael Graves naquit à Indianapolis en 1934. Il fit ses études à l'Université de Harvard, puis à Rome, comme lauréat du Prix de Rome ; en 1962, il fut nommé professeur d'architecture à l'Université de Princeton. Il acquit une renommée internationale avec la parution en 1972 de *Cinq Architectes*. En euxmêmes, ces faits sont de peu d'importance si l'on considère le développement de l'architecture dans son ensemble. Suffisamment d'oeuvres ont été réalisées pour faire l'objet de cette publication, dont les pages présentent une sorte d'oeuvre complète provisoire, et cela malgré une époque de crise économique : le mérite en revient entièrement à Graves. Il serait le premier à reconnaître qu'il s'agit d'un travail effectué en son nom et sous son nom, comme le prouvent les 'Remerciements' de cette publication. Les auteurs remercient également pour l'aide précieuse qu'elles ont apporté à l'établissement de cette publication, Karen Wheeler, qui travaille dans le bureau de Graves, et Carol Constant, qui n'y travaille plus, étant actuellement elle-même lauréate du Prix de Rome.

Alan Colquhoun et Peter Carl ont, dans leurs essais respectifs, des positions différentes vis-à-vis de l'oeuvre de Graves. Colquhoun considère que le caractère premier et essentiel de cette oeuvre est sa 'personnalité', soulignant que, malgré ses possibles relations avec les traditions aussi bien américaines qu'européennes, elle maintient une forte individualité qui ne pourrait échapper à l'accusation d'arbitraire. Carl pour sa part défend une approche plus universelle de l'oeuvre, suggérant qu'elle aborde en réalité certains problèmes de la perception, liés aux problèmes de la représentation et de la conceptualisation dans l'oeuvre d'art, que l'on retrouve chez Cézanne et, vraisemblablement, chez des peintres antérieurs, et qui furent à nouveau posés par Picasso, Le Corbusier et Duchamps.

Tous deux reconnaissent cependant que Graves a réalisé des progrès substantiels en s'attaquant à cette 'lacune' dans la théorie du Mouvement Moderne, qui est tout simplement le problème de l'articulation de l'entrée. En célébrant et 'exagérant' cet aspect, Graves semble avoir ouvert la voie pour ce qui est de l'articulation de ces parties de la construction d'un bâtiment, qui song susceptibles de ritualisation et qui peuvent, par la forme que l'on donne aux surfaces environnantes, marquer le caractère sacré de toute construction. Selon Colqhoun cependant, ces recherches manquent de cette passion qui fut à l'origine même du Mouvement Moderne, de cet extraordinaire désir de modeler, en plaçant un élément architectural à côté d'un autre, le monde tel qu'il devrait être, ou tel qu'il pourrait être. Carl de son côté voit dans l'oeuvre le résultat 'd'une passion réalisée et épuisée', le moment dans une continuité d'êtres et de constructions dont les origines remontent si loin dans le passé que seuls les aide-mémoires de l'archéologie pourraient aider à comprendre la condition originelle de l'homme et de son architecture.

Nous ne nous proposons pas ici de trouver un compromis entre ces deux interprétations. Les deux textes procèdent, au niveau de l'interprétation, d'hypothèses qui ne sont pas au fond en opposition ; l'hypothèse de Colquhoun est qu'un impératif moral doit inspirer l'architecture, même s'il serait le premier à reconnaître la difficulté d'une telle prémisse ; l'hypothèse de Carl est une position phénoménologique, qui considère dans l'acte architectural la potentialité d'une universalité de la condition humaine, et une position presque médiévale, dans sa capacité à voir la totalité dans la partie.

Graves a été admiré au moins autant pour la délicatesse et la précision de ses dessins que pour la complexité et le mystère de ses constructions. Cette constatation amène à poser la question des relations existant aux Etats-Unis entre les modes de constructions et les styles de design. Pour Carl, cette relation est purement légale. Mais la sensualité des matériaux et les limites techniques, entre ce qui est possible et ce qui ne l'est pas, jouent un rôle dans la réalisation de toute construction, pour aussi riche qu'ait été sa base conceptuelle. Peindre une surface dans un édifice peut être coder un espace, le Centre Georges Pompidou en est un exemple, peut-être le plus récent et le mieux connu. Exécuter une peinture murale, dont les antécédents stylistiques remontent à des conceptions sensiblement eloignees des conceptions actuelles de la peinture comme l'un des beaux-arts, c'est établir un champ d'interprétation entre la réalité de la construction et la représentation de l'image. Si l'image est placée à un point significatif dans le plan de l'édifice et qu'elle se réfère à des composants, ou plutôt à des éléments conceptuels de l'édifice, on présente simultanément à l'observateur l'édifice et un commentaire sur ses éléments. Mais ses éléments sont à la fois conceptuels, l'idée d'une architrave, et fonctionnels, le but d'une architrave. S'il n'est pas nécessaire pour l'architecte de ré-inventer chaque fois l'architrave, il faut cependant en un certain sens que l'architrave soit reconsidérée, aussi bien en tant qu'idée qu'en tant qu'objet, et comme partie nécessaire de la construction. On peut juger que l'oeuvre de Graves, dans ses dernières réalisations, opère un retour aux éléments de construction établis, et, en quelque sorte, démodés ; doit-on en conclure qu'il s'agit d'une acceptation de la validité de. ces éléments, parce qu'ils fournissent une articulation aux endroits où l'Architecture Moderne recherche une stricts neutralité, ou qu'il s'agit d'un refus délibéré de ré-inventer les éléments de construction ? Pour continuer avec l'exemple de l'architrave, le point crucial est le profil de la moulure ; comme Moretti le dit dans son article de 1951, publié à nouveau dans *Oppositions* 4, 'Les Valeurs des Profils', ' . . . les variations de lumière révèlent les palpitations continuelles d'une ancienne façade, qui changent d'heure en heure, tandis que le soleil dans sa course la (la corniche) modèle en harmonie avec le monde'. Il poursuit : ' . . . la forme d'une corniche donne les raisons d'une façade et les révèle avec énergie . . .'.

Pour revenir à notre sujet, en tenant compte du fait que le matériau utilisé dans les anciennes moulures l'est souvent d'une façon qui dépasse ses caractéristiques physiques propres, l'oeuvre de Graves n'opère pas un travail de recherche à partir de ces données classiques, pas plus qu'elle ne tente de trouver une tension sensuelle dans utilisation des matériaux. Elle se colore ainsi d'une certaine nostalgie, parce qu'elle accepte les éléments préfabriques du langage classique, même si les relations qu'elle introduit entre ces éléments entraînent, comme le souligne Carl avec raison, des progrès dans la conception de l'entrée et dans celle du plan par rapport au site. Cette nostalgie est inquiétante, en ce qu'elle implique une ré-jection, et non une re-lecture, des postulats du Mouvement Moderne en tout ce qui concerne l'utilisation des matériaux, tout en acceptant les techniques pour dresser les plans, qui sont la partie la plus généralement reconnue dans l'héritage de ce mouvement. Cette apparente contradiction ne représente cependant pas un échec, ouvrant au contraire pour le futur de l'architecture une problématique que Graves sera sûrement un des tous premiers à attaquer. Mais on peut conclure que cette discussion ne fait que souligner un fait évident, que, en publiant un ouvrage sur les oeuvres de Graves, alors que sa carrière en est encore à ses débuts, *Architectural Monographs* publie le dossier d'une 'Oeuvre à Suivre'.

Deutsche Zusammenfassung

Michael Graves wurde 1934 in Indianapolis geboren. Seiner Berufung als Professor für Architektur nach Princeton ging eine Ausbildung in Harvard in Rom als Rompreisträger voraus. Mit seiner Publikation *Fünf Architekten* im Jahr 1972 wurde er weltweit bekannt. So etwas — für sich genommen — hat im allgemeinen kaum Einfluß auf den Lauf der Architektur als Ganzes. Es ist ganz allein sein Verdienst, daß trotz Konjunkturflaute ein Werk produziert wurde, das umfangreich genug ist, um eine Veröffentlichung als eine Art Interim *oeuvre complète* auf diesen Seiten zu verdienen. Er wäre der Erste, einzugestehen, daß es sich um Arbeiten handelt, die unter dem Banner seines Namens fertiggestellt wurden, wie die Liste der Namen, denen sich verpflichtet fühlt, zeigt. Der Dank des Editors gilt Karen Wheeler aus seinem Büro und Carol Constant, die nun selbst Rompreisträgerin und deshalb ex officio ist, für ihre große Hilfe bei der Vorbereitung dieses Artikels.

Alan Colquhoun und Peter Carl nehmen in ihren jeweiligen Essays abweichende Positionen gegenüber Graves Werk ein. Für den ersteren ist das Werk in der Hauptsache persönlich, was heißt, daß es, obwohl es der amerikanischen wie auch der europäischen Tradition nahesteht, ein gewisses Quantum an Individualität enthüllt, das de facto nicht dem Vorwurf der Willkür entgehen kann. Der Letztere schlägt einen mehr universellen Zugang zu seinen Werk vor und ist der Meinung, daß Graves Probleme der Wahrnehmung anpackt, die auf einer Linie mit den Problemen der Repräsentation und der Konzeptualisierung des Kunstwerks liegen, was auf Césanne zurückgeht und vermutlich auch auf frühere Künstler bis hin zu Picasso, Le Corbusier und Duchamps.

Beide akzeptieren jedoch, daß Graves entscheidende Schritte unternommen hat, mit der Lacuna in der Theorie der Modernen Architektur zurande zu kommen, die ganz einfach in der Betonung des Eingangs besteht. Durch die Zelebrierung und 'Übertreibung' dieses Aspekts scheint Graves Mittel aufgetan zu haben, diejenigen Aspekte auszudrücken, die aufnahmefähig für Ritualisierung sind dort wo die Form der umgebenden Oberflächen in einer gewissen Weise die Heiligkeit markiert, die jeglichen Bauen innewohnt. Was ihm für Colquhoun fehlt, ist diese gewisse Leidenschaft, die die Moderne Architektur in erster Linie erzeugte, dieses außergewöhnliche Verlangen, durch Plazieren eines Architekturelementes neben einem anderen, ein Bild der Welt wie sie sein könnte, oder sein sollte, vorzusehen. Carl sieht auf der anderen Seite sein Werk als (verausgabte) Leidenschaft, 'als Beteiligter eines Stroms von Sein und Bauen', dessen Wurzeln so weit zurück in der Vergangenheit liegen, daß nur die Gedächtnisstützen der Archäologie helfen können, die Herkunft des Menschen zu erhellen.

Es ist nicht beabsichtigt, hier einen Kompromiss zwischen diesen beiden Interpretationen zustande zu bringen. Beide Texte gehen auf der Interpretationsebene von Prämissen aus, die in ihrer Essenz nicht entgegengesetzt sind. Colquhoun geht von dem Gefühl aus, daß ein moralischer Imperativ sich der Architektur mitteilen muß, obwohl er der erste wäre, die Schwierigkeit dieses Unterfangen einzugestehen, und Carl geht von einer phenomenologischen Position aus, die das Potential an Gemeingültigkeit, was die menschlichen Lebensbedingungen anbelangt, in der Tat des Architekten sieht, und von einer fast mittelalterlichen Fähigkeit, das Ganze in seinen Teil zu sehen.

Da Graves für die Feinheit und die Präzision seiner Graphik wenigstens genauso bewundert wird wie für die Komplexität und Rätselhaftigkeit seiner Bauten, kann man die Frage nach dem Verhältnis der Gepflogenheiten des Bauens in den USA zu der zeichnerischen Darstellung fragen. Carl sieht dieses Verhältnis als rein legal. Jedoch die Sinnlichkeit von Materialien und die technischen Beschränkungen von dem was möglich ist und was nicht, spielen eine Rolle bei der Fertigstellung eines jeden Bauwerks wie reich seine Entwurfsbasis auch immer sein mag. Eine Gebäudefassade anzumalen mag dazu dienen, einen Raum mit einem Code zu versehen; das Georges-Pompidou-Zentrum ist vielleicht das bekannteste und neueste Beispiel. Ein Wandgemälde zu malen, dessen stilistische Voraussetzungen es ganz klar abheben vom gegenwärtigen Stand des Malens als Schöner Kunst, heißt ein interpretatives Feld einzurichten, das zwischen der Realität des Gebäudes und der Repräsentation im Bild besteht. Wenn dieses Bild dann an einem bedeutungsvollen Punkt im Plan plaziert wird, und die Komponenten oder vielmehr die Entwurfselemente des Gebäudes zum Inhalt hat, dann ist der Betrachter gleichzeitig mit dem Gebäude und einem Komentar zu seinen Einzelteilen konfrontiert. Aber seine Einzelelemente sind sowohl begrifflich, nämlich die Idee eines Architravs, als auch gleichzeitig konstruktiv, nämlich der Zweck eines Architravs. Obwohl es für einen Architekten nicht nötig ist, jedesmal das Architrav neu zu erfinden, muß er es jedoch sowohl als Idee als auch als Objekt und Teil der Baustruktur noch einmal nachprüfen. Wenn man von Graves Werk denken kann, daß es zumindest in seinen späteren Bauten, zu den etebierten und in einem gewissen Maße altmodischen Konstruktionselementen zurückkehrt, könnte man dies als Akzeptieren der Gültigkeit dieser Elemente ansehen, da sie ja hervorheben, wo die Moderne Architektur nach exakter Einfachheit suchte — oder könnte es eine Weigerung darstellen, diese Konstruktionselemente noch einmal wiederzuentwerfen? Entscheidend wichtig wird das Profil der Kehlung, um bei dem Beispiel des Architravs zu bleiben, das wie Moretti in seinem Artikel 'Die Bedeutung von Profilen' 1951 sagt, der in *Oppositions* 4 neu veröffentlicht ist, mit 'Variationen von Licht zu tun hat und das den ewigen Herzschlag einer Fassade enthüllt, von Stunde zu Stunde wechselnd da der Sonnenstand es (das Karnies) in Harmonie mit der Welt formt.' Er fährt fort, 'die Form eines Karnies übermittelt die Begründung für eine Fassade und enthüllt sie vehement.' Zurückkehrend zur oben gestellten Frage und akzeptierend, daß das Material, aus dem alte Gesimse gemacht worden sind, über die eigenen physikalischen Eigenschaften hinausgeht, kann man sagen, daß Graves Werk diese klassische Ader nicht erneut erarbeitet, noch scheint es, daß eine sinnliche Spannung im Gebrauch der Materialien Teil seiner Bemühungen ist. Es muß dann einen Hauch von Nostalgie haben, denn es akzeptiert die Vorfertigungen der klassischen Sprache, selbst wenn das Verhältnis zwischen Elementen in seinem Werk, wie Carl beredt aufzeigt, zu Vervollkommnung auf der Ebene von Figur/Untergrund führt. Diese Nostalgie ist beängstigend, denn sie beinhaltet eine Ablehnung, nicht eine Neuinterpretation der Forderungen der Modernen Architektur was die Anwendung von Materialien anbelangt; wobei doch gleichzeitig die Planungstechniken akzeptiert werden, die doch das weitgehend gemeinhin anerkannte Erbe der Modernen Architektur darstellen. Diese Inkonsequenz ist jedoch in keiner Hinsicht ein Fehler, denn sie eröffnet für die Zukunft der Architektur eine Problematik, die Graves sicher als einer der ersten angreifen wird. Aber abschließend möchte der Autor bemerken, dieses Argument unterstreicht die offenkundige Tatsache, daß *Architectural Monographs*, indem es Graves Werk in einem so frühen Stadium seiner Karriere publiziert, einen Band aus der Reihe 'Werk im Entstehen' veröffentlicht.

Sommario in italiano

Michael Graves è nato a Indianapolis nel 1934. Una formazione a Harvard come borsista del Prix de Rome, ha preceduto la sua nomina nel 1962 a professore di architettura a Princeton. La pubblicazione di *Five Architects* nel 1972 gli ha dato fama internazionale. Tali fatti in se stessi hanno poca importanza rispetto al corso dell'architettura in generale. Invece, malgrado questi tempi di crisi economica, è interamente a suo credito di aver prodotto abbastanza lavoro da meritare la pubblicazione di una specie di 'opera completa' provvisoria in queste pagine. Egli sarebbe il primo a riconoscere che si tratta di lavoro d'equipe, compiuto sotto il suo nome. I ringraziamenti del redattore vanno a Karen Wheeler del suo studio, e a Carol Constant, che è attualmente borsista a Roma e quindi non più nello studio, per la loro contribuzione alla preparazione di questo numero.

Alan Colquhoun e Peter Carl nei loro rispettivi articoli assumono posizioni divergenti sull'opera di Graves. Per il primo quest' opera è soprattutto 'personale', cioè, pur con delle connessioni alla tradizione sia americana che europea, essa contiene una parte essenziale di individualismo e non può in realtà sfuggire all'accusa di arbitrarietà. Il secondo invece propende per un approccio più universalistico alla sua opera, suggerendo che ciò che Graves affronta sono certe soluzioni percettive nella linea dei problemi di rappresentazione e concettualizzazione nell'opera d'arte, derivate da Cezanne, e da più lontano nel tempo, attraverso Picasso, Le Corbusier e Duchamp.

Entrambi tuttavia ammettono che Graves ha fatto un passo sostanziale affrontando questa lacuna del movimento moderno, che è semplicemente il problema dell'articolazione dell'entrata. Attraverso l'esaltazione e l''esagerazione' di questo aspetto Graves sembra aver rivelato una maniera di articolare le parti del programma di un edificio suscettibili di ritualizzazione, quelle parti cioè in cui la forma delle superfici può in qualche modo marcare l'atto sacro del costruire. Ciò che manca secondo Colquhoun è questa passione, che fu all'origine del movimento moderno, questo straordinario desiderio di prevedere, attraverso l'accostamento degli elementi architettonici, un'immagine del mondo come dovrebbe o potrebbe essere. Carl invece vede l'opera di Graves come 'tutta passione', come partecipe di una corrente dell'essere e del costruire le cui radici rimontano così lontano nel passato, che solo i reperti archeologici possono aiutare a far luce sulle condizioni originarie dell'uomo.

Non è nelle nostre intenzioni di cercare un compromesso tra queste due interpretazioni. Entrambi partono per la loro interpretazione da presupposti non essenzialmente opposti: Colquhoun dall'idea che un imperativo morale deve guidare l'architettura, benché egli sarebbe il primo a riconoscere la difficoltà di una tale impresa; e Carl da una posizione fenomenologica che gli fa intravedere nell'atto architettonico una potenzialità più generale sulla condizione umana ed un'abilità quasi medioevale a vedere l'insieme nel particolare.

Poiché Graves è stato almeno altrettanto ammirato per la delicatezza e precisione del suo grafismo, che per la complessità ed il mistero dei suoi edifici, ci si può interrogare sul rapporto tra i modi di costruire negli Stati Uniti e la maniera di disegnare. Carl vede questa relazione come puramente legale. Ma la sensualità dei materiali e le restrizioni tecniche hanno un ruolo nella realizzazione di un edificio, per quanto ricche possano essere le sue basi concettuali. Dipingere la superficie di un edificio può essere un modo di codificare uno spazio, il Centro Georges Pompidou è forse l'esempio conosciuto e più recente. L'atto di dipingere un muro, atto i cui antecedenti stilistici si situano ad un significativo passaggio dell'idea attuale della pittura come arte, è creare un terreno di interpretazione tra la realtà dell'edificio ed il soggetto rappresentato. Se poi il dipinto si trova in un punto significativo della pianta, e 'rappresenta' le componenti o gli elementi concettuali dell'edificio, allora l'occhio è simultaneamente confrontato all'edificio stesso e ad un commento sui suoi elementi. Ma questi elementi sono al tempo stesso concettuali, l'idea di un'architrave, e costruttivi, la necessità di un'architrave. Benché non sia necessario per un architetto di riinventare l'architrave ad ogni progetto, ciò nonostante l'architrave deve essere riconsiderato come idea e come oggetto, e come parte della necessità costruttiva dell'edificio. Se l'opera di Graves può, almeno negli ultimi edifici, essere intesa come un ritorno ad elementi costruttivi stabiliti e forse fuori moda, può questa essere considerata un'accettazione di validità di tali elementi, da una parte perché essi articolano, laddove l'architettura moderna ricerca una precisa coerenza, o può allora un deliberato rifiuto di riinventare questi elementi costruttivi? Ecco che diventa essenziale, per proseguire nell'esempio dell'architrave, il profilo della modanatura, attraverso il quale, come Moretti dice nel suo articolo del 1951, ripubblicato in *Opposizioni* 4, dal titolo 'I valori dei profili', cioè 'le variazioni della luce rivelano le continue vibrazioni di una facciata antica, diverse di ora in ora, secondo come il corso del sole dà forma (alla cornice) in armonia col cosmo'. E ancora 'la forma di una cornice trasmette la logica di una facciata e la rivela con veemenza...'

Ritornando al nostro problema, ed accettando che la materia di cui sono fatte le antiche modanature è spesso spinta oltre le sue proprietà fisiche, il lavoro di Graves non riinventa in questo senso la tradizione classica, né apparirà che una tensione sensitiva nell'uso dei materiali è nelle sue intenzioni. Deve quindi avere una sfumatura di nostalgia, poiché accetta le acquisizioni del linguaggio classico, benché l'interrelazione tra gli elementi nella sua opera lo porti, come Carl sottolinea con precisione, ad avanzare la ricerca a livello dell'entrata e della forma della pianta. Questa nostalgia è inquietante, perché implica un rifiuto, e non una rilettura dei postulati del movimento moderno, almeno per quanto concerne l'uso dei materiali, pur accettando al tempo stesso le tecniche di progettazione che sono l'eredità più generalmente riconosciuta di questo movimento. Questa incongruenza comunque non è affatto un difetto, aprendo nel futuro dell'architettura una problematica che Graves sarà certamente tra i primi ad attaccare. Ma, per concludere, questo argomento conferma il fatto ovvio che, nel pubblicare l'opera di Graves in questa fase ancora iniziale della sua carriera, *Architectural Monographs* pubblica lo studio di un' 'Opera in evoluzione'.

Resumen en español

Michael Graves nació en Indianapolis en 1934. Estudió en Harvard y Roma como becario del Prix de Rome antes de ser profesor de arquitectura en 1962 en Princeton. Con la publicación de *Five Architects* en 1972 se convirtió en una figura internacional. Estos datos por sí sólos tienen poca pertinencia al curso de la arquitectura. A pesar de las dificultades económicas, se le puede conceder el mérito de haber producido suficiente trabajo para poder publicarlo como obra completa provisional. Debemos agradecer la ayuda de Karen Wheeler y Carol Constant, la cual es ahora una becaria en Roma, por su gran ayuda en preparar éste número de la revista.

Alan Colquhoun y Peter Carl toman dos atitudes hacia la obra de Graves. Para el primero, la obra es primariamente 'personal'. Es decir, que aunque se relacione con las tradiciones americanas y europeas, contiene individualidad que no se puede atribuir a arbitrariedad. El segundo discute un enfoque más universal a la obra, y sugiere que lo que Graves está resolviendo son ciertas decisiones perceptuales que paralelan los problemas de representación y conceptualización de una obra artística que prodede de Cezanne y tambien atraves de Picasso, Duchamps y Le Corbusier.

Pero los dos aceptan que Graves ha llegado a un arreglo con la *lacuna* en la teoría del Movimiento Moderno, que simplemente es el problema de la articulación de la entrada. Mediante ésta 'exageración' Graves ha creado una manera de articular los varios aspectos de la construcción de un edificio que son susceptibles a una ritualización, aspectos que se encuentran en la forma de las superficies que señalan la 'santidad' de cualquier construcción. Para Colquhoun, lo que carece la obra de Graves es el entusiasmo que engendró al Movimiento Moderno, ese deseo extraordinario de ver una imágen del mundo como debe o puede ser mediante la colocación de un elemento arquitectónico junto a otro. Carl ve la obra como 'toda pasión (consumida?)', como una parte de construcción y existencia que tiene raices que se han de buscar arqueológicamente.

Esencialmente, los dos escritos no se oponen; Colquhoun discute de un punto de vista que los imperativos morales se han de pasar a la arquitectura, aún conociendo las dificultades de tal condición; Carl toma una posición fenomenológica que comprende las posibilidades de generalizar sobre la condición humana en la arquitectura, y la abilidad de ver lo completo en una porción.

Graves puede admirarse por la delicacia y precisión de sus dibujos y tambien por la complejidad y mysterio de sus edificios. Debido a ésto se puede alzar la question sobre los distintos modos de construcción en los Estados Unidos y la manera de dibujar. Carl vé ésta relación en términos legales. Pero la sensualidad de los materiales y las restricciones técnicas toman gran parte en la realización de cualquier construcción por muy ricas que sean su bases conceptuales. En pintar las superficies de un edificio se puede dar un 'código' al un espacio. El centro Georges Pompidou es un ejemplo conocido y reciente. Pintando un mural (cuyos antecedentes estan ajenos al presente estado de pintura como bellas artes) es crear una esfera de interpretación que existe entre la realidad del edificio y su representación en el dioujo. Entonces, si se situa tal pintura en un punto significativo en el plan, y está entre los elementos conceptuales del edificio, se presenta simultáneamente al edificio y un comentario sobre sus elementos. Pero sus elementos son a la vez conceptuales (la idea de un arquitrabe) y estructurales (el propósito del arquitrabe). Mientras que no es necesario que el arquitecto reinvente el arquitrabe, cada vez que diseña uno, la idea del arquitrabe tiene que estudiarse de nuevo como idea, objeto y como parte necesaria del edificio. Si las obras mas recientes de Graves se pueden analizar como una vuelta a una manera de construir establecida y pasada de moda, ¿puede ésto ser una admisión de la validez de los elementos arquitectónicos porque articulan en donde la Arquitectura Moderna busca una suavidad? ¿o es que es un rechazo deliberado de la reinvención de los elementos de construcción? Lo decisivo, usando el ejemplo del arquitrabe, es el perfíl de la moldura, que es (segun Moretti en su articulo de 1951 en *Oppositions* 4 'The Values of Profiles' (Los Meritos del Perfil) 'la variación de la luz que revela las eternas palpitaciones de una antigua fachada, que varía de hora a hora, según la marcha del sol que da forma a la cornisa harmoniosamente con el mundo.' Y continúa 'la forma de la cornisa comunica las razones para la existencia de una fachada y lo revela vehementemente...'

Si aceptamos que la materia de las antiguas molduras se usaron más allá de los límites de las características físicas de la materia, la obra de Graves no sigue éste camino, ni usa la tensión de la materia como parte de su empeño. Entonces debe ser una cierta nostaligia ya que acepta lo ya hecho del lenguaje clásico, aún cuando la relación entre los elementos de su obra, según Carl, avanza el nivel de entrada y el nivel de 'figura/fondo' *(figure/ground)*. Ésta nostalgia es tremenda ya que implica un rechazo y no una re-lectura de los postulados del Movimiento Moderno (en lo que se refire al uso de materiales) y a la vez aceptando la técnica de planeamiento que es lo más aceptable de lo heredado de tal movimiento. Pero ésta contradicción no es un fallo, sino que abre un nuevo problema para la arquitectura que Graves tambien atacará. Pero, concluyendo, éste argumento se encuentra en el hecho que en publicar la obra de Graves que esta todavia en su principio, *Architectural Monographs* publica un 'Trabajo en Progreso'.